Poverty and Famines

An Essay on Entitlement and Deprivation

This study was prepared for the International Labour Office within the framework of the World Employment Programme. The World Employment Programme (WEP) was launched by the International Labour Organisation in 1969, as the ILO's main contribution to the International Development Strategy for the Second United Nations Development Decade.

The means of action adopted by the WEP have included the following:
- short-term high-level advisory missions;
- longer-term national or regional employment teams; and
- a wide-ranging research programme.

Through these activities the ILO has been able to help national decision-makers to reshape their policies and plans with the aim of eradicating mass poverty and unemployment.

A landmark in the development of the WEP was the World Employment Conference of 1976, which proclaimed inter alia that "strategies and national development plans should include as a priority objective the promotion of employment and the satisfaction of the basic needs of each country's population". The Declaration of Principles and Programme of Action adopted by the Conference have become the cornerstone of WEP technical assistance and research activities during the closing years of the Second Development Decade.

Poverty and Famines

*An Essay
on Entitlement
and Deprivation*

AMARTYA SEN

OXFORD
UNIVERSITY PRESS

OXFORD
UNIVERSITY PRESS

Great Clarendon Street, Oxford OX2 6DP

Oxford University Press is a department of the University of Oxford.
It furthers the University's objective of excellence in research, scholarship,
and education by publishing worldwide in

Oxford New York

Auckland Cape Town Dar es Salaam Hong Kong Karachi Kuala Lumpur
Madrid Melbourne Mexico City Nairobi New Delhi Shanghai Taipei Toronto

With offices in

Argentina Austria Brazil Chile Czech Republic France Greece
Guatemala Hungary Italy Japan South Korea Poland Portugal
Singapore Switzerland Thailand Turkey Ukraine Vietnam

Oxford is a registered trade mark of Oxford University Press
in the UK and in certain other countries

Published in the United States
by Oxford University Press Inc., New York

© International Labour Organisation 1981

First published 1981
First issued as a paperback 1982

The responsibility for opinion expressed in signed studies and other contributions
rest solely with their authors, and publication does not constitute an endorsement
by the International Labour Office of the opinions expressed in them.

The designations employed and the presentation of materials do not imply the expression
of any opinion whatsoever on the part of the International Labour Office concerning
the legal status of any country or territory or its authorities, or concerning the
delimitation of its frontiers.

British Library Cataloguing in Publication Data

Sen, Amartya
Poverty and famines.
1. Famines
I. Title
363.8 HC79.F3 80-42191

ISBN: 978-0-19-828463-5

16

Printed in Great Britain
on acid-free paper by
the MPG Books Group, Bodmin and King's Lynn

To Amiya Dasgupta
who introduced me to economics
and taught me what it is about

Preface

Much about poverty is obvious enough. One does not need elaborate criteria, cunning measurement, or probing analysis, to recognize raw poverty and to understand its antecedents. It would be natural to be impatient with long-winded academic studies on 'poor naked wretches' with 'houseless heads and unfed sides' and 'loop'd and windowed raggedness', to use King Lear's graphic description. And furthermore it may also be the case, as Lear told the blind Gloucester, that 'a man may see how this world goes with no eyes'. There is indeed much that is transparent about poverty and misery.

But not everything about poverty is quite so simple. Even the identification of the poor and the diagnosis of poverty may be far from obvious when we move away from extreme and raw poverty. Different approaches can be used (e.g. biological inadequacy, relative deprivation), and there are technical issues to be resolved within each approach. Furthermore, to construct an overall picture of poverty, it is necessary to go well beyond identifying the poor. To provide an aggregate profile based on the characteristics of those who are identified as poor, problems of aggregation have to be squarely faced. Finally—and most importantly—the *causation* of poverty raises questions that are not easily answered. While the 'immediate' antecedents of poverty may be too obvious to need much analysis, and the 'ultimate' causation too vague and open-ended a question to be settled fully, there are various intermediate levels of useful answers that are worth exploring. The problem is of particular relevance in the context of recent discussions on the causation of hunger and starvation.

This monograph is concerned with these questions. The main focus of this work is on the causation of starvation in general and of famines in particular. The basic approach, which involves analysing 'entitlement systems', is introduced in general terms in Chapter 1. This is done even before the concepts of poverty are examined in any detail, because that is where the thrust of this monograph lies. In Chapters 2 and 3 problems of conceptualization and measurement of poverty are examined. The specific problem of starvation is taken up in very general terms in Chapter 4, and the 'entitlement approach' is analysed in Chapter 5. This is followed by case studies of famines from different parts of the world: the Great Bengal Famine of 1943 (Chapter 6), the Ethiopian famines of 1973–75 (Chapter 7), famines in the Sahel region of Africa during the early 1970s (Chapter 8), and the Bangladesh famine of 1974 (Chapter 9). In Chapter 10 the entitlement approach is consolidated, taking up general issues of deprivation related to entitlement systems.

There are four technical appendices. Appendix A presents a formal analysis of the notion of exchange entitlement—an important aspect of entitlement systems. The relevance of failures of exchange entitlement for the development of famine situations is brought out in Appendix B in terms of some illustrative models. Appendix C provides an examination of the problem of poverty measurement, including a scrutiny of various measures that have been used or proposed. Finally, the pattern of famine mortality is discussed in Appendix D based on a case study of the Bengal famine of 1943.

This work has been prepared for the World Employment Programme of ILO. I am grateful for, among other things, their extraordinary patience; the work took a good deal longer than they—and for that matter I—imagined it would. I am also most grateful for helpful discussions with Felix Paukert and others involved in the Income Distribution and Employment Programme. I have also benefited greatly from detailed comments of Judith Heyer and Jocelyn Kynch on an earlier draft of this manuscript. For useful suggestions and advice, I am also grateful to Mohiuddin Alamgir, Sudhir Anand, Asit Bhattacharya, Robert Cassen, Dipankar Chatterjee, Pramit Chaudhuri, Amiya Dasgupta, Meghnad Desai, John Flemming, Madangopal Ghosh, David Glass, Ruth Glass, Terence Gorman, Keith Griffin, Carl Hamilton, Roger Hay, Julius Holt, Leif Johansen, J. Krishnamurti, Mukul Majumdar, Ashok Mitra, John Muellbauer, Suzy Paine, Debidas Ray, Debraj Ray, Samir Ray, Tapan Raychaudhuri, Carl Riskin, Joan Robinson, Suman Sarkar, John Seaman, Rehman Sobhan, K. Sundaram, Jaroslav Vanek and Henry Wan, among others.

I have drawn on my earlier writings, including articles

published in *Economic and Political Weekly* (1973, 1976), *Economet-rica* (1976, 1977), *Review of Economic Studies* (1976), *Cambridge Journal of Economics* (1977), *Scandinavian Journal of Economics* (1979), *Journal of Economic Literature* (1979), *World Development* (1980), and *Quarterly Journal of Economics* (1981).

Finally, a remark on presentation. While some mathematical concepts and notation have been used in Appendices A–C, the text of the monograph is almost entirely informal. Someone concerned with the detailed structures would have to consult the Appendices, but there should be no difficulty in following the main lines of the argument (including the case studies) without reference to them. I have tried to make the book accessible to as wide an audience as possible, since the subject matter of this work is important. I am also immodest enough to believe that the analysis presented in this monograph has a certain amount of relevance to matters of practical concern.

A. K. S.

Contents

Chapter 1

Poverty and Entitlements

1.1 ENTITLEMENTS AND OWNERSHIP

Starvation is the characteristic of some people not *having* enough food to eat. It is not the characteristic of there *being* not enough food to eat. While the latter can be a cause of the former, it is but one of many *possible* causes. Whether and how starvation relates to food supply is a matter for factual investigation.

Food supply statements say things about a commodity (or a group of commodities) considered on its own. Starvation statements are about the *relationship* of persons to the commodity (or that commodity group).[1] Leaving out cases in which a person may deliberately starve, starvation statements translate readily into statements of ownership of food by persons. In order to understand starvation, it is, therefore, necessary to go into the structure of ownership.

Ownership relations are one kind of *entitlement* relations. It is necessary to understand the entitlement systems within which the problem of starvation is to be analysed.[2] This applies *more generally* to poverty as such, and *more specifically* to famines as well.

An entitlement relation applied to ownership connects one set of ownerships to another through certain rules of legitimacy. It is a recursive relation and the process of connecting can be repeated. Consider a private ownership market economy. I own this loaf of bread. Why is this ownership accepted? Because I got it by exchange through paying some money I owned. Why is my ownership of that money accepted? Because I got it by selling a bamboo umbrella owned by me. Why is my ownership of the bamboo umbrella accepted? Because I made it with my own

[1] The contrast between commodities on the one hand and the relationship of commodities to persons on the other is central also to many other economic exercises. The evaluation of real national income is an important example, and for a departure from the traditional approaches to national income to a relationship-based evaluation in the light of this distinction, see Sen (1976b, 1979a).

[2] The 'entitlement approach' to starvation analysis was presented in Sen (1976c, 1977b), and is developed and extended in Chapter 5 and Appendix A, and applied to case studies in Chapters 6–9 below.

labour using some bamboo from my land. Why is my ownership of the land accepted? Because I inherited it from my father. Why is his ownership of that land accepted? And so on. Each link in this chain of entitlement relations 'legitimizes' one set of ownership by reference to another, or to some basic entitlement in the form of enjoying the fruits of one's own labour.[3]

Entitlement relations accepted in a private ownership market economy typically include the following, among others:

(1) *trade-based entitlement*: one is entitled to own what one obtains by trading something one owns with a willing party (or, multilaterally, with a willing set of parties);

(2) *production-based entitlement*: one is entitled to own what one gets by arranging production using one's owned resources, or resources hired from willing parties meeting the agreed conditions of trade;

(3) *own-labour entitlement*: one is entitled to one's own labour power, and thus to the trade-based and production-based entitlements related to one's labour power;

(4) *inheritance and transfer entitlement*: one is entitled to own what is willingly given to one by another who legitimately owns it, possibly to take affect after the latter's death (if so specified by him).

These are some entitlement relations of more or less straightforward kind, but there are others, frequently a good deal more complex. For example, one may be entitled to enjoy the fruits of some property without being able to trade it for anything else. Or one may be able to inherit the property of a deceased relation who did not bequeath it to anyone, through some rule of kinship-based inheritance accepted in the country in question. Or one may have some entitlements related to unclaimed objects on the basis of discovery. Market entitlements may even be supplemented by rationing or coupon systems, even in private ownership market economies, such as in Britain during the last war.[4]

---

[3] The interpretation of entitlement relations here is descriptive rather than prescriptive. In contrast, Robert Nozick's (1974) well-known exploration of 'the entitlement theory' of justice is prescriptive, discussing private property rights and other rights in normative terms. The two exercises are thus differently motivated, and must not be confused with each other.

[4] This may or may not be combined with price 'control', and that in its turn may or may not be combined with a flourishing 'black market'; see Dasgupta (1950) for an illuminating analysis of black market prices.

The scope of ownership relations can vary greatly with economic systems. A socialist economy may not permit private ownership of 'means of production', thereby rendering 'production-based entitlements' inoperative except when it involves just one's own labour and some elementary tools and raw materials. A capitalist economy will not only *permit* the private ownership of means of production; that is indeed one of its main *foundations*. On the other hand, a capitalist economy—like a socialist one—will not permit ownership of one human being by another, as a slave economy will. A socialist economy may restrict the employment of one person by another for production purposes, i.e. constrain the possibility of private trading of labour power for productive use. A capitalist economy will not, of course, do this, but may impose restrictions on binding contracts involving labour-power obligations over long periods of time. This, however, is the standard system under some feudal practices involving bonded labour, and also in some cases of colonial plantations.

1.2 EXCHANGE ENTITLEMENT

In a market economy, a person can exchange what he owns for another collection of commodities. He can do this exchange either through trading, or through production, or through a combination of the two. The set of all the alternative bundles of commodities that he can acquire in exchange for what he owns may be called the 'exchange entitlement' of what he owns.

The 'exchange entitlement mapping' is the relation that specifies the set of exchange entitlements for each ownership bundle. This relation—E-mapping for brevity—defines the possibilities that would be open to him corresponding to each ownership situation. A person will be exposed to starvation if, for the ownership that he actually has, the exchange entitlement set does not contain any feasible bundle including enough food. Given the E-mapping, it is in this way possible to identify those ownership bundles—call them collectively the starvation set— that must, thus, lead to starvation in the absence of non-entitlement transfers (e.g. charity). E-mappings, starvation sets, and related concepts are discussed in Chapter 5 and are formally analysed in Appendix A, and here we are concerned only with the underlying ideas.

Among the influences that determine a person's exchange

entitlement, given his ownership bundle (including labour power), are the following:

(1) whether he can find an employment, and if so for how long and at what wage rate;

(2) what he can earn by selling his non-labour assets, and how much it costs him to buy whatever he may wish to buy;

(3) what he can produce with his own labour power and resources (or resource services) he can buy and manage;

(4) the cost of purchasing resources (or resource services) and the value of the products he can sell;

(5) the social security benefits he is entitled to and the taxes, etc., he must pay.

A person's ability to avoid starvation will depend both on his ownership and on the exchange entitlement mapping that he faces. A general decline in food supply may indeed cause him to be exposed to hunger through a rise in food prices with an unfavourable impact on his exchange entitlement. Even when his starvation is *caused* by food shortage in this way, his immediate reason for starvation will be the decline in his exchange entitlement.

More importantly, his exchange entitlement may worsen for reasons other than a general decline of food supply. For example, given the same total food supply, other groups' becoming richer and buying more food can lead to a rise in food prices, causing a worsening of exchange entitlement. Or some economic change may affect his employment possibilities, leading also to worse exchange entitlement. Similarly, his wages can fall behind prices. Or the price of necessary resources for the production he engages in can go up relatively. These diverse influences on exchange entitlements are as relevant as the overall volume of food supply *vis-à-vis* population.

1.3 MODES OF PRODUCTION

The exchange entitlements faced by a person depend, naturally, on his position in the economic class structure as well as the modes of production in the economy. What he owns will vary with his class, and even if exactly the same E-mapping were to hold for all, the actual exchange entitlements would differ with his ownership position.

But even with the same ownership position, the exchange

entitlements will be different depending on what economic prospects are open to him, and that will depend on the modes of production and his position in terms of production relations.[5] For example, while a peasant differs from a landless labourer in terms of ownership (since he owns land, which the labourer does not), the landless share-cropper differs from the landless labourer not in their respective ownerships, but in the way they can use the only resource they own, viz. labour power. The landless labourer will be employed in exchange for a wage, while the share-cropper will do the cultivation and own a part of the *product*.

This difference can lead not merely to contrasts of the levels of typical remuneration of the two, which may or may not be very divergent, but also to sharp differences in exchange entitlements in distress situations. For example, a cyclone reducing the labour requirement for cultivation by destroying a part of the crop in each farm may cause some casual agricultural labourers to be simply fired, leading to a collapse of their exchange entitlements, while others are retained. In contrast, in this case the share-croppers may all operate with a lower labour input and lower entitlement, but no one may become fully jobless and thus incomeless.

Similarly, if the output is food, e.g. rice or wheat, the share-cropper gets his return in a form such that he can directly eat it without going through the vagaries of the market. In contrast, the agricultural labourer paid in money terms will have to depend on the exchange entitlement of his money wage. When famines are accompanied by sharp changes in relative prices—and in particular a sharp rise in food prices—there is much comparative merit in being a share-cropper rather than an agricultural labourer, especially when the capital market is highly imperfect. The greater production risk of the share-cropper compared with the security of a fixed wage on the part of the agricultural labourer has been well analysed (see, for example, Stiglitz, 1974); but a fixed money wage may offer no security at all in a situation of sharply varying food prices (even when employment is guaranteed). In contrast, a share of the food output does have some security advantage in terms of exchange entitlement.

---

[5] See Marx (1857–8, 1867) for the classic treatment of modes of production and their relevance to production and distribution.

Similarly, those who sell services (e.g. barbers or rickshaw-pullers) or handicraft products (e.g. weavers or shoemakers) are—like wage labourers—more exposed, in this respect, to famines involving unexpected rises of food prices than are peasants or share-croppers producing food crops. This is the case even when the *typical* standard of living of the latter is no higher than that of the former.

In understanding general poverty, or regular starvation, or outbursts of famines, it is necessary to look at both ownership patterns and exchange entitlements, and at the forces that lie behind them. This requires careful consideration of the nature of modes of production and the structure of economic classes as well as their interrelations. Later in the monograph, when actual famines are analysed, these issues will emerge more concretely.

1.4 SOCIAL SECURITY AND EMPLOYMENT ENTITLEMENTS

The exchange entitlements depend not merely on market exchanges but also on those exchanges, if any, that the state provides as a part of its social security programme. Given a social security system, an unemployed person may get 'relief', an old person a pension, and the poor some specified 'benefits'. These affect the commodity bundles over which a person can have command. They are parts of a person's exchange entitlements, and are conditional on the absence of other exchanges that a person might undertake. For example, a person is not entitled to unemployment benefit if he exchanges his labour power for a wage, i.e. becomes employed. Similarly, exchanges that make a person go above the specified poverty norm will make him ineligible for receiving the appropriate relief. These social security provisions are essentially supplementations of the processes of market exchange and production, and the two types of opportunities together determine a person's exchange entitlements in a private ownership market economy with social security provisions.

The social security arrangements are particularly important in the context of starvation. The reason why there are no famines in the rich developed countries is not because people are generally rich on the average. Rich they certainly are when they have jobs and earn a proper wage; but for large numbers of people this condition fails to hold for long periods of time, and the exchange entitlements of their endowments in the absence of social security arrangements could provide very meagre commodity bundles indeed. With the proportion of unemployment as high as it is, say, in Britain or America today, but for the social security arrangements there would be widespread starvation and possibly a famine. What prevents that is not the high average income or wealth of the British or the general opulence of the Americans, but the guaranteed minimum values of exchange entitlements owing to the social security system.

Similarly, the elimination of starvation in socialist economies —for example in China—seems to have taken place even without a dramatic rise in food availability per head, and indeed, typically the former has *preceded* the latter. The end of starvation reflects a shift in the entitlement system, both in the form of social security and—more importantly—through systems of guaranteed employment at wages that provide exchange entitlement adequate to avoid starvation.

1.5 FOOD SUPPLY AND STARVATION

There has been a good deal of discussion recently about the prospect of food supply falling significantly behind the world population. There is, however, little empirical support for such a diagnosis of recent trends. Indeed, for most areas in the world— with the exception of parts of Africa—the increase in food supply has been comparable to, or faster than, the expansion of population.[6] But this does not indicate that starvation is being systematically eliminated, since starvation—as discussed—is a function of entitlements and not of food availability as such. Indeed, some of the worst famines have taken place with no significant decline in food availability per head (see Chapters 6, 7, and 9).

To say that starvation depends 'not merely' on food supply but also on its 'distribution' would be correct enough, though not remarkably helpful. The important question then would be: what determines distribution of food between different sections of the community? The entitlement approach directs one to questions dealing with ownership patterns and—less obviously

[6] See Aziz (1975), Sinha (1976a, 1976b, 1977), Sinha and Gordon Drabek (1978), Interfutures (1979), and also the FAO *Production Yearbooks* and FAO *Monthly Bulletins* (e.g., vol. 3, No. 4, 1980, pp. 15–16). See also chapters 5 and 10 below.

but no less importantly—to the various influences that affect exchange entitlement mappings (see Appendices A and B, and Chapters 5–10). In so far as food supply itself has any influence on the prevalence of starvation, that influence is seen as working *through* the entitlement relations. If one person in eight starves regularly in the world,[7] this is seen as the result of his inability to establish entitlement to enough food; the question of the physical availability of the food is not directly involved.

The approach of entitlements used in this work is very general and—I would argue—quite inescapable in analysing starvation and poverty. If, nevertheless, it appears odd and unusual, this can be because of the hold of the tradition of thinking in terms of what *exists* rather than in terms of who can *command* what. The mesmerizing simplicity of focusing on the ratio of food to population has persistently played an obscuring role over centuries, and continues to plague policy discussions today much as it has deranged anti-famine policies in the past.[8]

---

[7] See Aziz (1975), pp. 108 and 123.
[8] See Chapters 6, 7, 9 and 10.

Chapter 2

Concepts of Poverty

2.1 REQUIREMENTS OF A CONCEPT OF POVERTY

On his deathbed in Calcutta, J. B. S. Haldane wrote a poem called 'Cancer's a funny thing'.[1] Poverty is no less funny. Consider the following view of poverty:

> People must not be allowed to become so poor that they offend or are hurtful to society. It is not so much the misery and plight of the poor but the discomfort and cost to the community which is crucial to this view of poverty. We have a problem of poverty to the extent that low income creates problems for those who are not poor.[2]

To live in poverty may be sad, but to 'offend or [be] hurtful to society', creating 'problems for those who are not poor' is, it would appear, the real tragedy. It isn't easy to push much further the reduction of human beings into 'means'.

The first requirement of the concept of poverty is of a criterion as to *who* should be the focus of our concern. The specification of certain 'consumption norms', or of a 'poverty line', may do part of the job: 'the poor' are those people whose consumption standards fall short of the norms, or whose incomes lie below that line. But this leads to a further question: is the concept of poverty to be related to the interests of: (1) only the poor, (2) only the non-poor, or (3) both the poor and the non-poor?

It seems a bit grotesque to hold that the concept of poverty should be concerned only with the non-poor, and I take the liberty of dropping (2)—and the 'view' quoted in the first paragraph—without further ado. Alternative (3) might, however, appear to be appealing, since it is broad-based and unrestrictive. There is little doubt that the penury of the poor does, in fact, affect the well-being of the rich. The real question is whether such effects should enter into the concept of poverty as

---

[1] *Oxford Book of 20th Century English Verse*, ed. P. Larkin, Oxford, 1973, p. 271.

[2] Rein (1971), p. 46. I hasten to add that here Professor Rein is describing one of the *three* 'broad concepts' of poverty, viz. (1) 'subsistence', (2) 'inequality', and (3) 'externality'; the view quoted corresponds to 'externality'.

such, or whether they should figure under the possible *effects* of poverty. I believe a good case can be made for choosing the latter alternative, since in an obvious sense poverty must be a characteristic of the poor rather than of the non-poor. One can, for instance, argue that, if one considers a case of reduction of real income and increase in the suffering of all the poor, it *must* be described as an increase of poverty, no matter whether this change is accompanied by a reduction in the adverse effects on the rich (e.g. whether the rich are less 'offended' by the sight of penury).

This conception of poverty based on (1) does not, of course, imply any denial of the fact that the suffering of the poor themselves may depend on the condition of the non-poor. It merely asserts that the focus of the concept of poverty has to be on the well-being of the poor as such, no matter what influences affect their well-being. *Causation* of poverty and *effects* of poverty will be important issues to study on their own rights, and the conceptualization of poverty in terms of the conditions only of the poor does not affect the worthwhileness of studying these questions. Indeed, there will be much to say on these questions later on in the book.

It is perhaps worth mentioning in this context that in some discussions one is concerned not with the prevalence of poverty in a country in the form of the suffering of the *poor*, but with the relative opulence of the nation *as a whole*.[3] In those discussions it will, of course, be entirely legitimate to be concerned with the well-being of all the people in the nation, and the description of a nation as 'poor' must obviously relate to such a broader concept. These are *different* exercises, and so long as this fact is clearly recognized there need not be any confusion.

Even after we have identified the poor and specified that the concept of poverty is concerned with the conditions of the poor, much remains to be done. There is the problem of aggregation— often important—over the group of the poor, and this involves moving from the description of the poor to some over-all measure of 'poverty' as such. In some traditions, this is done very simply by just counting the number of the poor, and then expressing poverty as the ratio of the number of the poor to the total number of people in the community in question.

[3] See, for example, Paul Streeten, 'How Poor Are the Poor Countries and Why?' in

This 'head-count measure'—*H* for short—has at least two serious drawbacks. First, *H* takes no account of the *extent* of the short-fall of incomes of the poor from the 'poverty line': a reduction in the incomes of all the poor without affecting the incomes of the rich will leave this head count measure completely unchanged. Second, it is insensitive to the distribution of income among the poor; in particular, no transfer of income from a poor person to one who is richer can increase this head count measure. Both these defects make the measure *H*, which is by far the most widely used measure, quite unacceptable as an indicator of poverty, and the conception of poverty that lies implicit in it seems eminently questionable.

In this chapter I am not concerned with problems of measurement as such, which will be taken up in the next two chapters and in Appendix C. But behind each measure lies an analytical concept, and here I am concerned with the general ideas on the conception of poverty. If the preceding argument is right, then the requirements of a concept of poverty must include two distinct—but not unrelated—exercises, namely (1) a method of identifying a group of people as poor ('identification'); and (2) a method of aggregating the characteristics of the set of poor people into an over-all image of poverty ('aggregation'). Both these exercises will be performed in the next two chapters, but before that we need to study the kinds of considerations that may be used in choosing the operations (both identification and aggregation). The rest of the chapter will be concerned with these issues.

The underlying considerations come out most sharply in the alternative approaches to the concept of poverty that one can find in the literature. Some of these approaches have been subjected to severe attacks recently, while others have not been examined sufficiently critically. In attempting an evaluation of these approaches in the following sections, I shall try to assess the approaches as well as their respective critiques.

2.2 THE BIOLOGICAL APPROACH

In his famous study of poverty in York, Seebohm Rowntree (1901) defined families as being in 'primary poverty' if their 'total earnings are insufficient to obtain the minimum necessities for the maintenance of merely physical efficiency'. It is not surprising that biological considerations related to the requirements of survival or work efficiency have been often used in defining the poverty line. Starvation, clearly, is the most telling aspect of poverty.

The biological approach has come under rather intense fire recently.[4] There are indeed several problems with its use. First, there are significant variations related to physical features, climatic conditions and work habits.[5] In fact, even for a specific group in a specific region, nutritional requirements are difficult to define precisely. People have been known to survive with incredibly little nutrition, and there seems to be a cumulative improvement of life expectation as the dietary limits are raised. In fact, physical opulence seems to go on increasing with nutrition over a very wide range; Americans, Europeans and Japanese have been growing measurably in stature as their diets have continued to improve. There is difficulty in drawing a line somewhere, and the so-called 'minimum nutritional requirements' have an inherent arbitrariness that goes well beyond variations between groups and regions.

Second, the translation of minimum *nutritional* requirements into minimum *food* requirements depends on the choice of commodities. While it may be easy to solve the programming exercise of a 'diet problem', choosing a minimum cost diet for meeting specified nutritional requirements from food items sold at specified costs, the relevance of such a minimum cost diet is not clear. Typically, it turns out to be very low-cost indeed,[6] but monumentally boring, and people's food habits are not, in fact, determined by such a cost minimization exercise. The actual incomes at which specified nutritional requirements are met will depend greatly on the consumption habits of the people in question.

Third, for non-food items such minimum requirements are not easy to specify, and the problem is usually solved by assuming that a specified proportion of total income will be spent on food. With this assumption, the minimum food costs can be used to derive minimum income requirements. But the proportion spent on food varies not merely with habits and culture, but also with relative prices and availability of goods and services. It is not

---

[4] See, for example, Townsend (1971, 1974) and Rein (1971).
[5] See Rein (1971), Townsend (1974), Sukhatme (1977, 1978), and Srinivasan (1977a, 1979).
[6] See, for example, Stigler's (1945) astonishing estimates of 'the cost of subsistence'. See also Rajaraman (1974).

surprising that the assumptions made often turn out to be contradicted by actual experience; for example, Lord Beveridge's estimate of subsistence requirements of income during the Second World War proved to be far from correct, since the British were spending a much lower proportion of their income on food than was assumed (see Townsend, 1974, p. 17).

In view of these problems, one may well agree with Martin Rein's (1971) assertion that 'almost every procedure in the subsistence-level definition of poverty can be reasonably challenged' (p. 61). But the question that does remain is this: after we have challenged every one of the procedures used under the biological approach, what do we do *then*? Do we simply ignore that approach,[7] or do we examine whether something remains in it to be salvaged? I would argue that there does remain something.

First, while the concept of nutritional requirements is a rather loose one, there is no particular reason to suppose that the concept of poverty must itself be clear-cut and sharp. In fact, a certain amount of vagueness is implicit in both the concepts, and the really interesting question is the extent to which the areas of vagueness of the two notions, as commonly interpreted, tend to coincide. The issue, thus, is not whether nutritional standards are vague, but whether the vagueness is of the required kind.

Second, to check whether someone is getting a specified bundle of nutrition, one need not necessarily go through the procedure of examining whether that person has the income level that would generate that bundle. One can simply examine whether the person is, in fact, meeting that nutritional requirement or not. Even in poor countries, direct nutritional information of this type can be collected through sample surveys of consumption bundles and can be extensively analysed (see, for example, Srinivasan and Bardhan, 1974, especially the paper by Chatterjee, Sarkar and Paul, and Panikar *et al.*, 1975); and the 'identification' exercise under the nutritional approach need not go through the intermediary of income at all.

---

[7] Much depends on what the alternatives are. Rein (1971) himself recommends that 'other' conceptions 'deserve more attention and developments' (p. 62). Since 'subsistence' is one of his three 'broad concepts' of poverty, we are left with 'externality' and 'inequality'. Inequality—though related to poverty in terms of both causation and evaluation—is, however, a *distinct* issue from poverty, as will be presently argued (see Section 2.3). 'Externality', in terms of the effects of poverty on the *non-poor*, is an approach that we have already discussed (in Section 2.1), critically.

Third, even when we do go through the intermediary of income, the translation of a set of nutritional norms (or of alternative sets of such norms) into a 'poverty line' income (or poverty-line *incomes*) may be substantially simplified by the wide prevalence of particular patterns of consumption behaviour in the community in question. Proximity of *actual* habits and behaviour makes it possible to derive income levels at which the nutritional norms will be 'typically' met. (This question is discussed further in Chapter 3.)

Finally, while it can hardly be denied that malnutrition captures only one aspect of our idea of poverty, it is an important aspect, and one that is particularly important for many developing countries. It seems clear that malnutrition must have a central place in the conception of poverty. How exactly this place is to be specified remains to be explored, but the recent tendency to dismiss the whole approach seems to be a robust example of misplaced sophistication.

2.3 THE INEQUALITY APPROACH

The idea that the concept of poverty is essentially one of inequality has some immediate plausibility. After all, transfers from the rich to the poor can make a substantial dent on poverty in most societies. Even the poverty line to be used for identifying the poor has to be drawn with respect to contemporary standards in the community in question, so that poverty may look very like inequality between the poorest group and the rest of the community.

Arguments in favour of viewing poverty as inequality are presented powerfully by Miller and Roby, who conclude:

Casting the issues of poverty in terms of stratification leads to regarding poverty as an issue of inequality. In this approach, we move away from efforts to measure poverty lines with pseudo-scientific accuracy. Instead, we look at the nature and size of the differences between the bottom 20 or 10 per cent and the rest of the society. Our concern becomes one of narrowing the differences between those at the bottom and the better-off in each stratification dimension.[8]

There is clearly quite a bit to be said in favour of this approach. But one can argue that inequality is fundamentally a different

---

[8] Miller and Roby (1971, p. 143). Also Miller, Rein, Roby and Cross (1967). See Wedderburn (1974) for discussions of alternative approaches.

issue from poverty. To try to analyse poverty 'as an issue of inequality', or the other way round, would do little justice to either. Inequality and poverty are not, of course, unrelated. But neither concept subsumes the other. A transfer of income from a person in the top income group to one in the middle income range must *ceteris paribus* reduce inequality; but it may leave the perception of poverty quite unaffected. Similarly, a general decline in income that keeps the chosen measure of inequality unchanged may, in fact, lead to a sharp increase in starvation, malnutrition and obvious hardship; it will then be fantastic to claim that poverty is unchanged. To ignore such information as starvation and hunger is not, in fact, an abstinence from 'pseudo-scientific accuracy', but blindness to important parameters of the common understanding of poverty. Neither poverty nor inequality can really be included in the empire of the other.[9]

It is, of course, quite a different matter to recognize that inequality and poverty are *associated* with each other, and to note that a different distribution system may cure poverty even without an expansion of the country's productive capabilities. Recognizing the distinct nature of poverty as a concept permits one to treat it as a matter of interest and involvement in itself. The role of inequality in the prevalence of poverty can then figure in the analysis of poverty without making the two conceptually equivalent.

2.4 RELATIVE DEPRIVATION

The concept of 'relative deprivation' has been fruitfully used in the analysis of poverty,[10] especially in the sociological literature. Being poor has clearly much to do with being deprived, and it is natural that, for a social animal, the concept of deprivation will be a relative one. But within the uniformity of the term 'relative deprivation', there seem to exist some distinct and different notions.

One distinction concerns the contrast between *'feelings* of

[9] It is also worth noting that there are many measures of inequality, of which the gap 'between the bottom 20 or 10 per cent and the rest' is only one. See Atkinson (1970), Sen (1973a), Kolm (1976a, 1976b), and Blackorby and Donaldson (1978, 1980b). Also, inequality is not just a matter of the *size distribution* of income but one of investigating contrasts between different sections of the community from many different perspectives, e.g. in terms of *relations of production*, as done by Marx (1859, 1867).

[10] See Runciman (1966) and Townsend (1971), presenting two rather different approaches to the concept.

deprivation' and '*conditions* of deprivation'. Peter Townsend has argued that 'the latter would be a better usage'.[11] There is indeed much to be said for a set of criteria that can be based on concrete conditions, so that one could use 'relative deprivation' 'in an objective sense to describe situations where people possess less of some desired attribute, be it income, favourable employment conditions or power, than do others'.[12]

On the other hand, the choice of '*conditions* of deprivation' can not be independent of '*feelings* of deprivation'. Material objects cannot be evaluated in this context without reference to how people view them, and even if 'feelings' are not brought in explicitly, they must have an implicit role in the selection of 'attributes'. Townsend has rightly emphasized the importance of the 'endeavour to define the style of living which is generally shared or approved in each society and find whether there is . . . a point in the scale of the distribution of resources below which families find it increasingly difficult . . . to share in the customs, activities and diets comprising that style of living'.[13] One must, however, look also at the feelings of deprivation in deciding on the style and level of living the failure to share which is regarded as important. The dissociation of 'conditions' from 'feelings' is, therefore, not easy, and an objective diagnosis of 'conditions' requires an objective understanding of 'feelings'.

A second contrast concerns the choice of 'reference groups' for comparison. Again, one has to look at the groups with which the people in question actually compare themselves, and this can be one of the most difficult aspects of the study of poverty based on relative deprivation. The horizon of comparison is not, of course, independent of political activity in the community in question,[14] since one's sense of deprivation is closely related to one's expectations as well as one's view of what is fair and who has the right to enjoy what.

These different issues related to the general notion of relative deprivation have considerable bearing on the social analysis of

[11] Townsend (1974), pp. 25–6.
[12] Wedderburn (1974), p. 4.
[13] Townsend (1974), p. 36.
[14] For example, Richard Scase (1974) notes that Swedish workers tend to choose rather wider reference groups than British workers, and relates this contrast to the differences in the nature of the two trade union movements and of political organization generally.

poverty. It is, however, worth noting that the approach of relative deprivation—even including all its variants—cannot really be the *only* basis for the concept of poverty. A famine, for example, will be readily accepted as a case of acute poverty no matter what the relative pattern within the society happens to be. Indeed, there is an irreducible core of *absolute* deprivation in our idea of poverty, which translates reports of starvation, malnutrition and visible hardship into a diagnosis of poverty without having to ascertain first the relative picture. Thus the approach of relative deprivation supplements rather than supplants the analysis of poverty in terms of absolute dispossession.

2.5 A VALUE JUDGEMENT?

The view that 'poverty is a value judgement' has recently been presented forcefully by many authors. It seems natural to think of poverty as something that is disapproved of, the elimination of which is regarded as morally good. Going further, it has been argued by Mollie Orshansky, an outstanding authority in the field, that 'poverty, like beauty, lies in the eye of the beholder'.[15] The exercise would, then, seem to be primarily a subjective one: unleashing one's personal morals on the statistics of deprivation.

I would like to argue against this approach. It is important to distinguish between different ways in which the role of morals can be accommodated into the exercise of poverty measurement. There is a difference between saying that the exercise *is itself* a prescriptive one and saying that the exercise must *take note* of the prescriptions made by members of the community. To describe a prevailing prescription is an act of description, not prescription. It may indeed be the case that poverty, as Eric Hobsbawm (1968) puts it, 'is always defined according to the conventions of the society in which it occurs' (p. 398). But this does not make the exercise of poverty assessment in a given society a value judgement. Nor a subjective exercise of some kind or other. For the person studying and measuring poverty, the conventions of society are matters of fact (what *are* the contemporary standards?), and not issues of morality or of subjective search (what *should be* the contemporary standards? what *should be* my values? how do I *feel* about all this?).[16]

---

[15] Orshansky (1969), p. 37. For a critique of this position, see Townsend (1974).

[16] This does not, of course, in any way deny that one's values may implicitly affect one's

The point was brought out very clearly by Adam Smith more than two hundred years ago:

By necessaries I understand not only the commodities which are indispensably necessary for the support of life, but what ever the custom of the country renders it indecent for creditable people, even the lowest order, to be without. A linen shirt, for example, is, strictly speaking, not a necessary of life. The Greeks and Romans lived, I suppose, very comfortably though they had no linen. But in the present times, through the greater part of Europe, a creditable day-labourer would be ashamed to appear in public without a linen shirt, the want of which would be supposed to denote that disgraceful degree of poverty which, it is presumed, nobody can well fall into without extreme bad conduct. Custom, in the same manner, has rendered leather shoes a necessary of life in England. The poorest creditable person of either sex would be ashamed to appear in public without them.[17]

In a similar vein Karl Marx (1867) argued that, while 'a historical and moral element' enters the concept of subsistence, 'nevertheless, in a given country, at a given period, the average quantity of the means of subsistence necessary for the labourer is practically known' (p. 150).

It is possible that Smith or Marx may have overestimated the extent of uniformity of views that tends to exist in a community on the content of 'subsistence' or 'poverty'. Description of 'necessities' may be very far from ambiguous. But the presence of ambiguity in a description does not make it a prescriptive act—only one of ambiguous description. One may be forced to be arbitrary in eliminating the ambiguity, and if so that arbitrariness would be worth recording. Similarly, one may be forced to use more than one criteria because of non-uniformity of accepted standards, and to look at the *partial* ordering generated by the criteria taken together (reflecting 'dominance' in terms of all the criteria).[18] But the partial ordering would still reflect a descript-

---

assessment of facts, as indeed they very often do. The statement is about the *nature* of the exercise, viz. that it is concerned with assessment of facts, and not about the way it is typically performed and the psychology that lies behind that performance. (The doctor attached to the students' hostel in which I stayed in Calcutta would refuse to diagnose influenza on the powerful ground that 'flu shouldn't be a reason for staying in bed'.) The issue is, in some respects, comparable to that of one's interests influencing one's values; for an important historical analysis of various different aspects of that relationship, see Hirschman (1977).

[17] Smith (1776), pp. 351–2.
[18] Sen (1973a), Chapters 2 and 3.

ive statement rather than a prescriptive one. Indeed, the statement would be rather like saying, 'Nureyev may or may not be a better dancer than Nijinsky, but he dances better than this author, according to contemporary standards', a descriptive statement (and sadly non-controversial).

2.6 A POLICY DEFINITION?

A related issue is worth exploring in this context. The measurement of poverty may be based on certain given standards, but what kind of statements do these standards themselves make? Are they standards of public policy, reflecting either the objectives of actual policy *or* views on what the policy should be? There is little doubt that the standards must have a good deal to do with some broad notions of acceptability, but that is not the same thing as reflecting precise policy objectives—actual *or* recommended. On this subject too a certain amount of confusion seems to exist. For example, the United States President's Commission on Income Maintenance (1969) argued thus for such a 'policy definition' in its well-known report, *Poverty amid Plenty*:

If society believes that people should not be permitted to die of starvation or exposure, then it will define poverty as the lack of minimum food and shelter necessary to maintain life. If society feels some responsibility for providing to all persons an established measure of well-being beyond mere existence, for example, good physical health, then it will add to its list of necessities the resources required to prevent or cure sickness. At any given time a policy definition reflects a balancing of community capabilities and desires. In low income societies the community finds it impossible to worry much beyond physical survival. Other societies, more able to support their dependent citizens, begin to consider the effects that pauperism will have on the poor and non-poor alike.[19]

There are at least two difficulties with this 'policy definition'. First, practical policy-making depends on a number of influences, going beyond the prevalent notions of what should be done. Policy is a function of political organization, and depends on a variety of factors including the nature of the government, the sources of its power, and the forces exerted by other organizations. In the public policies pursued in many countries, it is, in fact, hard to detect a concern with the elimination of deprivation in any obvious sense. If interpreted in terms of actual

[19] US President's Commission on Income Maintenance (1969), p. 8.

policy, the 'policy definition' may fail to catch the political issues in policy-making.

Second, even if 'policy' is taken to stand not for actual public policy, but for policy recommendations widely held in the society in question, there are problems. There is clearly a difference between the notion of 'deprivation' and the idea of what should be eliminated by 'policy'. For one thing, policy recommend-ations must depend on an assessment of feasibilities ('ought implies can'[20]), but to concede that some deprivations cannot be immediately eliminated is not the same thing as conceding that they must not currently be seen as deprivations. (Contrast: 'Look here, old man, you aren't really poor even though you are starving, since it is impossible in the present economic circumst-ances to maintain the income of everyone above the level needed to eliminate starvation.') Adam Smith's notion of subsistence based on 'the commodities which are indispensably necessary for the support of life' and 'what ever the custom of the country renders it indecent' for someone 'to be without' is by no means identical with what is generally accepted as could and should be provided to all as a matter of policy. If in a country suddenly impoverished, say, by war it is agreed generally that the income maintenance programme must be cut down to a lower level of income, would it be right to say that the country does not have any greater poverty since a reduction of incomes has been *matched* by a reduction of the poverty line?

I would submit that the 'policy definiton' is based on a fundamental confusion. It is certainly true that with economic development there are changes in the notion of what counts as deprivation and poverty, and there are changes also in the ideas as to what should be done. But while these two types of changes are interdependent and also intertemporally correlated with each other, neither can be *defined* entirely in terms of the other. Oil-rich Kuwait may be 'more able to support their dependent citizens' with its new prosperity, but the notion of what is poverty may not go up immediately to the corresponding level. Similarly, the war-devastated Netherlands may keep up its standard of what counts as poverty and not scale it down to the level commensurate with its predicament.[21]

[20] Cf. Hare (1963), Chapter 4.
[21] For an account of that predicament, see Stein, Susser, Saenger, and Marolla (1975).

If this approach is accepted, then the measurement of poverty must be seen as an exercise of description assessing the predicament of people in terms of the prevailing standards of necessities. It is primarily a factual rather than an ethical exercise, and the facts relate to what is regarded as deprivation, and not directly to what policies are recommended. The deprivation in question has both absolute and relative aspects (as argued in Sections 2.2 and 2.4 above).

2.7 STANDARDS AND AGGREGATION

This still leaves two issues quite untouched. First, in comparing the poverty of two societies, how can a common standard of necessities be found, since such standards would vary from society to society? There are actually two quite distinct types of exercises in such inter-community comparisons. One is aimed at comparing the extent of deprivation in each community in relation to their respective standards of minimum necessities, and the other is concerned with comparing the predicament of the two communities in terms of some given minimum standard, e.g. that prevalent in one community. There is, indeed, nothing contradictory in asserting both of the following pair of statements:

(1) There is *less* deprivation in community A than in community B in terms of some *common* standard, e.g. the notions of minimum needs prevailing in community A.

(2) There is *more* deprivation in community A than in community B in terms of their *respective* standards of minimum needs, which are a good deal higher in A than in B.[22]

It is rather pointless to dispute which of these two senses is the 'correct' one, since it is quite clear that both types of questions are of interest. The important thing to note is that the two questions are quite distinct from each other.

Second, while the exercise of 'identification' of the poor can be based on a standard of minimum needs, that of 'aggregation' requires some method of combining deprivations of different people into some overall indicator. In the latter exercise some relative scaling of deprivations is necessary. The scope for

---

[22] There is also no necessary contradiction in asserting that community A has less deprivation in terms of one community's standards (e.g. A's itself), while community B is less deprived in terms of another community's standards (e.g. B's).

arbitrariness in this is much greater, since conventions on this are less firmly established and the constraints of acceptability would tend to leave one with a good deal of freedom. The problem is somewhat comparable with the criteria for making *aggregative descriptive statements* in such fields as, say, comparisons of sporting achievements of different groups. While it is clear that certain circumstances would permit one to make an aggregative statement like 'Africans are better at sprint than Indians' (e.g. the circumstance in which the former group keeps winning virtually all sprint events over the Indians), and other circumstances would force one to deny this, there are intermediate cases in which either of the two aggregative descriptive statements would be clearly disputable.

In this context of arbitrariness of 'aggregate description', it becomes particularly tempting to redefine the problem as an 'ethical' exercise, as has indeed been done in the measurement of economic inequality.[23] But the ethical exercises involve exactly similar ambiguities, and furthermore end up answering a different question from the descriptive one that was originally asked.[24] There is very little alternative to accepting the element of arbitrariness in the description of poverty, and making that element as clear as possible. Since the notion of the poverty of a nation has some inherent ambiguities, one should not have expected anything else.

2.8 CONCLUDING REMARKS

Poverty is, of course, a matter of deprivation. The recent shift in focus—especially in the sociological literature—from *absolute* to *relative* deprivation has provided a useful framework of analysis (Section 2.4). But relative deprivation is essentially incomplete as an approach to poverty, and supplements (but cannot supplant) the earlier approach of absolute dispossession. The much maligned biological approach, which deserves substantial reformulation but not rejection, relates to this irreducible core of absolute deprivation, keeping issues of starvation and hunger at the centre of the concept of poverty (Sections 2.2 and 2.4).

To view poverty as an issue in inequality, as is often recommended, seems to do little justice to either concept.

[23] See Dalton (1920), Kolm (1969), and Atkinson (1970).
[24] See Bentzel (1970), Hansson (1977), and Sen (1978b).

Poverty and inequality relate closely to each other, but they are distinct concepts and neither subsumes the other (Section 2.3).

There is a good case for viewing the measurement of poverty not, as is often asserted, as an ethical exercise, but primarily as a descriptive one (Section 2.5). Furthermore, it can be argued that the frequently used 'policy definition' of poverty is fundamentally flawed (Section 2.6). The exercise of describing the predicament of the poor in terms of the prevailing standards of 'necessities' does, of course, involve ambiguities, which are inherent in the concept of poverty; but ambiguous description isn't the same thing as prescription.[25] Instead, the arbitrariness that is inescapable in choosing between permissible procedures and possible interpretations of prevailing standards requires recognition and appropriate treatment.

[25] The underlying methodological issues have been discussed in Sen (1980a).

Chapter 3

Poverty: Identification and Aggregation

3.1 COMMODITIES AND CHARACTERISTICS

It was argued in the last chapter that the measurement of poverty can be split into two distinct operations, viz. the *identification* of the poor, and the *aggregation* of their poverty characteristics into an over-all measure. The identification exercise is clearly prior to aggregation. The most common route to identification is through specifying a set of 'basic'—or 'minimum'—needs,[1] and regarding the inability to fulfil these needs as the test of poverty. It was claimed in the last chapter that considerations of relative deprivation are relevant in specifying the 'basic' needs, but attempts to make relative deprivation the *sole* basis of such specification is doomed to failure since there is an irreducible core of absolute deprivation in the concept of poverty. Within the general perspective that was presented in the last chapter, some detailed—and more technical—issues are taken up in this chapter before moving from identification to aggregation.

Are the basic needs involved in identifying poverty better specified in terms of commodities, or in terms of 'characteristics'? Wheat, rice, potatoes, etc., are commodities, while calories, protein, vitamins, etc., are characteristics of these commodities that the consumers seek.[2] If each characteristic could be obtained from only one commodity and no others, then it would be easy to translate the characteristics needs into commodity needs. But this is very often not the case, so that characteristics requirements do not specify commodity requirements. While calories are necessary for survival, neither wheat nor rice is.

[1] The literature on basic needs is vast. For some of the main issues involved, see ILO (1976a, 1976b), Haq (1976), Jolly (1976), Stewart and Streeten (1976), Beckerman (1977), Bhalla (1977), Ghai, Khan, Lee and Alfthan (1977), Streeten (1977), Balogh (1978), Griffin and Khan (1978), Perkins (1978), Singh (1978), and Streeten and Burki (1978). On related issues, see also Adelman and Morris (1973), Chenery, Ahluwalia, Bell, Duloy and Jolly (1974), Morawetz (1977), Reutlinger and Selowsky (1976), Drewnowski (1977), Grant (1978), Chichilnisky (1979), Morris (1979), and Fields (1980).
[2] For analyses of consumer theory in terms of characteristics, see Gorman (1956, 1976), and Lancaster (1966).

The characteristics needs are, in an obvious sense, prior to the needs for commodities, and translation of the former to the latter is possible only under special circumstances. Multiplicity of sources is, however, not uniform. Many commodities provide calories or proteins; rather few commodities provide shelter. Literacy comes almost entirely from elementary schooling, even though there are, in principle, other sources. In many cases, therefore, it is possible to move from characteristics requirements to commodity requirements—broadly defined—with rather little ambiguity. It is for this reason that 'basic' or 'minimum' needs are often specified in terms of a hybrid *vector*—e.g. amounts of calories, proteins, housing, schools, hospital beds—some of the components being pure characteristics while others are un-abashed commodities. While there is some evidence that such mongrelism disconcerts the purist, it is quite economic, and typically does little harm.

An interesting intermediate case arises when a certain charac-teristic can be obtained from several different commodities, but the tastes of the community in question guarantee that the characteristic is obtained from one commodity only. A com-munity may, for example, be wedded to rice, and may not treat the alternative sources of calories (or carbohydrates) as acceptable. A formal way of resolving the issue is to define the characteristic 'calories from rice' as the thing sought by the consumer in question, so that rice and rice alone can satisfy this. This is analytically adequate if a little underhand. But there are also other ways of handling the problem, e.g. the assumption that the group seeks calories as such but treats rice as its only *feasible* source. While these conceptual distinctions may not have much immediate practical importance, they tend to suggest rather different approaches to policy issues involving taste variations.

The role of knowledge accumulation in reforming ideas of feasible diets may in fact be an important part of nutritional planning. The knowledge in question includes both information about nutrition as such and experience of how things taste (once one breaks out of the barrier spotted by the old Guinness ad: 'I have never tasted it because I don't like it').

Dietary habits of a population are not, of course, immutable, but they have remarkable staying power. In making inter-community comparisons of poverty, the contrast between formulating needs in terms of characteristics and formulating needs in terms of commodities may turn out to be significant. For example, the ranking of rural living standards in different states in India changes significantly when the basis of comparison is shifted from command over commodities to command over characteristics such as calories and protein.[3] There is little doubt that ultimately characteristics provide the more relevant basis for specification of basic needs, but the relative inflexibility of taste factors makes the conversion of these basic needs into minimum cost diets a function not merely of prices but also of consumption habits.[4] Explicit account would have to be taken of this issue in completing the identification exercise. This last question is further discussed in the next section.

3.2 THE DIRECT METHOD VERSUS THE INCOME METHOD

In identifying the poor for a given set of 'basic needs', it is possible to use at least two alternative methods.[5] One is simply to check the set of people whose actual consumption baskets happen to leave some basic need unsatisfied. This we may call the 'direct method', and it does not involve the use of any income notion, in particular not that of a poverty-line income. In contrast, in what may be called the 'income method', the first step is to calculate the minimum income π at which all the specified minimum needs are satisfied. The next step is to identify those whose actual incomes fall below that poverty line.

In an obvious sense the direct method is superior to the income method, since the former is not based on particular assumptions of consumption behaviour which may or may not be accurate. Indeed, it could be argued that *only* in the absence of direct information regarding the satisfaction of the specified needs can there be a case for bringing in the intermediary of income, so that the income method is at most a second best.

There is much to be said for such a view, and the income method can indeed be seen as a way of approximating the results

[3] See Sen (1976d) on this general issue, and Rath (1973), Bhattacharya and Chatterjee (1974, 1977), and Sen (1976b), on the underlying empirical studies.

[4] While dietary habits are not easy to change, they do, of course, undergo radical transformation in a situation of extreme hunger, for example in famine conditions. In fact, one of the more common causes of death during a famine is diarrhoea caused by eating unfamiliar food—*and* non-food (see Appendix D below).

[5] The distinction relates closely to Seebohm Rowntree's (1901) contrast between 'primary' and 'secondary' poverty.

of the direct method. However, this is not all there is to the contrast of the two methods. The income method can also be seen as a way of taking note of individual idiosyncrasies without upsetting the notion of poverty based on deprivation. The ascetic who fasts on his expensive bed of nails will be registered as poor under the direct method, but the income method will offer a different judgement in recognition of his level of income, at which typical people in that community would have no difficulty in satisfying the basic nutritional requirements. The income of a person can be seen not merely to be a rough aid to predicting a person's actual consumption, but also as capturing a person's *ability* to meet his minimum needs (whether or not he, in fact, chooses to use that ability).[6]

There is a difficult line to draw here. If one were to look merely for the ability to meet minimum needs without being bothered by tastes, then one would, of course, set up a cost-minimizing programming problem and simply check whether someone's income falls short of that minimum cost solution. Such minimum cost diets are typically very inexpensive but exceedingly dull, and are very often regarded as unacceptable. (In Indira Rajaraman's (1974) pioneering work on poverty in Punjab, in an initial round of optimization, unsuspecting Punjabis were subjected to a deluge of Bengal grams.) Taste factors can be introduced through constraints (as Rajaraman did, and others do), but it is difficult to decide how pervasive and severe these constraints should be. In the extreme case the constraints determine the consumption pattern entirely.

But there is, I believe, a difference in principle between taste constraints that apply broadly to the entire community and those that essentially reflect individual idiosyncrasies. If the poverty-level income can be derived from typical behaviour norms of society, a person with a higher income who is choosing to fast on a bed of nails can, with some legitimacy, be declared to be non-poor. The income method does, therefore, have some merit of its own, aside from its role as a way of approximating what would have been yielded by the direct method had all the detailed consumption data been available.

The 'direct method' and the 'income method' are not, in fact,

---

[6] The income method has close ties with the welfare economics of real income comparisons; see Hicks (1958).

two alternative ways of measuring the same thing, but represent two alternative *conceptions* of poverty. The direct method identifies those whose actual consumption fails to meet the accepted conventions of minimum needs, while the income method is after spotting those who do not have the ability to meet these needs within the behavioural constraints typical in that community. Both concepts are of some interest on their own in diagnosing poverty in a community, and while the latter is a bit more remote in being dependent on the existence of some typical behaviour pattern in the community, it is also a bit more refined in going beyond the observed choices into the notion of ability. A poor person, on this approach, is one whose income is not adequate to meet the specified minimum needs in conformity with the conventional behaviour pattern.[7]

The income method has the advantage of providing a metric of numerical distances from the 'poverty line', in terms of income short-falls. This the 'direct method' does not provide, since it has to be content with pointing out the short-fall of each type of need. On the other hand, the income method is more restrictive in terms of preconditions necessary for the 'identification' exercise. First, if the pattern of consumption behaviour has no uniformity, there will be no specific level of income at which the 'typical' consumer meets his or her minimum needs. Second, if prices facing different groups of people differ, e.g. between social classes or income groups or localities, then the poverty line will be group-specific, even when uniform norms and uniform consumption habits are considered.[8] These are real difficulties and cannot be wished away. That the assumption of a uniform poverty line for a given society distorts reality seems reasonably certain. What is much less clear, however, is the *extent* to which reality is thus distorted, and the seriousness of the distortion for the purposes for which the poverty measures may be used.

3.3 FAMILY SIZE AND EQUIVALENT ADULTS

Another difficulty arises from the fact that the family rather than the individual is the natural unit as far as consumption behaviour

---

[7] The income method is based on *two* distinct sets of conventions, viz. (1) those used to identify the minimum needs, and (2) those used to specify behaviour and taste constraints.

[8] For evidence of sharp differences in income-group-specific price deflators in India, see Bardhan (1973), Vaidyanathan (1974) and Radhakrishna and Sarma (1975), among others. See also Osmani (1978).

is concerned. In calculating the income necessary for meeting the minimum needs of families of different size, some method of correspondence of family income with individual income is needed. While the simplest method of doing this is to divide the family income by the number of family members, this overlooks the economies of large scale that operate for many items of consumption, and also the fact that the children's needs may be quite different from those of adults. To cope with these issues, the common practice for both poverty estimation and social security operations is to convert each family into a certain number of 'equivalent adults' by the use of some 'equivalence scale', or, alternatively, to convert the families into 'equivalent households'.[9]

There tends to be a lot of arbitrariness in any such conversion. Much depends on the exact consumption pattern of the people involved, which varies from family to family and with age composition. Indeed, both the minimum needs of children as well as variations of consumption behaviour of families with variations of the number and age composition of children are complex fields for empirical investigation. The question of maldistribution *within* the family is also an important issue requiring a good deal more attention than it has received so far.

There are also different bases for deriving appropriate equivalence of needs.[10] One approach is to take the nutritional requirements for each age group separately and then to take the ratios of their costs, given established patterns of consumer behaviour. .The acceptability of this approach depends not merely on the validity of the nutritional standards used, but also on the assumption that family behaviour displays the same concern for fulfilling the respective nutritional requirements of members of different age groups in the family.[11] It also ignores economies of scale in consumption which seem to exist even for such items as food.

A second approach is to examine how the people involved regard the equivalence question themselves, viz. how much extra

[9] See Orshansky (1965), Abel-Smith and Townsend (1965), and Atkinson (1969), among others. See also Fields (1980).

[10] For an illuminating account of these methods and their underlying logic, see Deaton and Muellbauer (1980).

[11] Another important variable is the work load, including that of the children, which too can be high in many poor economies; see Hansen (1969) and Hamilton (1975).

income they think is needed to make a larger family have the same standard of well-being as a smaller one. Empirical studies of these 'views' (e.g., Goedhart, Halberstadt, Kapteyn, and van Praag, 1977) have shown considerable regularities and consistency.

A third way is to examine the actual consumption behaviour of families of different size and to treat some aspect of this behaviour as an indicator of welfare. For example, the fraction spent on food has been treated as an indicator of poverty: two families of different size are regarded as having 'equivalent' incomes when they spend the same proportion of their incomes on food.[12]

No matter how these equivalent scales are drawn up, there remains the further issue of the weighting of families of different size. Three alternative approaches may be considered: (1) put the same weight on each *household*, irrespective of size; (2) put the same weight on each *person*, irrespective of the size of the family to whom they belong; and (3) put a weight on each *family* equal to the number of equivalent adults in it.

The first method is clearly unsatisfactory since the poverty and suffering of a large family is, in an obvious sense, greater than that of a small family at a poverty level judged to be equivalent to that of the former. The third alternative might look like a nice compromise, but is, I believe, based on a confusion. The scale of 'equivalent adults' indicates conversion factors to be used to find out how well off members of that family are, but ultimately we are concerned with the sufferings of *everyone* in the family and not of a hypothetical equivalent number. If two can live as cheaply as one and a half and three as cheaply as two, these facts must be taken into account in comparing the relative well-beings of two-member and three-member families; but there is no reason why the suffering of two three-member families should receive any less weight than that of three two-member families at the same level of illfare. There is, thus, a good case for using procedure (2), after the level of well-being or poverty of each person has been ascertained by the use of equivalent scales taking note of the size and composition of the families to which they belong.

[12] See Muellbauer (1977b) and Deaton and Muellbauer (1980), Chapter 8. The method goes back to Engel (1895). On this approach and others addressed to the problem of comparing well-beings of households, see Friedman (1952), Brown (1954), Prais and Houthakker (1955), Barten (1964), Theil (1967), Nicholson (1976), Muellbauer (1977a), Deaton and Muellbauer (1980), Fields (1980), Kakwani (1980a), and Marris and Theil (1980).

3.4 POVERTY GAPS AND RELATIVE DEPRIVATION

The income short-fall of a person whose income is less than the poverty-line income can be called his 'income gap'. In the aggregate assessment of poverty, these income gaps must be taken into account. But does it make a difference whether or not a person's short-fall is unusually large compared with those of others? It seems reasonable to argue that any person's poverty cannot really be independent of how poor the others are.[13] Even with exactly the same absolute short-fall, a person may be thought to be 'poorer' if the other poor have short-falls smaller than his, in contrast with the case in which his short-fall is less than that of others. Quantification of poverty would, thus, seem to need the marrying of considerations of absolute and relative deprivation even *after* a set of minimum needs and a poverty line have been fixed.

The question of relative deprivation can be viewed also in the context of a possible transfer of a unit of income from a poor person—call him 1—to another—christened 2—who is richer but still below the poverty line and remains so even after the transfer. Such a transfer will increase the absolute short-fall of the first person by exactly the same amount by which the absolute short-fall of person 2 will be reduced. Can one then argue that the over-all poverty is unaffected by the transfer? One can dispute this, of course, by bringing in some notion of diminishing marginal utility of income, so that the utility loss of the first may be argued to be greater than the utility gain of the second. But such cardinal utility comparisons for different persons involves the use of a rather demanding informational structure with well-known difficulties. In the absence of cardinal comparisons of marginal utility gains and losses, is it then impossible to hold that the overall poverty of the community has increased? I would argue that this is not the case.

Person 1 is relatively deprived compared with 2 (and there may be others in between the two who are more deprived than 2 but less so than 1). When a unit of income is transferred from 1 to 2, it increases the absolute short-fall of a *more* deprived person and reduces that of someone *less* deprived, so that in a straightforward

[13] Cf. Scitovsky (1976) and Hirsch (1976). See also Hirschman and Rothschild (1973).

sense the over-all relative deprivation is increased.[14] And this is
the case quite irrespective of whether absolute deprivation is
measured by income short-falls, or—taking utility to be an
increasing function of income—by utility short-falls, from the
break-even poverty line. One does not, therefore, have to
introduce an interpersonally comparable *cardinal* welfare scale to
be able to say that the transfer specified will increase the extent of
relative deprivation.

In the 'aggregation' exercise the magnitudes of absolute
deprivation may have to be supplemented by considerations of
relative deprivation. Before this exercise is studied, it will be
useful to review the standard measures of poverty used in the
literature and to examine their shortcomings.

3.5 CRITIQUE OF STANDARD MEASURES

The commonest measure of over-all poverty, already discussed in
Chapter 2, is the head-count measure H, given by the proportion
of the total population that happens to be identified as poor, e.g.
as falling below the specified poverty-line income. If q is the
number of people who are identified as being poor and n the total
number of people in the community, then the head-count
measure H is simply q/n.

This index has been widely used—explicitly or by im-
plication—ever since quantitative study and measurement of
poverty began (see Booth, 1889; Rowntree, 1901). It seems to be
still the mainstay of poverty statistics on which poverty programmes are based (see Orshansky, 1965, 1966; Abel-Smith and
Townsend, 1965). It has been extensively utilized recently both
for intertemporal comparisons as well as for international
contrasts.[15]

Another measure that has had a fair amount of currency is the

[14] A complex problem arises when the transfer makes person 2 cross the poverty line—
a possibility that has been deliberately excluded in the postulated case. This case involves
a reduction in one of the main parameters of poverty, viz. the identification of the poor,
and while there is an arbitrariness in attaching a lot of importance to whether a person
actually crosses the poverty line, this is an arbitrariness that is implicit in the concept of
poverty itself based on the use of a break-even line. The question is investigated further in
Section C. 3, pp. 192–4.

[15] See, for example, the lively debate on the time trend of Indian poverty: Ojha (1970),
Dandekar and Rath (1971), Minhas (1970, 1971), Bardhan (1970, 1971, 1973),
Mukherjee, Bhattacharya and Chatterjee (1972), Bhatty (1974), Kumar (1974),
Vaidyanathan (1974), Lal (1976), Ahluwalia (1978), and Dutta (1978). For inter-
national comparisons, see Chenery, Ahluwalia, Bell, Duloy and Jolly (1974).

so-called 'poverty gap', which is the aggregate short-fall of income of all the poor from the specified poverty line.[16] The index can be normalized by being expressed as the percentage short-fall of the average income of the poor from the poverty line. This measure—denoted *I*—will be called the 'income-gap ratio'.

The income-gap ratio *I* is completely insensitive to transfers of income among the poor so long as nobody crosses the poverty line by such transfers. It also pays no attention whatever to the number or proportion of poor people below the poverty line, concentrating only on the aggregate short-fall, no matter how it is distributed and among how many. These are damaging limitations.[17]

The head-count measure *H* is, of course, not insensitive to the number below the poverty line; indeed, for a given society it is the only thing to which *H* is sensitive. But *H* pays no attention whatever to the extent of income short-fall of those who lie below the poverty line. It matters not at all whether someone is just below the line or very far from it, in acute misery and hunger.

Furthermore, a transfer of income from a poor person to one who is richer can never increase the poverty measure *H*—surely a perverse feature. The poor person from whom the transfer takes place is, in any case, counted in the value of *H*, and no reduction of his income will make him count any more than he does already. On the other hand, the person who *receives* the income transfer cannot, of course, move below the poverty line as a consequence of this. *Either* he was rich and stays so or was poor and stays so, in both of which cases the *H* measure remains unaffected; *or* he was below the line but is pulled above it by the transfer, and this makes the measure *H* fall rather than rise. So a transfer from a poor person to one who is richer can *never* increase poverty as represented by *H*.

There are, thus, good grounds for rejecting the standard poverty measures in terms of which most of the analyses and debates on poverty have traditionally taken place. The head-count measure in particular has commanded implicit support of a kind that is quite astonishing. Consider A. L. Bowley's (1923) famous assertion: 'There is, perhaps, no better test of the progress

[16] The poverty gap has been used by the US Social Security Administration; see Batchelder (1971). See also Kakwani (1978) and Beckerman (1979a, 1979b).
[17] The underlying issues have been discussed in Sen (1973b, 1976a). See also Fields (1980).

of the nation than that which shows what proportion are in poverty' (p. 214). The spirit of the remark is acceptable enough, but surely not the gratuitous identification of poverty with the head-count measure H.

What about a combination of these poverty measures? The head-count measure H ignores the extent of income short-falls, while the income-gap ratio I ignores the numbers involved: why not a combination of the two? This is, alas, still inadequate. If a unit of income is transferred from a person below the poverty line to someone who is richer but who still is (and remains) below the poverty line, then both the measures H and I will remain completely unaffected. Hence any 'combined' measure based only on these two must also show no response whatsoever to such a change, despite the obvious increase in aggregate poverty as a consequence of this transfer in terms of relative deprivation.

There is, however, a special case in which a combination of H and I might just about be adequate. Note that, while individually H is insensitive to the extent of income short-falls and I to the numbers involved, we could criticize the *combination* of the two only for their insensitivity to variations of distribution of income among the poor. If we were, then, to confine ourselves to cases in which all the poor have precisely the same income, it may be reasonable to expect that H and I together may do the job. Transfers of the kind that have been considered above to show the insensitivity of the combination of H and I will not then be in the domain of our discourse.

The interest of the special case in which all the poor have the same income does not arise from its being a very likely occurrence. Its value lies in clarifying the way absolute deprivation *vis-à-vis* the poverty line may be handled when there isn't the additional feature of relative deprivation *among* the poor.[18] It helps us to formulate a condition that the required poverty measure P should satisfy when the problem of distribution among the poor is assumed away by postulating equality. It provides *one* regularity condition to be satisfied among others.

[18] As was discussed in Section 2.1, the question of relative deprivation *vis-à-vis* the rest of the community is involved also in the fixing of minimum needs on which the choice of the poverty line is based, so that the estimation of 'absolute' deprivation *vis-à-vis* the poverty line involves implicitly some considerations of *relative* deprivation as well. The reference in the text here is to issues of relative deprivation that remain even after the poverty line has been drawn, since there is the further question of one's deprivation compared with others who are also deprived.

3.6 AXIOMATIC DERIVATION OF A POVERTY MEASURE AND VARIANTS

We may require the poverty measure P to be a weighted sum of the short-falls of all people who are judged to be poor. This is done in a very general way with weights that can be functions of other variables. If we wished to base the poverty measure on some quantification of the sum-total loss of utility arising from the penury of the poor, then the weights should be derived from the familiar utilitarian considerations. If, additionally, it is assumed that the utility of each person depends only on his own income, then the weight on each person's income gap will depend only on the income of that person, and not also on the incomes of others. This will provide a 'separable' structure, each person's component of the overall poverty being derived without reference to the conditions of the others. But this use of the traditional utilitarian model will miss the idea of relative deprivation, which—as we have already argued—is rather central to the notion of poverty. Furthermore, there are difficulties with such cardinal comparisons of utility gains and losses, and even if these were ignored, it is no easy matter to secure agreement on using one particular utility function among so many that can be postulated, all satisfying the usual regularity conditions (such as diminishing marginal utility).

Instead, the concentration can be precisely on aspects of relative deprivation. Let $r(i)$ be the rank of person i in the ordering of all the poor in the decreasing order of income; e.g. $r(i) = 12$ if i is the twelfth worst off among the poor. If more than one person has the same income, they can be ranked in any arbitrary order: the poverty measure must be such that it should not matter which particular arbitrary order is chosen among those with the same income. Clearly, the poorest poor has the largest rank value q, when there are q people altogether on this side of the poverty line, while the least poor has the rank value of *1*. The greater the rank value, the more the person is deprived in terms of relative deprivation with respect to others in the same category.[19] It is, thus, reasonable to argue that a poverty measure capturing this aspect of relative deprivation must make the weight on a person's income short-fall increase with his rank value $r(i)$.

[19] Cf. Runciman (1966) and Townsend (1971).

A rather distinguished and simple case of such a relationship is to make the weight on any person i's income gap equal the rank value $r(i)$. This makes the weights equidistanced, and the procedure is in the same spirit as Borda's (1781) famous argument for the rank-order method of voting, choosing equal distances in the absence of a convincing case for any alternative assumption. While this too is arbitrary, it captures the notion of relative deprivation in a simple way, and leads to a transparent procedure, making it quite clear what precisely is being assumed.[20]

This axiom of 'Ranked Relative Deprivation' (axiom R) focuses on the distribution of income among the poor, and may be combined with the kind of information that is presented by the head-count measure H and the income-gap ratio I in the special case in which everyone below the poverty line has the same income (so that there is no distribution problem among the poor). H presents the proportion of people who are deprived in relation to the poverty line, and I reflects the proportionate amount of absolute income deprivation *vis-a-vis* that line. It can be argued that H catches one aspect of overall deprivation, viz. how many (never mind how much), while I catches another aspect of it, viz. how much on the average (never mind suffered by how many). In the special case when all the poor have the same income, H and I together may give us a fairly good idea of the extent of poverty in terms of over-all deprivation. Since the problem of relative distribution among the poor does not arise in this special case, we may settle for a measure that boils down to some function of only H and I under these circumstances. A simple representation of this, leading to a convenient normalization, is the product HI. This may be called the axiom of 'Normalized Absolute Deprivation' (axiom A).[21]

If these two axioms are imposed on a quite general format of

---

[20] It is, in fact, possible to derive the characteristic of equidistance from other—more primitive—axioms (see Sen, 1973b, 1974).

[21] It should be remembered that in fixing the poverty line considerations of relative deprivation have already played a part, so that absolute deprivation *vis-à-vis* the poverty line is non-relative only in the limited context of the 'aggregation' exercise. As was discussed earlier, the concepts of absolute and relative deprivation are both relevant to *each* of the two exercises in the measurement of poverty, viz. identification and aggregation. Axioms A and R are each concerned exclusively with the aggregation exercise.

the poverty measure being a weighted sum of income gaps, then a precise measure of poverty emerges (as shown in Sen, 1973b, 1976a). When G is the Gini coefficient of the distribution of income among the poor, this measure is given by $P = H\{I + (1-I)G\}$. The precise axiomatic derivation is discussed in Appendix C. When all the poor have the same income, then the Gini coefficient G of income distribution among the poor equals zero, and P equals HI. Given the same average poverty gap and the same proportion of poor population in total population, the poverty measure P increases with greater inequality of incomes below the poverty line, as measured by the Gini coefficient. Thus, the measure P is a function of H (reflecting the number of poor), I (reflecting the aggregate poverty gap), and G (reflecting the inequality of income distribution below the poverty line). The last captures the aspect of 'relative deprivation', and its inclusion is indeed a direct consequence of the axiom of Ranked Relative Deprivation.

Many interesting empirical applications of this approach to the measurement of poverty have been made,[22] and several variants of it have also been considered in the literature,[23] which will be discussed in Appendix C. While the measure P has certain unique advantages which its axiomatic derivation brings out, several of the variants are certainly permissible interpretations of the common conception of poverty. There is nothing defeatist or astonishing in the acceptance of this 'pluralism'. Indeed, as argued in Chapter 2, such pluralism is inherent in the nature of the exercise. But the important point to recognize is that the assessment of overall poverty has to take note of a variety of considerations capturing different features of absolute and relative deprivation. Such simplistic measures as the commonly used head-count ratio H, or the poverty-gap ratio I, fail to do justice to some of these features. It is necessary to use complex measures such as the index P to make the measurement of

[22] See, for example, Ahluwalia (1978), Alamgir (1976, 1978a), Anand (1977), Bhatty (1974), Clark, Hemming and Ulph (1979), Dutta (1978), Fields (1979), Ginneken (1980), Kakwani (1978, 1980), Osmani (1978), Pantulu (1980), Sastry (1977, 1980), Seastrand and Diwan (1975), Szal (1977), among others.

[23] See Anand (1977), Blackorby and Donaldson (1980a), Clark, Hemming and Ulph (1979), Hamada and Takayama (1978), Kakwani (1978, 1980), Osmani (1978), Pyatt (1980), Szal (1977), Takayama (1979), Thon (1979, 1980), Fields (1980), and Chakravarty (1980a, 1980b), among others.

poverty sensitive to the different features that are implicit in our ideas on poverty. In particular, the question of distribution remains relevant even when incomes *below* the poverty line are considered. It will be necessary to go into this question further in the context of analysing starvation and famines, as is done in the chapters that follow.[24]

[24] The relevance of this aspect of the distributional question is brought out in the empirical studies of starvation and famine (Chapters 6–9), and the general argument is assessed in that light (Chapter 10).

Chapter 4

Starvation and Famines

4.1 FAMINES

Famines imply starvation, but not vice versa. And starvation implies poverty, but not vice versa. The time has come for us to move from the general terrain of poverty to the disastrous phenomenon of famines.

Poverty, as was discussed in Chapter 2, can reflect relative deprivation as opposed to absolute dispossession. It is possible for poverty to exist, and be regarded as acute, even when no serious starvation occurs. Starvation, on the other hand, does imply poverty, since the absolute dispossession that characterizes starvation is more than sufficient to be diagnosed as poverty, no matter what story emerges from the view of *relative* deprivation.

Starvation is a normal feature in many parts of the world, but this phenomenon of 'regular' starvation has to be distinguished from violent outbursts of famines. It isn't just regular starvation that one sees in 436 BC, when thousands of starving Romans 'threw themselves into the Tiber'; or in Kashmir in AD 918, when 'one could scarcely see the water of Vitasta [Jhelum] entirely covered as the river was with corpses'; or in 1333–7 in China, when—we are told—four million people died in one region only; or in 1770 in India, when the best estimates point to ten million deaths; or in 1845–51 in Ireland, when the potato famine killed about one-fifth of the total Irish population and led to the emigration of a comparable number.[1] While there is quite a literature on how to 'define' famines,[2] one can very often

[1] For some absorbing accounts of the phenomenon of famines in different parts of the world and some comparative analysis, see Mallory (1926), Ghosh (1944), Woodham-Smith (1962), Masefield (1963), Stephens (1966), Bhatia (1967), Blix, Hofvander and Vahlquist (1971), Johnson (1973), Aykroyd (1974), Hussein (1976), Tudge (1977), and Alamgir (1978b, 1980), among a good many other studies. Early accounts of famines in the Indian subcontinent can be found in Kautilya (*circa* 320 BC) and Abul Fazl (1592), among other documents.

[2] A few of the many definitions: 'On balance it seems clear that any satisfactory definition of famine must provide that the food shortage is either widespread or extreme if not both, and that the degree of extremity is best measured by human mortality from starvation' (Masefield, 1963, pp. 3–4). 'An extreme and protracted shortage of food

diagnose it—like a flood or a fire—even without being armed with a precise definition.[3]

In distinguishing between starvation and famine, it is not my intention here to attribute a sense of deliberate harming to the first absent in the second, as intended by the Irish American Malone in Bernard Shaw's *Man and Superman*:

Malone: Me father died of starvation in the black 47. Maybe you've heard of it?
Violet: The Famine?
Malone: No, the starvation. When a country is full o food and exporting it, there can be no famine. Me father was starved dead; and I was starved out to America in me mother's arms.[4]

The history of famines as well as of regular hunger is full of blood-boiling tales of callousness and malevolence—and I shall have something to say on this—but the distinction between starvation and famine used in this work does not relate to this. Starvation is used here in the wider sense of people going without adequate food, while famine is a particularly virulent manifestation of its causing widespread death; that is, I intend to use the two words in their most common English sense.[5]

4.2 THE TIME CONTRAST

In analysing starvation in general, it is important to make clear distinctions between three different issues. (1) *lowness of the typical level* of food consumption; (2) *declining trend* of food consumption;

resulting in widespread and persistent hunger, evidenced by loss of body weight and emaciation and increase in the death rate caused either by starvation or disease resulting from the weakened condition of the population' (Johnson, 1973, p. 58). 'In statistical term, it can be defined as a severe shortage of food accompanied by a significant increase in the local or regional death rate' (Mayer, 1975). 'Famine is an economic and social phenomenon characterised by the widespread lack of food resources which, in the absence of outside aid, leads to death of those affected' (UNRISD, 1975). I hope the reader has got the point.

[3] The definitional exercise is more interesting in providing a pithy description of what happens in situations clearly diagnosed as one of famine than in helping us to do the diagnosis—the traditional function of a definition. For example, Gale Johnson's (1973) pointer to disease in addition to starvation directs our attention to an exceptionally important aspect of famines (see Chapter 8 and Appendix D below). See also Morris (1974).

[4] G. Bernard Shaw, *Man and Superman*, Penguin, Harmondsworth, 1946, p. 196.

[5] The meaning of 'starve' as 'to cause to die, to kill, destroy' is described by *The Shorter Oxford English Dictionary* as 'obsolete' (with its latest recorded use being placed in 1707), but—of course—the meaning 'to cause to perish of hunger' or 'to keep scantily supplied with food' survives, and—alas—has much descriptive usage in the modern world.

and (3) *sudden collapse* of the level of food consumption. Famine is chiefly a problem of the third kind, and while it can—obviously—be helped by the first two features, it often does not work that way.

For example, in dealing with the trend of foodgrains availability in India in this century, S. R. Sen (1971) notes the following dichotomy between the trend of the moving average and the level of the minimal values (pp. 2–3):

A study of these data shows that during the first 24 years of the century foodgrains production increased at an average annual rate of 0.81 per cent per annum on the average, the trough points showed a declining trend of 0.14 per cent per annum on the average and there was a growing divergence. Thus, while the foodgrains production showed a rising trend, the instability was also on the increase. . . . The next 24 years, however, presented a completely different picture. During this period, foodgrains production showed a declining trend of 0.02 per cent per annum on the average, in spite of the fact that droughts turned out to be relatively moderate and less frequent. In contrast with the previous period, while the peak points reached showed a declining trend of 0.04 per cent, the trough points recorded a rising trend of 0.10 per cent per annum on the average and the two were converging.

A similar contrast has been suggested for Japan in comparing food consumption in the Meiji period with that in the Tokugawa period by Nakamura (1966).[6] He argues:

In fact food consumption picture of the Tokugawa period (and earlier) is that of periodic food shortages and famine owing to the high incidence of natural calamities. In view of this, it is even possible that the Japanese *ate more regularly but consumed less food on the average* in the later Meiji era than they did in late Tokugawa before food imports became available to relieve shortages.[7]

There is, of course, nothing in the least bit surprising about a rising trend being accompanied by bigger fluctuations, or a falling trend going with greater stability.[8] Even more obvious is

---

[6] The underlying empirical generalisation about trends of food availability has been, however, the subject of some controversy. See also Ohkawa (1957) and Ohkawa and Rosovsky (1973).

[7] Nakamura (1966), p. 100; italics added. See also a similar contrast in Eric Hobsbawm's analysis of the British standard of living during 1790–1850 (Hobsbawm, 1957, especially p. 46).

[8] The empirical issue as to whether the quoted views of the Indian or Japanese economic history are correct is, of course, a different question.

the fact that a rising trend need not *eliminate* big fluctuations. Indeed, there are good reasons to think that the trend of food availability per head in recent years has been a rising one in most parts of the world,[9] but nevertheless acute starvation has occurred quite often, and there is some evidence of intensification of famine threats.[10] While this is partly a problem of distribution of food between different groups in a nation—an issue to which I shall turn presently—there is also the time contrast (in particular, the problem of sharp falls against a generally rising trend). Famines can strike even when regular starvation is on firm decline.

The food crisis of 1972 is a global example of this time contrast. Colin Tudge (1977) describes the development in dramatic terms:

The 1960s brought good harvests, augmented by the Third World's 'green revolution', based on American-developed dwarf strains of wheat and rice. The world's food problem was not shortage, apparently, but over-production, leading to low prices and agricultural depression. The US took land out of production, and in the early 1970s both the US and Canada ran down their grain stores. Then the bad weather of 1972 brought dismal harvests to the USSR, China, India, Australia and the Sahel countries south of Sahara. Russia bought massively in the world grain markets before others, including the US, realized what was happening. By mid-1974 there was only enough grain left in store to feed the world's population for three-and-a-half weeks; terrifying brinkmanship.[11]

In all this the focus has been on the *total* availability of food—for the nation as a whole, or even for the world as a whole. But exactly similar contrasts hold for food availability to a particular section of a given community. A sudden collapse of the command of a group over food can go against a rising trend (or against a typically high level of food consumption). Problems of (i) existence of much regular starvation, (ii) worsening trend of regular starvation, and (iii) sudden outbreak of acute starvation, are quite distinct. While they can accompany each other, they need not, and often do not, do so.

[9] See FAO (1979). See also Aziz (1975), p. 116, Table 2; and Sinha (1976a), p. 6, Table 1.
[10] See Blix, Hofvander and Vahlquist (1971); UNRISD (1975, 1978); Aziz (1975); and Tudge (1977)
[11] Tudge (1977), p. 2.

4.3 THE GROUP CONTRAST

While famines involve fairly widespread acute starvation, there is
no reason to think that it will affect all groups in the famine-
affected nation. Indeed, it is by no means clear that there has ever
occurred a famine in which all groups in a country have suffered
from starvation, since different groups typically do have very
different commanding powers over food, and an over-all shortage
brings out the contrasting powers in stark clarity.

There has been some speculation as to whether such a
comprehensive famine was not observed in India in 1344–5 (see
Walford 1878, and Alamgir 1980, p. 14). There is indeed some
evidence for this famine being a very widespread one. In fact, the
authoritative *Encyclopaedia Britannica* saw the famine as one in
which even 'the Mogul emperor was unable to obtain the
necessaries for his household' (Eleventh Edition, 1910–1, vol. X,
p. 167). This is most unlikely since the Mogul empire was not
established in India until 1526! But it is also doubtful that the
Tughlak king then in power—Mohammad Bin Tughlak—was
really unable to obtain his household necessities, since he had the
resources to organize one of the most illustrous famine relief
programmes, including remitting taxes, distributing cash, and
opening relief centres for the distribution of cooked food (see
Loveday, 1916). One has to be careful about anecdotal history,
just as a companion volume of the same Encyclopaedia points
out: 'the idea that Alfred, during his retreat at Athenley, was a
helpless fugitive rests upon the foolish legend of the cakes'. This is,
however, not to deny that some famines are much more
widespread than others, and Alamgir is certainly right that the
Dutch famine during 1944 was very widely shared by the Dutch
population.[12]

The importance of inter-group distributional issues rests not
merely in the fact that an over-all shortage may be very
unequally shared by different groups,[13] but also in the recognition that some groups can suffer acute absolute deprivation

[12] See Aykroyd (1974), Chapter 10, and Stein, Susser, Saenger and Marolla (1975).
[13] One contrast that has received much professional attention recently is that between
urban and rural population (see particularly Lipton, 1977). This contrast is indeed
relevant to conflicts implicit in some famines (see for example Chapter 6 below), but there
are other, more specialized, group conflicts which deserve more attention (some of these
contrasts are taken up in Chapters 6, 7, 8, and 9).

even when there is no over-all shortage. There is no reason whatsoever to think that the food consumption of different groups must vary in the same *direction* (even if by different proportions and amounts), and in later chapters cases will be encountered in which different groups' fortunes moved sharply in opposite directions.

Chapter 5

The Entitlement Approach

5.1 ENDOWMENT AND EXCHANGE

The entitlement approach to starvation and famines concentrates on the ability of people to command food through the legal means available in the society, including the use of production possibilities, trade opportunities, entitlements *vis-à-vis* the state, and other methods of acquiring food. A person starves *either* because he does not have the ability to command enough food, *or* because he does not use this ability to avoid starvation. The entitlement approach concentrates on the former, ignoring the latter possibility. Furthermore, it concentrates on those means of commanding food that are legitimized by the legal system in operation in that society. While it is an approach of some generality, it makes no attempt to include all possible influences that can in principle cause starvation, for example illegal tranfers (e.g. looting), and choice failures (e.g. owing to inflexible food habits).

Ownership of food is one of the most primitive property rights, and in each society there are rules governing this right. The entitlement approach concentrates on each person's entitlements to commodity bundles including food, and views starvation as resulting from a failure to be entitled to a bundle with enough food.

In a fully directed economy, each person i may simply get a particular commodity bundle which is assigned to him. To a limited extent this happens in most economies, e.g. to residents of old people's homes or of mental hospitals. Typically, however, there is a menu—possibly wide—to choose from. E_i is the entitlement set of person i in a given society, in a given situation, and it consists of a set of alternative commodity bundles, any one of which the person can decide to have. In an economy with private ownership and exchange in the form of trade (exchange with others) and production (exchange with nature), E_i can be characterized as depending on two parameters, viz. the *endowment* of the person (the ownership bundle) and the *exchange entitlement mapping* (the function that specifies the set of alternative commodity bundles that the person can command respectively for each endowment bundle).[1] For example, a peasant has his land, labour power, and a few other resources, which together make up his endowment. Starting from that endowment he can produce a bundle of food that will be his. Or, by selling his labour power, he can get a wage and with that buy commodities, including food. Or he can grow some cash crops and sell them to buy food and other commodities. There are many other possibilities. The set of all such available commodity bundles in a given economic situation is the exchange entitlement of his endowment. The exchange entitlement *mapping* specifies the exchange entitlement set of alternative commodity bundles respectively for each endowment bundle. The formal relations are analysed in Appendix A.

The exchange entitlement mapping, or E-mapping for short, will depend on the legal, political, economic and social characteristics of the society in question and the person's position in it. Perhaps the simplest case in terms of traditional economic theory is one in which the endowment bundle can be exchanged in the market at fixed relative prices for any bundle costing no more, and here the exchange entitlement will be a traditional 'budget set'.

Bringing in production will make the E-mapping depend on production opportunities as well as trade possibilities of resources and products. It will also involve legal rights to apportioning the product, e.g. the capitalist rule of the 'entrepreneur' owning the produce. Sometimes the social conventions governing these rights can be very complex indeed—for example those governing the rights of migrant members of peasant families to a share of the peasant output (see Sen, 1975).

Social security provisions are also reflected in the E-mapping, such as the right to unemployment benefit if one fails to find a job, or the right to income supplementation if one's income would fall otherwise below a certain specified level. And so are employment guarantees when they exist—as they do in some socialist economies—giving one the option to sell one's labour power to the government at a minimum price. E-mappings will depend also on provisions of taxation.

[1] Formally, an exchange entitlement mapping $E_i(.)$ transforms an endowment vector of commodities $\mathbf{x}$ into a set of alternative availability vectors of commodities $E_i(\mathbf{x})$.

Let the set of commodity bundles, each of which satisfies person i's minimum food requirement, be F_i. Person i will be forced to starve because of unfavourable entitlement relations if and only if he is not entitled to any member of F_i given his endowment and his exchange entitlement mapping. The 'starvation set' S_i of endowments consists of those endowment bundles such that the exchange entitlement sets corresponding to them contain no bundles satisfying his minimum food requirements.[2]

5.2 STARVATION AND ENTITLEMENT FAILURES

Person i can be plunged into starvation if his endowment collapses into the starvation set S_i either through a fall in the endowment bundle, or through an unfavourable shift in the exchange entitlement mapping. The distinction is illustrated in Figure 5.1 in terms of the simple case of pure trade involving only two commodities, food and non-food. The exchange entitlement mapping is taken to assume the simple form of constant price exchange. With a price ratio p and a minimum food requirement OA, the starvation set S_i is given by the region OAB. If the endowment vector is $\mathbf{x}$, the person is in a position to avoid starvation. This ability can fail either (1) through a lower endowment vector, e.g. $\mathbf{x}^*$, or (2) through a less favourable exchange entitlement mapping, e.g. that given by p^*, which would make the starvation set OAC.

It is easy to see that starvation can develop for a certain group of people as its endowment vector collapses, and there are indeed many accounts of such endowment declines on the part of sections of the poor rural population in developing countries through alienation of land, sale of livestock, etc. (see, for example, Griffin, 1976, 1978; Feder, 1977; and Griffin and Khan, 1977).[3] Shifts in exchange entitlement mappings are rather less palpable, and more difficult to trace, but starvation can also develop with *unchanged* asset ownership through move-

---

[2] For formalities, see Appendix A. For applications see Chapters 6–10 and Appendix B. See also Sen (1976c, 1977b, 1979c); Griffin (1978); Hay (1978b); Ghosh (1979); Penny (1979); Shukla (1979); Seaman and Holt (1980); and Heyer (1980).

[3] Asset loss affects not merely the ability to exchange the asset directly with food, but also the ability to borrow against one's future earning power. Given the nature of the capital markets, substantial borrowing is typically impossible without tangible securities. The limitations of the capital markets often constitute an important aspect of famine conditions.

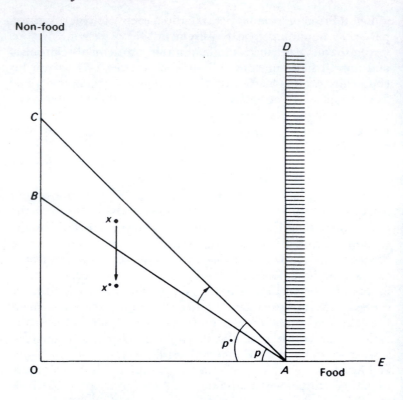

FIG. 5.1 Illustration of Endowment and Entitlement

ments of exchange entitlement mapping.[4] This would be impossible only if the endowment vector itself contained enough food, for example, in figure 5.1, if it belonged to the region *DAE*. The characteristics of commodities in most people's endowment bundles rule out this possibility.

5.3 LIMITATIONS OF THE ENTITLEMENT APPROACH

Before proceeding to the use of the entitlement approach, a few of the limitations may be briefly noted. First, there can be

---

[4] Shifts in E-mapping may arise from different sources, e.g. growth of unemployment, changes in relative prices and terms of trade, variations in social security (see Chapter 1 and Appendix A). For an insightful analysis of the role of terms of trade in economic development, see Mitra (1977).

ambiguities in the specification of entitlements. Even in capitalist market economies, entitlements may not be well defined in the absence of a market-clearing equilibrium,[5] and in pre-capitalist formations there can be a good deal of vagueness on property rights and related matters.[6] In many cases the appropriate characterization of entitlements may pose problems,[7] and in some cases it may well be best characterized in the form of 'fuzzy' sets and related structures— taking precise note of the vagueness involved.[8] In empirical studies of actual famines the question of precision is compromised by data problems as well, and the focus here will be not on characterizing entitlements with pretended exactitude, but on studying shifts in some of the main ingredients of entitlements. Big shifts in such ingredients can be decisive in causing entitlement failures, even when there is some 'fuzziness' in the entitlement relations.

Second, while entitlement relations concentrate on rights within the given legal structure in that society, some transfers involve violation of these rights, such as looting or brigandage. When such extra-entitlement transfers are important, the entitlement approach to famines will be defective. On the other hand, most recent famines seem to have taken place in societies with 'law and order', without anything 'illegal' about the processes leading to starvation. In fact, in guarding ownership rights against the demands of the hungry, the legal forces uphold entitlements; for example, in the Bengal famine of 1943 the people who died in front of well-stocked food shops protected by the state[9] were denied food because of *lack* of legal entitlement, and not because their entitlements were violated.[10]

[5] See Hicks (1939), Debreu (1959), and Arrow and Hahn (1971).

[6] There are also legal and economic ambiguities in an *open* 'black market' (see Dasgupta, 1950).

[7] There is also the critique by Ronald Dworkin (1977) of 'legal positivism', disputing the view of law as a set of 'rules', and emphasizing the role of 'principles, policies, and other sorts of standards' (p. 22), which are, of course, inherently more ambiguous.

[8] A similar problem arises from the ambiguity of values in economic planning, requiring 'range'—rather than 'point'—specification of shadow prices leading to partial orders (see Sen, 1975). Correspondingly here, the possible set of endowment vectors may be partitioned into three subsets, viz. definitely starvation set, definitely non-starvation set, and neither.

[9] See Ghosh (1944) and also Famine Inquiry Commission (1945a).

[10] Cf. 'A concept of law which allows the invalidity of law to be distinguished from its immorality, enables us to see the complexity and variety of these separate issues' (Hart, 1961, p. 207).

Third, people's actual food consumption may fall below their entitlements for a variety of other reasons, such as ignorance, fixed food habits, or apathy.[11] In concentrating on entitlements, something of the total reality is obviously neglected in our approach, and the question is: how important are these ignored elements and how much of a difference is made by this neglect?

Finally, the entitlement approach focuses on starvation, which has to be distinguished from famine mortality, since many of the famine deaths—in some cases *most* of them—are caused by epidemics, which have patterns of their own.[12] The epidemics are, of course, induced partly by starvation but also by other famine characteristics, e.g. population movement, breakdown of sanitary facilities.

5.4 DIRECT AND TRADE ENTITLEMENT FAILURES

Consider occupation group j, characterized as having only commodity j to sell or directly consume. Let q_j be the amount of commodity j each member of group j can sell or consume, and let the price of commodity j be p_j. The price of food per unit is p_f. The maximum food entitlement of group j is F_j, given by $q_j p_j / p_f$, or $q_j a_j$, where a_j is occupation j's *food exchange rate* (p_j/p_f).

Commodity j may or may not be a *produced* commodity. The commodity that a labourer has to sell is labour power. It is his means of survival, just as commodities in the shape of baskets and jute are the means of survival of the basket-maker and the jute-grower, respectively.[13]

A special case arises when the occupation consists of being a producer of food, say rice, which is also what members of that

---

[11] Also, people sometimes choose to starve rather than sell their productive assets (see Jodha, 1975, for some evidence of this in Indian famines), and this issue can be accommodated in the entitlement approach using a relatively long-run formulation (taking note of future entitlements). There is also some tendency for asset markets to collapse in famine situations, making the reward from asset sales rather puny.

[12] See Appendix D for a study of the pattern of mortality in the Great Bengal Famine. See also McAlpin (1976).

[13] In general, it may be necessary to associate several different commodities, rather than one, with the same occupation, but there is not much difficulty in redefining q_j and p_j appropriately.

[14] Given the selective nature of calamities such as floods and droughts, affecting one group but not another, it will be sometimes convenient to partition the occupation f into a number of subgroups (f, i) for famine analysis. With $q_{f,i}$ the food grown by subgroup (f, i), we have: $F_{f,i} = q_{f,i}$.

occupation live on. In this case $p_j = p_f$, and $a_f = 1$. Thus $F_f = q_f$.[14]

It is worth emphasizing that this drastically simple modelling of reality makes sense only in helping us to focus on some important parameters of famine analysis; it does not compete with the more general structure outlined earlier (and more formally in Appendix A). Furthermore, these simplifications will be grossly misleading in some contexts, for example in analysing entitlements in an industrialized economy, because of the importance of raw materials, intermediate products, asset holdings, etc. Even in applying this type of structure to analyse rural famines in developing countries, care is needed that the distortions are not too great.

For any group j to start starving *because of* an entitlement failure, F_j must decline, since it represents the *maximum* food entitlement. F_j can fall either because one has produced less food for own consumption, or because one can obtain less food through trade by exchanging one's commodity for food. The former will be called a 'direct entitlement failure', and the latter a 'trade entitlement failure'. The former can arise for food-producing groups, while the latter can occur for others (i.e. for those who sell their commodities to buy food), because of a fall in a_j, or a fall in q_j. Such a fall in q_j can occur either owing to an autonomous production decline (e.g. a cash crop being destroyed by a drought), or owing to insufficiency of demand (e.g. a labourer being involuntarily unemployed, or a basket-maker cutting down the output as the demand for baskets slackens).

It is, in fact, possible for a group to suffer both direct entitlement failure and trade entitlement failure, since the group may produce a commodity that is both directly consumed and exchanged for some other food. For example, the Ethiopian pastoral nomad both eats the animal products directly and also sells animals to buy foodgrains (thereby making a net gain in calories), on which he is habitually dependent.[15] Similarly, a Bengali fisherman does consume some fish, though for his survival he is dependent on grain-calories which he obtains at a favourable calorie exchange rate by selling fish—a luxury food for most Bengalis.[16]

[15] See Chapter 7.
[16] See Chapter 6.

Chapter 6

The Great Bengal Famine

6.1 A BRIEF OUTLINE

The official Famine Inquiry Commission reporting on the Bengal famine of 1943 put its death toll at 'about 1.5 million'.[1] W. R. Aykroyd, who as a member of the Commission was primarily responsible for the estimation, has said recently: 'I now think it was an under-estimate, especially in that it took little account of roadside deaths, but not as gross an under-estimate as some critics of the Commission's report, who preferred three to four million, declared it to be' (Aykroyd, 1974, p. 77). In fact, it can be shown that the Commission's own method of calculation does lead to a figure around three million deaths, and there will be an occasion to go into this demographic issue in Appendix D. But for the present purpose it does not really matter which of the estimates we accept. Our chief concern here is with the causation of the Bengal famine, and in particular with the role of food supply and that of exchange entitlements in the genesis of the famine.[2]

First, a bit of background. There are three rice crops in Bengal: (1) *aman*, sown in May and June, harvested in November and December (the winter crop); (2) *aus*, sown around April and harvested in August and September (the autumn crop); and (3) *boro*, planted in November and harvested in February and March (the spring crop). The winter crop is by far the most important, and the respective shares of the three crops during the five years 1939–43 were: 73, 24, and 3 per cent. In 1942 the autumn crop was a little less than normal (97 per cent of the preceding four years), and the winter crop quite a bit less (83 per cent of the average preceding four years). This was largely the result of a cyclone in October, followed by torrential rain in some parts of Bengal and a subsequent fungus disease. Further, the Japanese occupation of Burma in 1942—Rangoon fell on 10 March 1942—cut off rice imports from there, which affected the

---

[1] Famine Inquiry Commission, India (1945a), pp. 109–10.
[2] This chapter relies heavily on an earlier paper, viz. Sen (1977b).

supply to Bengal. Since the famine hit Bengal in 1943, it is quite natural, in view of the cyclone, flooding, fungus diseases, the disruption of the war, and the loss of Burma rice, that its primary cause should be seen in 'the serious shortage in the total supply of rice available for consumption in Bengal as compared with the total supply normally available' (Famine Inquiry Commission, India, 1945a, p. 77). This thesis will be examined presently.

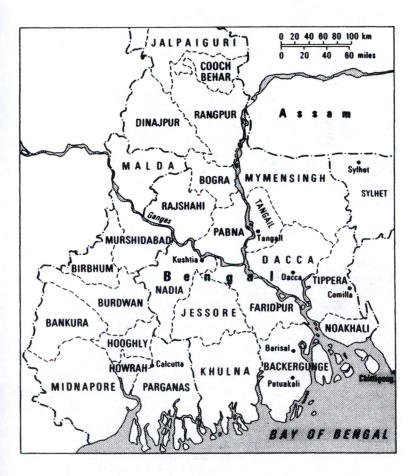

FIG. 6.1 Bengal, 1943

The wholesale price of rice, which had been between Rs. 13 and Rs. 14 per 'maund' (about 82.3 lbs.) on 11 December 1942, rose to Rs. 21 by 12 March 1943 and to above Rs. 30 by 21 May; by 20 August it had risen to Rs. 37 (see Table 6.1). Because of a government order fixing a maximum price, quotations for rice transactions are difficult to obtain from September 1943

TABLE 6.1

*Wholesale Price of Rice in Calcutta, 1942 and 1943
(rupees per maund)*

Date	Ballam no. 1 Price (Rs.)	Index	Kalma no. 1 Price (Rs.)	(mill-cleaned) Index
1941				
19 December	7.00–7.25	100	(not quoted)	
1942				
16 January	6.25–6.50	90	(not quoted)	
20 February	6.13–6.38	88	(not quoted)	
20 March	6.13–6.38	88	(not quoted)	
17 April	6.25	88	(not quoted)	
15 May	6.25–6.38	89	(not quoted)	
19 June	8.00	112	(not quoted)	
31 July	7.75–8.00	111	(not quoted)	
21 August	9.25	130	(not quoted)	
18 September	9.88–10.38	142	(not quoted)	
30 October	9.88–10.38	142	(not quoted)	
13 November	9.25–9.75	133	(not quoted)	
11 December	13.00–14.00	190	(not quoted)	
1943				
15 January	14.00–15.00	204	(not quoted)	
12 February	14.00–15.00	204	(not quoted)	
12 March	21.00	295	(not quoted)	
16 April	(not quoted)		22.00–23.00	306
21 May	30.00–31.00	428	31.00	428
18 June	(not quoted)		32.00–33.00	442
16 July	(not quoted)		32.00–33.00	442
20 August	(not quoted)		37.00	503

Notes
1 The price quotations are taken from the respective numbers of the *Indian Trade Journal*, a weekly publication, for 1942 and 1943.
2 Price data are given in the *Indian Trade Journal* typically either for Ballam no. 1 variety or for Kalma no. 1 variety, and very rarely for both. The index for Ballam no. 1 is constructed by setting the price on 19 December 1941 as 100. Since there is no quotation for Kalma no. 1 at that time, the index value of Kalma is equated to that of Ballam on 21 May 1943, when *both* prices are reported *for the first time* in the period covered. This provides the base for the Kalma index.

onwards, but there are non-official reports of further rises, especially in retail markets, such as in October that rice was being sold in Chittagong at Rs. 80 per maund (see *The Statesman*, 5 November 1943; Bhatia, 1967, p. 323), and in Dacca at Rs. 105 per maund (see Ghosh, 1944, p. 42).

The economic experience of Bengal leading to and during the famine can be split into three phases:

Phase I: from the beginning of 1942 to March 1943;
Phase II: from March 1943 to November 1943;
Phase III: From November 1943 through most of 1944.

The death rate reached its peak only in Phase III, but the most acute period of starvation had by then passed; epidemics were raging in a famine-devastated country. Phase II is when starvation death reached its peak. In contrast, what I am calling Phase I is usually taken to be a period when the famine had not yet begun. In a sense that view is correct, since starvation deaths were still relatively rare, but the economic distress that paved the way for the famine had already gripped a substantial part of the population.

The famine revealed itself first in the districts away from Calcutta, starting early in 1943. Its progress can be watched in the reports of the commissioners and district officers all over the province. Beginning with descriptions of 'hunger marches organized by communists' on 28 December 1942, a selection of the reports include: 'people having to go without food' (10 February); 'indications of distress among local people' (27 February); 'acute distress prevails' (26 March); 'crime against property increasing and paddy looting cases have become frequent' (28 March); 'major economic catastrophe apprehended' (27 April); 'economic conditions approach a crisis' (13 May); 'bands of people moving about in search of rice' (12 June); 'deaths in streets' (12 June); 'town filled with thousands of beggars who are starving' (17 July); 'passing through the most acute stage of distress' (10 August); 'deaths still occurring' (9 September); 'disposal of dead bodies . . . a problem' (27 September); 'supplies arriving but no hope of saving those who are starving' (25 October).[3] Mortality reached its peak only in December 1943 and stayed up for quite a while longer, but this was mostly the result of famine-induced epidemics, e.g. of

[3] See Famine Inquiry Commission (1945a), Appendix VI.

cholera, malaria, and smallpox. Death directly from starvation and 'famine diarrhoea' had passed its peak in late summer and autumn of 1943.[4]

The experience was quite different in Calcutta. The official policy was based on the firm conviction that 'the maintenance of essential food supplies to the industrial area of Calcutta must be ranked on a very high priority among their [the government's] war time obligations', and as early as August 1942 the Bengal government had explained to the Bengal Chamber of Commerce that as far as Calcutta was concerned the government promised to do 'all in their power to create conditions under which essential supplies may be obtainable in adequate quantities and at reasonable prices'.[5] The 'Bengal Chamber of Commerce Foodstuffs Scheme', guaranteeing essential items of food to the grain shops of industrial concerns connected with the Chamber, came into existence with the government's help in August 1942; it covered 620,000 employees by December of that year. The other chambers of commerce developed similar schemes with government backing, covering another 170,000 employees. Public arrangements for provision of supplies to those employed by the central and provincial governments, the railways, the Port Trust, and the Calcutta Corporation covered another 300,000 employees. These schemes guaranteed freedom from starvation to more than a million employees and their dependants. In addition, 'controlled shops' were started in Calcutta in August and September 1942, supplemented in 1943 by a scheme of 'approved markets' by which government stocks were made available to selected private shops for sale to the public. The government helped to feed Calcutta through three successive schemes of procurement at controlled prices between December 1942 and March 1943, but since they did not prove to be very successful, free purchase at market prices was resumed in the districts from March 1943, leading to very sharp rises in the price of rice in the districts.[6]

---

[4] See Sen (1977b, 1980b). An illuminating and insightful account of the Bengal famine in the economic, social and cultural perspective of Bengal has recently been provided by Greenough (1979).

[5] Famine Inquiry Commission (1945a), p. 30.

[6] See *The Calcutta Gazette* Supplements over this period; also Famine Inquiry Commission (1945a), p. 40.

Calcutta saw the famine mainly in the form of masses of rural destitutes, who trekked from the districts into the city; by July 1943 the streets were full. To start with, relief was confined to personal charity and to kitchens organized by charitable organizations, but by August relief for destitutes in Calcutta was accepted as an official policy. While cautious parsimony prevailed—meals were given 'at the same time of day in all kitchens, to prevent destitutes from getting more than one meal'[7]—there is little doubt that a destitute who had found his way into Calcutta had a much better chance of survival than anywhere else in Bengal. Nevertheless, since the relief offered was quite inadequate, unattended dead bodies could be found everywhere in the city—3,363 had to be disposed of by relief organizations in October alone.[8]

The number of starving and sick destitutes in Calcutta was estimated to be 'at least 100,000' in October. A decision was taken by the end of the month to remove the destitutes from the city. The Bengal Destitute Persons (Repatriation and Relief) Ordinance, passed on 28 October, was a rather controversial piece of legislation, since it was alleged that 'repatriation' was rather more firmly achieved than 'relief' in the many 'destitute homes' and 'camps' set up outside Calcutta.[9] For Calcutta, however, the worst of the famine was over, and the death rate came down sharply.[10] In fact, the situation in the districts also eased as some relief reached there directly, and with the harvesting of a good autumn crop and an outstanding winter one. The continued increase in the death rates in the districts was largely the result of famine-induced epidemics (see Appendix D).

6.2 A FOOD SUPPLY CRISIS?

The most common approach to famines is to propose explanations in terms of *food availability decline* (FAD). This FAD approach has been extensively used to analyse and explain the Bengal famine. The Famine Inquiry Commission's view that the primary cause of the famine was 'a serious shortage in the total supply of rice available for consumption in Bengal' provides the

[7] Famine Inquiry Commission (1945a), p. 71.
[8] See Ghosh (1944), pp. 119–20.
[9] See Famine Inquiry Commission (1945a), p. 71–2.
[10] See Ghosh (1944), p. 121.

standard explanation of the famine. As Blyn notes in his authoritative account of 'agricultural trends in India' (1966), referring to the Report of the Famine Inquiry Commission and to the *Census of India 1951*:[11] 'In 1942–43 cyclones and floods reduced the Bengal rice crop by about a third; this, coupled with the absence of exports from Japanese-controlled Burma, and inadequate relief, led to famines, epidemics (malaria, cholera and smallpox), aggravated by widespread starvation' (p. 98).

But is this explanation really supported by the facts—even by data to be found in the body of the *Report* of the Famine Inquiry Commission itself? First, consider what the Commission calls the 'current supply' for a given year, obtained by adding the winter crop of the *preceding* year (harvested in December, and usually sold in the following three months) to the spring and autumn crops of the year in question, plus net imports. Calculated from data given in the *Report* of the Famine Inquiry Commission (1945a), these are presented in columns (2), (3), and (4) of Table 6.2 below. While 1943 was not a very good year in terms of crop availability, it was not by any means a disastrous year either. The current supply for 1943 was only about 5 per cent lower than the average of the preceding five years. It was, in fact, 13 per cent *higher* than in 1941, and there was, of course, no famine in 1941.

However, certain further calculations are needed before the FAD view can be rejected.

Correction 1: Adjustment of official production estimates

The official estimates of agricultural production in India have been criticized for a long time, e.g. by P. C. Mahalanobis. Among recent contributions, Blyn (1966) provides fairly comprehensive estimates of agricultural trends in India, though yield data are not given separately for Bengal, only for 'Greater Bengal', including Bengal, Bihar, and Orissa. But the picture of a better food production situation in 1943 compared with 1941 is confirmed (see his Appendices 3A and 4C). Even the rice yield *per acre*, which is given separately for the Bengal province (Appendix Table 7A), is shown to have been higher in the year 1942–3 than in 1940–1, despite the fact that the acreage in 1942–3 was known to be much higher than in 1940–1.

[11] *Census of India*, 1951, vol. 1, pp. 291–92. See also the *Census of Pakistan*, 1951, vol. 3; and Bhatia's well-known book on Indian famines (1967), pp. 231–4.

Some corrections to the official estimates were carried out by the Famine Inquiry Commission itself, on the lines suggested by Mahalanobis and others. These included corrections also to the trade data, to increase coverage of 'movements across the frontier by road or by country-boat'. The Commission's 'adjusted' figures from their Statement III (p. 215) are presented in columns (5) and (6) in Table 6.2 below. Once again, the 1943 figure for current supply is not exceptionally low, and is higher than that for 1941.

Correction 2: Changes in wheat imports

While rice is by far the dominant food in Bengal, wheat is also consumed in considerable amounts, so that foodgrains availability should reflect variations in both rice and wheat. Very little wheat is grown in Bengal, but a fair amount is imported. The net imports of wheat and wheat flour into Bengal by rail and river-borne trade for 1938 to 1943 are calculated from *Accounts Relating to the Inland (Rail and Riverborne) Trade of India*, a then-current monthly publication of the Department of Commercial Intelligence and Statistics, Government of India.[12] These statistics do not, however, include road-based trade. The Famine Inquiry Commission's (1945a) figure of net arrivals in Bengal in 1943 (p. 54) is 36 per cent higher than the rail and river net imports, and its statement that in the 'five years ending 1941–42, [Bengal] imported from outside the province an average of 21,000 tons a month' (p. 3) makes the total for this period 33 per cent higher than the total of the rail and river net imports. To cover the gaps in the trade statistics from the rail and river data, these amounts have been raised by 36 per cent to get the total net imports of wheat into Bengal. This is almost certainly an overestimate for 1941 *vis-à-vis* 1943, but this is an acceptable bias as it favours the thesis we are rejecting.

The rice and wheat current supply figures are given in column (7) together with indices based on 1941 = 100 in column (8) in Table 6.2 below. The supply in 1943 was 11 per cent higher than in 1941.

[12] The figures for Calcutta are given separately from Bengal in these *Accounts* and the net figures presented here are computed as 'imports into Bengal' plus 'imports into Calcutta', less 'exports out of Bengal' and 'exports out of Calcutta'. Note also that 'wheat' and 'wheat flour' are given separately and have to be added together for each month.

Correction 3: Per capita supply

Since population of Bengal was growing over this period, the availability figure must be scaled down correspondingly to arrive at an index of *per capita* availability. The annual rate of *natural increase* in population in West Bengal was calculated to be 0.46 per cent per year during 1941–50 in the *Census of India* 1951 (vol. VI, part 1B, p. 2). But this is an underestimate for our period since the decade average reflects the impact of the famine itself; also, the 1941 figure was acknowledged to have been overstated owing to excessive registration of both the Hindu and Muslim communities to exaggerate their respective strengths in pre-partition India. A figure of 1 per cent per year is, however, a reasonably safe overestimate, and it is chosen here with a bias *in favour* of the thesis to be rejected. In the last column of Table 6.2, the *per capita* indices of food availability (rice and wheat) are presented with an assumed population growth of 1 per cent per year, again with 1941 being taken as 100. The *per capita* availability index for 1943 is higher by about 9 per cent than that for 1941.

Correction 4: Late availability of imported food in 1943

It can be argued that the availability of foodgrains was particularly bad in the earlier part of 1943; imports of rice and wheat were rather lower then and rose sharply in the last quarter of 1943. While the death rate seems to have reached its peak only in December 1943, there is evidence that starvation was at its peak in the third quarter of 1943.

During the last quarter of 1943, Bengal imported 100 thousand tons of rice (as opposed to an average of 55 thousand tons per quarter earlier in the year), and 176 thousand tons of wheat (as opposed to an earlier average of 54 thousand tons).[13] To bias the figures as much as possible against 1943, the extra amounts of rice and wheat imports during the last quarter of 1943 over the averages for the three previous quarters may be simply deducted from the total 1943 figure. This yields a current supply of rice and wheat of 9.068 million tons in 1943, with an index value of 109 of foodgrains supply and of 107 of *per capita* food grains availability. The former is, thus, fully 9 per cent higher and the latter nearly 7

[13] See Famine Inquiry Commission, India (1945a), p. 54.

TABLE 6.2
Foodgrains Availability in Bengal, 1938–43

Period	Output of rice (official estimates)	Net imports of rice (official estimates)	Current supply of rice (official)	Adjusted output of rice	Adjusted current supply of rice	Rice and wheat: adjusted current supply	Index of total foodgrains supply	Index of per capita foodgrains availability
	(1)	(2)	(3)	(4)	(5)	(6)	(7)	(8)
I Annual data								
1938	8.474	0.033	8.507	9.848	9.981	10.217	123	127
1939	7.922	0.382	8.304	9.114	9.596	9.787	118	120
1940	8.223	0.258	8.481	9.524	9.882	10.196	122	123
1941	6.768	0.223	6.991	7.631	7.954	8.332	100	100
1942	9.296	−0.102	9.194	10.776	10.774	10.947	131	130
1943	7.628	0.264	7.892	8.632	8.896	9.235	111	109
II Moving averages: *2 years*								
1938–39			8.406		9.789	10.002	120	123
1939–40			8.393		9.739	9.992	120	122
1940–41			7.736		8.918	9.264	111	112
1941–42			8.093		9.364	9.640	116	115
1942–43			8.543		9.835	10.091	121	119
III Moving averages: *3 years*								
1938–40			8.431		9.820	10.067	121	123
1939–41			7.925		9.144	9.438	113	114
1940–42			8.222		9.537	9.825	118	118
1941–43			8.026		9.208	9.505	114	113

Note
Unit = 1 million tons for columns (1)–(6); 1941 value = 100 for columns (7) and (8).

per cent larger than the values for 1941, for which no deduction whatsoever for the last quarter is made.

Correction 5:   The so-called 'carry-over' of old rice

The figures presented so far take no account of the 'carry-over' stock from before the December harvest of the previous year. The Famine Inquiry Commission (1945a) thought that one cause of the famine was 'a shortage in the stock of old rice carried forward from 1942 to 1943' (p. 77). Indeed, it argued that the 'carry-over' was substantially smaller than in 1941 (p. 15), and gave this an important role in precipitating the famine (p. 77). But it gave no data on this, and as Mr M. Afzal Hussain, a member of the Commission, noted in his 'Minute', 'absolutely no data are available regarding the stock position of rice (or any other food grain) from month to month, or year to year, in Bengal, or any other part of India' (p. 179). The Commission's majority view that 'the carry-over at the beginning of 1943 was probably sufficient for about six weeks' requirements' (p.15) is just as much a pure surmise as is Husain's view that 'a carry-over in the sense of surplus over consumption must have vanished years ago' (p. 182).[14]

A reasonable way of looking at the carry-over problem in the absence of direct information is to examine moving averages over two or three years ending in the year in question. This will indicate the build-up to the year under examination. Moving averages for two-year and three-year periods are given in rows under II and III for the main columns in Table 6.2. As it happens, the two-year average ending in 1943 is the *highest* in the series for total foodgrains availability—hardly the build-up for a famine. The three-year average ending in 1943 takes a dip from the preceding average, but it is still of the same order of magnitude as the average ending in 1941—indeed, it is just a bit higher. For *per capita* figures, even with our deliberately raised population growth assumption, the three-year average ending in 1943 is only just a shade lower than that ending in 1941, and the two-year average ending in 1943 is, in fact, quite a bit higher than that for 1941.

---

[14] Husain's scepticism regarding carry-over was directed towards arguing that the *absolute* shortage in 1943 was larger that the Commission thought. The scepticism, however, naturally extends to *relative* positions in 1943 *vis-à-vis* 1941.

It seems safe to conclude that the disastrous Bengal famine was not the reflection of a remarkable over-all shortage of foodgrains in Bengal.[15]

6.3 EXCHANGE ENTITLEMENTS

The Bengal famine was essentially a rural phenomenon. Urban areas, especially Calcutta, substantially insulated from rising food prices by subsidized distribution schemes, saw it mainly in the form of an influx of rural destitutes. Is the growth of rural destitution understandable in terms of shifting exchange entitlements? In what follows exchange entitlements will be

[15] This general conclusion, presented earlier in Sen (1977b), has been questioned by Alamgir (1980), pp. 81–3. His arguments seem to centre on three points: (1) *regional* distribution: 'many districts suffered more relative to others' (p. 81); (2) *temporal* distribution: 'between April and October of 1943, many parts of Bengal witnessed a drastic shortfall in foodgrain availability per capita, which is not entirely captured by the aggregate annual index of per capita foodgrain availability calculated by Sen' (p. 82); and (3) *redefinition* of availability: 'foodgrain availability' can be 'defined broadly' so as to 'subsume the contending hypotheses presented by Sen and others' (p. 83). These are all important issues, but I do not believe they affect my general conclusion and the rejection of FAD. First, so far as (1) is concerned, while there were inter-regional variations, the famine was a comprehensive one affecting every region of Bengal. Alamgir (1980) himself notes that 'all subdivisions of Bangladesh were affected with various intensities' (p. 92), and this is true of all regions of the rest of Bengal also, as is readily checked from Table D. 4 below (Appendix D). Of course, food moved out of rural Bengal into urban areas, notably Calcutta, but that is not a question of over-all availability but of the operation of market and political forces affecting 'entitlements' and they were analysed as such in Sen (1977b), and are further analysed below. Second, so far as (2) is concerned, the reported shortage during April to October, i. e., during the famine, is of course a picture of shortage for some but not for others, and that is indeed how entitlement forces operate. How regions like Calcutta with greater market command pulled foodgrains out of the rest of Bengal over this period is a part of the economic analysis of the famine. The over-all availability did, of course, also have some variations over the year. But the annual availability figures calculated and presented in Sen (1977b), and here, include the *aman* harvest of December-January 1942–43 and excludes that of December-January 1943–44 (as already explained) and thus the issue of 'late arrival' would not arise with production. So far as import of foodgrains from *outside* Bengal is concerned, there was indeed 'late arrival' of central supplies, but that has already been corrected under 'Correction 4' above, without changing the general conclusion. Finally, the general conclusion I have put forward here (and in Sen, 1977b) deals with 'availability' as conventionally defined (e.g., as used in Malthus's analyses), viz., total available supply, rather than with marketing and disposal of the over-all availability. Alamgir (1980) is certainly right in emphasizing such issues as 'panic hoarding by producers, consumers and traders', 'favourable treatment of Calcutta as opposed to the rest of Bengal', 'inefficiency of the administration in storage and distribution of foodgrains to districts', 'delayed action since there was emphasis on a "wait and see" policy', etc. (pp. 81–3), but it seems unhelpful to lump them all together in some redefined figure of 'food availability'. FAD is a specific hypothesis—much used in the literature—and deserves to be examined on its own terms, rather than being rescued by *redefinition*. On its own terms, FAD stands rejected.

viewed in terms of entitlement to rice—the main source (indeed, the overwhelmingly dominant source) of calories to the population of Bengal. (It can be checked that the entitlement trends would be substantially similar if the exchange entitlements were calculated for other cereals, e.g. wheat.)

Consider first the class of agricultural labourers. While agricultural wage data are not available on a regular basis over this period, in the Final Report of the Famine Inquiry Commission (1945b) some indices were given for 'the province generally' (p. 484–5). These are presented in Table 6.3 below along with indices of exchange rates of agricultural labour *vis-à-vis* foodgrains. The wages, however, are given for financial years (April–March), while food prices refer to calendar years. Since wages earned are typically spent subsequently, and the main peak period of earning is around December, the exchange rates have been calculated with the wage in each financial year (ending in March) being related to the price of the calendar year (ending in the following December)—except for 1943–4, where the wage of the first six months of the financial year (April–September) has been related to the price in that calendar year.

TABLE 6.3

Indices of Exchange Rates between Agricultural Labour and Foodgrains in Bengal, 1939–44

Year	Wage index	Foodgrains price index	Index of exchange rate
1939–40 (1940)	100	100	100
1940–1 (1941)	110	109	101
1941–2 (1942)	115	160	72
1942–3 (1943)	125	385	32
1st half of 1943–4 (1943)	130	385	34

Source: Based on the data presented in Appendix IV of Famine Inquiry Commission (1945b).

This is not satisfactory, but no other information on this is given by the Commission.

A dramatic decline in the exchange rate against labour emerges from Table 6.3. It is quite clear that agricultural labour did not share in the inflationary rise enjoyed by many other sections of the community in the war economy of Bengal. Table 6.3 is, however, somewhat inconclusive, since the level of aggregation involved and the difference in the periods covered make the exchange rate indices difficult to interpret. One would have preferred a monthly series with data on wages and prices contemporary to each other. This the Famine Inquiry Commission did not provide.

While the Agro-Economic Research Centre for East India (1960) gives wage data in Birbhum from January 1939 to December 1941, and again from January 1946, the data for the intermediate period are not presented. But the sources of the wage data—the log books of the Sriniketan Farm and the Sriniketan Dairy—are still available for certain parts of the period, and using these it has been possible to obtain the local daily wage rate for male unskilled labour from September 1942 to January 1944. Treating the figures of unskilled male wage and the price of rice (no. 2 quality) for December 1941 as 100 respectively, the indices of both prices and of the exchange rate for labour against rice are given in Table 6.4.

While in September 1942 the wage stood where it was in December 1941 and the price of rice stood only a bit higher, a wild upsurge in the rice price followed thereafter, without a matching movement of the wage rate. In fact, while the price index of rice rose to 221 by November, the wage rate actually fell in absolute terms—against the usual seasonal pattern—and the index of the exchange rate declined to 38. After a partial recovery during the harvest months and immediately thereafter, the exchange rate fell some more and stood at 24 in May 1943. By July the index of the exchange rate had been below 30 for three months in succession.

In understanding the significance of the wage price data in Table 6.4, it is also worth bearing in mind that agricultural labourers tend to earn a great part of their incomes in the peak seasons of planting and harvesting of the main crop; and even if

TABLE 6.4

Daily Wage of Agricultural, Male, Unskilled Labour and the Price of Rice and Indices of Exchange Rates: Birbhum District around Bolpur

Mid-month	Rice (no. 2): Rs. per seer	Rice: price index	Wage: Rs. per day	Wage index	Exchange rate index: labour vis-à-vis rice
1941					
December	0.14	100	0.37	100	100
1942					
September	0.16	114	0.37	100	88
October	0.25	179	0.37	100	56
November	0.31	221	0.31	84	38
December	0.25	179	0.44	119	66
1943					
January	0.27	193	0.50	135	70
February	0.25	179	0.50	135	75
March	0.38	271	0.44	119	44
April	0.52	371	0.50	135	36
May	0.78	557	0.50	135	24
June	0.72	514	0.50	135	26
July	0.73	521	0.53	143	27
August	0.75	536	0.62	168	31
September	0.50	357	0.50	135	38
October	0.56	400	0.56	151	38
November	0.44	314	0.56	151	48
December	0.33	236	0.69	186	79
1944					
January	0.36	257	0.62	168	65

Sources: (1) Log books of contemporary wage records in Sriniketan Dairy and Sriniketan Farm;
(2) Log books of contemporary retail prices kept at the Agro-Economic Research Centre for East India;
(3) Agro-Economic Research Centre for East India (1960); the rice price in August 1943 is, however, corrected using (2). See also Sen (1977b).

wages had kept pace with the current rice prices, there would have been distress owing to the failure of the peak wages to anticipate the rise of food prices following the peak. The system of wage payments in Bengal had been geared to the experience of largely stable prices over the preceding decades, and there was no reflection at all in the peak wage rate of December–January of the tripling of rice prices that was to follow before the next peak in May–June.

We have rather little direct information on employment. The counter-seasonal decline in money wages in November 1942 and the low level of real wages through the winter harvesting period and post-harvest months may reflect some decline in employment. This would have been natural given the partial destruction of the winter crop of 1942 from cyclone, floods, and fungus disease. However, the lack of solid data on employment makes this part of the analysis rather speculative, even though there is some direct evidence of a fall in employment compared with the normal pattern (see Mahalanobis, Mukherjea and Ghosh, 1946, pp. 33–4; and Das, 1949, pp. 65–6).

Turning now from agricultural labour to other occupations, the exchange rates *vis-à-vis* rice of a number of commodities are presented in Table 6.5 based on retail prices in Bolpur in the Birbhum district, obtained from contemporary records. While some items, e.g. wheat flour, cloth, and mustard oil, more or less kept pace with rice in terms of price movements in Phase I, fish and bamboo umbrellas fell behind, and milk and haircuts declined sharply in value *vis-à-vis* rice.[16] In Phase II, these declines became more dramatic; for example, by summer the value of a haircut in units of rice had dropped to less than a fifth of what it was in December 1941.

As far as fish is concerned, after an early decline it seems to recover in the middle of Phase I (June–September 1942), to slump again. The temporary recovery was due partly to seasonal factors in the catching of fish (see June–September prices for other years in Agro-Economic Research Centre for East India, 1960, p. 49 onwards), but it may have also been connected with the general rise in fish price in Bengal as a consequence of the 'boat denial' policy carried through for military reasons. By Orders issued in May boats capable of carrying more than ten passengers were removed from a vast area of river-based Bengal to 'deny' them to the possibly-arriving Japanese, and this interfered with both river transport and fishing (see Famine Inquiry Commission, 1945a, pp. 26–7).[17] Thus the distress of

[16] See also the relative prices of other commodities covered in Agro-Economic Research Centre for East India (1960), pp. 73–4.

[17] The 'boat denial' policy was coupled with a 'rice denial' policy initiated in May 1942, aimed also at the elusive Japanese; rice stocks were removed from certain coastal districts (viz. Bakarganj, Khulna, and Midnapore). While the amount involved was not very large—about 40,000 tons altogether—and the rice thus bought and removed was later sold mostly within Bengal (chiefly in Calcutta), it did contribute to local scarcities.

TABLE 6.5

Indices of Exchange Rates vis-à-vis *Rice at Retail Prices: Bolpur in Birbhum District*

Mid-Month	Wheat flour	Mustard oil	Cloth	Bamboo umbrellas	Milk	Fish (pona)	Haircut
1941							
December	100	100	100	100	100	100	100
1942							
January	121	93	108	114	108	95	108
February	112	93	108	127	108	95	108
March	121	100	108	152	108	95	108
April	109	88	113	145	88	88	88
May	91	74	142	134	74	74	74
June	98	89	169	160	88	132	88
July	92	82	165	150	83	124	83
August	83	94	165	129	74	110	74
September	130	125	197	145	88	132	88
October	99	80	126	92	56	84	56
November	79	71	102	69	45	68	45
December	125	95	134	85	66	84	56
1943							
January	116	88	132	85	61	65	52
February	168	95	142	98	66	70	56
March	111	74	94	69	44	46	37
April	108	59	68	60	32	34	27
May	72	51	46	43	21	27	18
June	78	50	49	48	23	39	19
July	77	49	49	47	23	38	19
August	75	64	47	44	22	37	19
September	112	95	76	66	33	56	28
October	100	85	68	57	30	50	25
November	95	118	86	73	47	80	32
December	75	145	118	90	62	106	42
1944							
January	64	127	111	91	57	97	58

Sources: As in Table 6.4, (2) and (3). Note that the cloth index is based on the price of rural handwoven towels (*gamcha*), the only cotton good for which data are available.

fishermen cannot be judged by looking only at the fish–rice exchange rate. However, even that exchange rate declined sharply afterwards. Since Bolpur is a rather small market for fish, the fish–rice exchange rates in Calcutta are presented in Table 6.6; here the decline took place a bit later and somewhat less severely than in Bolpur.

TABLE 6.6
Indices of Retail Prices of Rice and Fish and of Fish–Rice Exchange Rates: College Street Market in Calcutta

	Price of rice (dhekichata)	Price of fish: rohi (cut pieces)	Price of whole fish	Exchange rate index: rohi fish vis-à-vis rice	Exchange rate index: whole fish vis-à-vis rice
1941					
December	100	100	100	100	100
1942					
January	100	100	100	100	100
February	100	100	100	100	100
March	100	100	100	100	100
April	100	100	100	100	100
May	100	110	140	110	140
June	119	110	140	92	118
July	130	130	180	100	138
August	137	150	160	109	117
September	133	150	180	113	135
October	147	140	180	95	122
November	154	170	180	110	117
December	170	170	180	100	106
1943					
January	228	150	180	66	79
February	218	150	180	69	83
March	219	150	180	68	82
April	330	n.a	n.a		
May	435	210	180	48	41
June	435	220	240	51	55
July	435	300	280	69	64
August	491	280	320	57	65

Sources: Calculated from data collected from the weekly *Calcutta Municipal Gazette* during 1941–3. The data refer to the mid-range value for the last observation in each month. Rice prices are discontinued from September, when 'price control' made higher market quotations illegal.

One group that could not have suffered a deterioration of exchange entitlement *vis-à-vis* rice would have been the rice producers. This category would include large farmers as well as peasants. To some extent this would apply to share-croppers as well, since the share is fixed as a proportion of the output, which in this case is rice. There can, of course, be a decline in employment opportunities of share-croppers, but in terms of exchange rates their position would have been distinctly less vulnerable than that of wage labourers, especially since most wages were fixed in money terms. The exchange entitlement approach would, therefore, tend to predict a lower impact of the famine on peasants and share-croppers than on agricultural labourers and sellers of certain commodities and services (fishermen, craftsmen, barbers, etc., who suffered sharp deteriorations of exchange entitlements).

6.4 THE CLASS BASIS OF DESTITUTION

Who were the famine victims? From which occupation categories did the destitutes come?

Data about famines are never plentiful. However, there are at least three important surveys of famine victims conducted during and just after the Bengal famine. First, P. C. Mahalanobis, R. Mukherjea and A. Ghosh (1946) have published the results of a detailed sample survey conducted in collaboration with K. P. Chattopadhyaya during 1944–5 covering 20 per cent of the families in 386 villages in rural Bengal.[18] The subdivisions of Bengal were chosen for the survey with an eye to the 'intensity of incidence' of the famine (41 subdivisions out of a total of 86), and then the villages in each subdivision, and 20 per cent of the population in each village, were chosen on a random basis. The occupational status of the families were recorded for three points of time: in January 1939 (before the famine), January 1943 (immediately preceding the famine—in fact, in terms of our phase structure towards the end of Phase I of the famine), and in May 1944 (after the famine). Second, K. Mukerji (1965) studied the economic conditions of five villages in the Faridpur district immediately after the famine in early 1944, and the results of that survey are of relevance to that particular region of East Bengal much affected by the famine. Third, while these two studies were conducted after the famine was over, a study of the destitutes in Calcutta during the famine was carried out in September 1943 by T. Das (1949), with the help of others, covering 820 destitute family units.

Data from the study by Mahalanobis, Mukherjea and Ghosh (1946) can be used to construct transition matrices in the period immediately preceding the famine, including Phase I of it (January 1939–January 1943), as well as over the severe phase of

[18] See also Chattopadhyaya and Mukherjea (1946).

the famine (January 1943–May 1944), and these are presented in Tables 6.9 and 6.10 at the end of the chapter. It should be observed that there is a fairly close relation between the inter-occupational orderings of pauperization in the 'immediate pre-famine' and the 'famine' periods.[19] (The value of Spearman's rank correlation happens to be 0.75.) It seems possible to argue that the destitution that took place during the famine was similar to what had been happening in the immediate pre-famine period. The extent of the pauperization rose sharply during the famine, and every occupation category—other than paupers themselves—experienced greater destitution in the period than in the four years preceding it (see Table 6.7, columns marked A), but the ranking of occupations in terms of pauperization rates remained similar.

In the famine period, the worst affected groups seem to have been fishermen, transport workers, paddy huskers, agricultural labourers, those in 'other productive occupations', craftsmen,

TABLE 6.7

Transition to (A) Destitution and (B) Destitution or Husking Paddy for Different Occupations

| | Between January 1939 and January 1943 | | Between January 1943 and May 1944 | |
	A	B	A	B
	%	%	%	%
Peasant cultivation and share-cropping	0.7	0.9	1.3	1.5
Part peasant, part labour	0.9	1.1	1.4	2.0
Non-cultivating owners	0.7	1.3	1.6	2.4
Profession and services	1.4	1.9	2.1	2.6
Trade	1.1	1.5	2.2	2.6
Craft	3.0	3.1	3.8	4.3
Non-agricultural labour	1.8	1.8	3.7	4.5
Other productive occupations	1.9	2.2	4.6	4.6
Agricultural labour	1.7	2.5	4.6	6.1
Transport	2.4	30.6	6.0	6.9
Fishing	1.6	1.6	9.6	10.5
Husking paddy	3.6	–	4.7	–

Source: Calculated from the data presented in Mahalanobis, Mukherjea and Ghosh (1946).

[19] As explained earlier, these terms are somewhat deceptive since the 'immediate pre-famine period' includes much of Phase I of it.

and non-agricultural labourers, in that order. The least affected were peasant cultivators and share-croppers. They were also the least affected group in the pre-famine period (including what we have been calling Phase I of the famine).

One of the occupation categories,—'paddy husking'— displays certain interesting features. It happens to be one of those marginal occupations that many rural families pass through on the way to total destitution. It has rather easy entry, and it is a lowly paid occupation done almost exclusively by women.[20] While—the destitution rates in husking paddy are so high—3.6 and 4.7 per cent respectively in the pre-famine and famine periods—the proportion of rural families dependent on these activities *rose* substantially both in the immediate pre-famine period as well as during the famine. It is interesting, in this connection, to note that, on the basis of the detailed information on sex, family status, and personal history obtained from the survey, Chattopadhyaya and Mukherjea (1946) observed that, while 'many of these women husking paddy are unattached persons . . . who have been following this occupation for making a livelihood for themselves', others with 'children dependent on them have been reduced to rely entirely on this occupation through death of earners and finally brought to destitution' (p. 7). Despite a high rate of destitution during 1939–43 as well as 1943–4, the number of families dependent on husking paddy showed a net increase by a little over 66 per cent between January 1939 and May 1944.

Treating entry into paddy husking as typically a sign of distress, columns marked B in Table 6.7 present the proportions of each occupation group moving to destitution *or* to living on husking paddy, in the immediate pre-famine period and during the famine. Again, the rank-ordering of this redefined index of distress in the pre-famine period is quite close to that during the famine (e.g., Spearman's rank correlation coefficient of the two series works out at 0.78).

In terms of recruitment to economic distress (defined as destitution or husking paddy), 'fishing', 'transport' and

[20] See Chattopadhyaya and Mukherjea (1946), p. 7. Note also that in a period of rice shortage, paddy husking also becomes a more lucrative occupation (in relative terms), permitting entry of labour thrown out from other walks of life. The fact that husking can be carried out on an extremely small scale is also relevant to this phenomenon of easy entry.

'agricultural labour' have the highest frequencies among the occupations. It is a bit difficult to conclude anything firmly about transport workers since the sample size was rather small, and there is also some relation between the distress of the fishermen and that of rural transport workers, since river transport 'is largely looked after by members of the fishermen caste' (Chattopadhyaya and Mukherjea, 1946, p. 7). But there is little doubt about fishermen and agricultural labourers being among the hardest hit by the famine. Other hard-hit groups were 'other productive occupations', 'non-agricultural labour', and 'craft'.

In absolute numbers, by far the largest group of destitutes came from the category of agricultural labourers, according to the data presented by Mahalanobis, Mukherjea and Ghosh (1946). Similarly, in his survey of the destitutes who had trekked to Calcutta at the height of the famine, conducted in September 1943, it was found by T. Das (1949) that about 41 per cent of those destitutes—the largest group—were from families of agricultural labour. It is not, however, possible to calculate the proportionate incidence of destitution from Das's data.

Finally, in Mukherji's survey of Faridpur villages, the highest rate of proportionate destitution is observed among agricultural labourers (a destitution rate of 52 per cent compared with an over-all average destitution rate of 29 per cent). The proportion of families 'wiped off during 1943' is also the highest among the agricultural labourers (40 per cent compared with an over-all average of 15 per cent; indeed, 77 per cent of those agricultural labourers who were destituted by the famine got 'wiped off'). The relative rates for the different occupation categories are given in Table 6.8. Next to agricultural labourers, the highest destitution rate is displayed in a category named 'unproductive', which is a bit deceptive since it includes people who traditionally live by beggary in these villages, and of course were easily destituted further. The next highest group is 'artisan' (35 per cent destitution and 10 per cent 'wiped off'). The peasant cultivators and share-croppers had a relatively lower famine incidence (18 per cent destitution and 6 per cent wiped off), higher only than office employees and landlords.

The picture that emerges from these data seems to be entirely in line with what one would expect from the use of the entitlement approach. The high incidence among agricultural

TABLE 6.8

Destitution in Five Surveyed Villages in Faridpur

Occupation on 1/1/43	Total nos. of families on 1/1/43	Nos. of destitute families in each group on 1/1/43	Proportion of destitution (%)	Nos. of families in each group 'wiped off' during 1943	Proportion being 'wiped off' during 1943 (%)
Peasant cultivation and share-cropping	266	49	18.4	17	6.4
Agricultural labour	124	65	52.4	50	40.3
Artisan	20	7	35.0	2	10.0
Petty trader	107	34	31.8	15	14.0
Crop-sharing landlord	16	1	6.3	0	0.0
Priest and petty employee	11	3	27.3	3	27.3
Office employee	20	2	10.0	0	0.0
Landlord	10	0	0.0	0	0.0
'Unproductive'	18	8	44.4	3	16.7
Total	592	169	28.5	90	15.2

Source: Based on Mukerji (1965), Table 63, p. 178.

labourers *vis-à-vis* the low impact on peasants and share-croppers
was to be expected. The food entitlements had, indeed, de-
teriorated sharply for the former, but not so much for the latter.[21]
The relatively large effects on fishermen, non-agricultural
labour, craftsmen, etc., are also consistent with the observed
pattern of shifts in entitlement relations.

6.5 CAUSES OF THE SHARP MOVEMENTS OF EXCHANGE ENTITLEMENTS

What caused the exchange entitlements to move so violently?
While data limitations rule out definitive discrimination between
alternative causal hypotheses, some tentative diagnoses seem
possible.

First, the increase in rice price in Phase I was essentially
related to demand factors; supply was exceptionally high in 1942
(see Table 6.2). The price increase in the Phase I period, while
not confined to Bengal, was much more acute in Bengal than
elsewhere (see Singh, 1965, pp. 95–9; Palekar, 1962). This was, to
a great extent, a result of general inflationary pressure in a war
economy. Bengal saw military and civil construction at a totally
unprecedented scale, and the war expenditures were financed to
a great extent by printing notes. While a substantial part—
indeed, more than half from 1941 to 1942—of the total war
expenditure incurred by India was 'recoverable' as sterling
balances owed by Britain, this did not reduce the immediate
inflationary pressure, since the 'recovery' took place much later.
Indeed, given the Indian monetary system, these sterling
balances were treated as assets against which the Reserve Bank of
India was 'entitled to print notes worth about two and a half
times their total value', so that the recoverable war expenditure
tended to have a *stronger* inflationary impact than expenditure on
India's own account (see Gadgil and Sovani, 1943, pp. 12–14).
The 1943 famine can indeed be described as a 'boom famine'
related to powerful inflationary pressures initiated by public
expenditure expansion.

[21] Indeed, peasants growing rice and living on exchanging rice for other commodities
might be thought to have had an *improvement* in exchange entitlements in terms of other
commodities. But the high retail price of food was often not correspondingly reflected in
the price paid to the peasant. Furthermore, at the initial post-harvest high price many
peasants sold off more rice than their surplus and had to repurchase some rice later at a
very much higher price still.

Second, in Phase II the demand forces were reinforced by the 'indifferent' winter crop and by vigorous speculation and panic hoardings. The hoarding was financially profitable on the basis of even 'static expectations': rice prices had more than doubled in the preceding year, while the 'bazar bill rate' in Calcutta still stood around 7 per cent per year (the bank deposit rate was below 2 per cent per annum).[22] There was a abnormally higher withholding of rice stock by farmers and traders from the winter harvest of 1942–3; the normal release following the harvest did not take place.[23] A moderate short-fall in *production* had by then been translated into an exceptional short-fall in *market release*. The 'current supply' figures of the Famine Inquiry Commission no longer reflected supply to the market.

Third, speculative withdrawal and panic purchase of rice stocks was encouraged by administrative chaos,[24] especially the inept handling of three procurement schemes, tried and hurriedly abandoned between December and March, ending with the sudden abolition of price control in the wholesale market on 11 March.[25] But the expectation of a famine and further price rises were most forcefully fed by the sight of distress and hunger that had already developed by the end of Phase I and the beginning of Phase II.[26] Many of the groups had already suffered severe declines in exchange entitlements in Phase I itself (see Tables 6.3–6.5) and had helped to fill the distress reports of commissioners and district officers (discussed earlier). The speculative price increase in rice in Phase II led to further deterioration of exchange entitlements, covering additional occupation groups. The Bengal government's propaganda drive that 'the supply position did not justify the high prices prevailing' failed totally.[27]

[22] Gadgil and Sovani (1943), p. 24.

[23] See Ghosh (1944), pp. 33–48; Famine Inquiry Commission, India (1945a), pp. 33-4, 38–41 and 83–5; and Das (1949), p. 119.

[24] Including a change of ministry in Bengal. The old Bengal government under the premiership of Fazlul Haq fell on 31 March, and a new ministry under Khwaza Nazimmuddin was sworn in on 23 April.

[25] See Famine Inquiry Commission (1945a), pp. 36–50. Similarly, the scheme to requisition traders' stocks in Calcutta a few months earlier had yielded little except the belief that not much stock existed to be requisitioned.

[26] See Ghosh (1944), Das (1949), and Famine Inquiry Commission, India (1945a), Appendix VI.

[27] The ineptness of the propaganda drive was exceptional. On 18 May the Finance Minister, T. C. Goswami, offered the following remarkable explanation of events,

Fourth, the prohibition of export of cereals in general and of rice in particular from each province, which had come into operation during 1942 with the consent of the government of India, prevented the price spiral in Bengal being broken by imports from the other provinces.[28] After much fumbling with various all-India schemes of food distribution, the government of India eventually ordered free trade in the eastern region of the country towards the middle of May 1943. But this was abandoned in July since the prices in these neighbouring provinces soon reached the 'maximum' levels laid down by the provincial governments. A 'Basic Plan' of centralized inter-state grain movements eventually came into operation in late summer, improving the supply position in Bengal in the last quarter of 1943.

Fifth, an important aspect of the famine was its association with an uneven expansion in incomes and purchasing powers. Those involved in military and civil defence works, in the army, in industries and commerce stimulated by war activities, and almost the entire normal population of Calcutta covered by distribution arrangements at subsidized prices (see Section 6.1) could exercise strong demand pressures on food, while others excluded from this expansion or protection simply had to take the consequences of the rise in food prices. Agricultural labour did not in general share in the war-based expansion, except 'in certain areas . . . where military or civil defence works were in progress'.[29] The abundance of labour in the agricultural sector (see Mahalanobis, Mukherjea and Ghosh, 1946; and Chattopadhyaya and Mukherjea, 1946) made the economic position of the labourers in the agricultural sector weak. The weakness of their position is also reflected in the fact that, while the famine killed millions, with agricultural labourers forming by far the

---

backing up a cheerful prediction: 'Before long the price will come down. The speculators were in their last grasp   [*sic*] and the reason why the prices were not coming down could be assigned to their last desperate attempt to keep prices up' (quoted in Ghosh, 1944, pp. 40–1). See also Famine Inquiry Commission, India (1945a), p. 55.

[28] The price difference between Bengal and its neighbouring provinces had already become substantial by the end of 1942. Compared with a mean harvest price of winter rice in Assam of Rs. 8.81, in Bihar of Rs. 8.00 and in Orissa of Rs. 6.19, the mean price of winter rice in Bengal was Rs. 14.00, and even the 1942 autumn harvest mean price had been Rs. 13.88 (see *Indian Agricultural Statistics 1939–40 to 1942–43*, Government of India, New Delhi, 1950, vol. 1, Table VII).

[29] Famine Inquiry Commission, India (1945b), p. 485.

largest group of those killed, Bengal was producing the largest rice crop in history in 1943. While I resist the temptation to propose a 'test' of the surplus labour hypothesis along Schultzian lines,[30] which rejected the surplus labour hypothesis on grounds of declines in agricultural output following the influenza epidemic of 1918, it is remarkable that agricultural operations could take place on such a gigantic scale despite deaths, debilitating diseases and migration in search of food, affecting a large part of the agricultural labour force.

Sixth, as far as occupation groups involving crafts, services, 'superior' foods (e.g. fish, milk) are concerned, Phase II could have created problems of its own. As distress developed generally in the rural economy of Bengal, the demand for these 'luxury' goods declined sharply—a phenomenon that has been observed in other famines as well.[31] This feedback helped to plunge additional groups of people into destitution.

Finally, it is perhaps significant that the Bengal famine stood exactly at the borderline of two historical price regimes. Prices had been more or less stationary for decades (the 1941 rice price was comparable to that in 1914), and the price rises (especially of food) that started off in 1942 were to become a part of life from then on. Institutional arrangements, including wage systems, were slow to adjust to the new reality.

6.6 THE ROLE OF THEORY IN POLICY FAILURES

The inadequacy of official policy in tackling the Bengal famine has been widely noted and criticized. The Famine Inquiry Commission (1945a) provided a detailed analysis of the policy failures both of the Bengal government as well as of the Indian government (see especially Chapters X and XI). The famine became a focal point of nationalist criticism of British imperial policy in India (for a classic work on this, see Ghosh, 1944), and official complacency came under particular attack. The refusal of the British government to permit more food imports into India through reallocation of shipping as an emergency measure to tackle the famine was severely criticized.[32] Lord Wavell, who

[30] See Schultz (1964); for a critique, see Sen (1967b), followed by Schultz's reply.

[31] See, for example, Wrigley (1969), p. 68, on the seventeenth-century famine in Mouy in France.

[32] For the international—especially American—reaction, see the interesting study of Venkataramani (1973).

became the new Viceroy at the last stage of the famine and who had to battle hard for increasing food imports into India, went on record in this context that he felt that 'the vital problems of India are being treated by His Majesty's Government with neglect, even sometimes with hostility and contempt'.[33]

Does our thesis that the Bengal famine did not arise from a drastic decline in food availability negate these criticisms? I don't believe it does, since no matter how a famine is *caused*, methods of *breaking* it call for a large supply of food in the public distribution system. This applies not only to organizing rationing and control, but also to undertaking work programmes and other methods of increasing purchasing power for those hit by shifts in exchange entitlements in a general inflationary situation. (One curious aspect of the Bengal famine was that it was never officially 'declared' as a famine, which would have brought in an obligation to organize work programmes and relief operations specified by the 'Famine Code', dating from 1883; Sir T. Rutherford, the Governor of Bengal, explained to the Viceroy: 'The Famine Code has not been applied as we simply have not the food to give the prescribed ration.'[34] A large food stock would have also helped in breaking the speculative spiral that ushered in the Phase II of the famine. Thus there is no reason to revise the criticisms made of the official failure to obtain more food in the public distribution system through greater procurement and larger imports from outside Bengal. Nor are there reasons to dispute the Famine Inquiry Commission's indictment of the Bengal government for administrative bungling and of the government of India for its failure to evolve an integrated food policy for India as a whole.

But the conspicuous failure of the Government to anticipate the famine and to recognise its emergence does appear in a new light. When the existence of the famine was eventually acknowledged officially in Parliament by the Secretary of State for India in a statement in October 1943, the influential Calcutta daily *The Statesman* wondered why 'the speech contained no direct admission of grave misjudgement on the higher authorities' part or even of error', overlooking 'previous official assertions in London and New Delhi that there existed virtually no food problem in

---

[33] Letter to Winston Churchill, dated 24 October 1944; quoted in Wavell (1973), p. 95.

[34] Document no. 158 in Mansergh (1973), p. 363.

India.'[35] In view of what we have discussed earlier (Section 6.2), one can argue that the Raj was, in fact, fairly right in its estimation of overall food availability, but disastrously wrong in its theory of famines.

The government's thinking on the nature of the food problem seems to have been persistently influenced by attempts to estimate the size of the 'real shortage' based on 'requirements' and 'availability'; it was a search in a dark room for a black cat which wasn't there. The approach provided no warning of the development of a gigantic famine arising from shifting exchange entitlements. The approach also contributed to some reluctance to accept the magnitude of the disaster even after the famine had in fact appeared.

Estimates of food shortages were periodically made by the Government of India. An estimate of 'shortage of rice' was made in December 1942, taking full note of 'loss of Burma rice, floods in Sind, cyclones in rice growing areas of Bengal and Orissa and an *indifferent* rice crop generally in Bengal'.[36] But the shortage seemed absorbable, and the Government of India used this 'rice shortage' estimate only to supplement its request to London for shipping allocation to meet the existing 'wheat shortage', viz., shipping facilities to import 'an additional 600,000 tons of wheat'.[37] In his 'memorandum' on this request, the Secretary of State for India observed:

No account is taken in it of the statistical shortage of 140,000 tons of rice and 650,000 tons of millets which is the background against which the Government of India have to view their wheat difficulties. *These shortages, serious as they are, would not from the statistical standpoint bear a catastrophic proportion of the Indian cereal crop of 60/70 million tons.*[38]

[35] "Seen from a distance", editorial, *The Statesman*, 14 October 1943; see also the editorial on 16 October following, entitled "The death-roll". *The Statesman*, a British-owned newspaper, had carried out a powerful campaign with news reports, photographs and editorial comments on the calamity – a role that would be praised later by the Famine Inquiry Commission. For the editor's account of the campaign and also for an interesting, anecdotal account of the Bengal famine, see Stephens (1966, chs. 13 and 14). Recognition of the reality of the famine seemed to decrease step by step in the move from the local administration via Calcutta and New Delhi to Whitehall.

[36] Document no. 265 in Mansergh (1971), p. 357; italics added. Note that the rice crop in Bengal was recognized to be 'indifferent' rather than exceptionally bad (cf. Section 6.2 above).

[37] Document no. 265 in Mansergh (1971), p. 358; see also Documents nos 282, 297, and 332 in the same volume.

[38] Document no. 330 in Mansergh (1971), p. 474; italics added.

While taking an essentially FAD approach, the Secretary's detailed memorandum went also into 'aggravating factors', particularly the problems of the urban population, who 'are dependent on the marketed part of the crop, who are the first to experience any shortage and . . . on whose labour the Indian munitions and supply industries depend'.[39] The distress of the rural population, especially of agricultural labour, arising from shifting exchange entitlements, which—as we have seen in Section 6.3—had already been quite substantial by then, was not noted. The reference to 'distribution' was only in the context of 'the strain put upon the railways by military and other loadings'.[40] (The tendency to view 'distribution' essentially as a transport problem rather than as one involving purchasing power and exchange was, incidentally, a persistent feature of official thinking on the subject.)[41]

As it happens, even the request for permission to import 600,000 tons of wheat was turned down in London on 16 January, only a small part of it being met.[42] This was received, it appears, with equanimity, since the government itself did not take its 'shortage' estimates too seriously in the context of over-all supply. The government immediately proceeded to decontrol the wholesale price of wheat, set up a government Purchasing Agency, and prohibit 'the export of foodgrains beyond Provincial and State boundaries on private account', and it issued a communiqué promising 'imports from abroad' and confiding that 'the Government of India believed that the food shortages were mainly due to hoarding'.[43]

On 26 January, the Viceroy wrote to the Secretary of State for India: 'Mindful of our difficulties about food I told him [the

---

[39] ibid. Even when the Bengal countryside was gripped by the famine and rural destitutes were pouring into relatively well-fed Calcutta, the government of India was concentrating chiefly on 'signs that difficulty is likely to arise in the non-rural and industrial districts' (see War Cabinet Paper WP (43) 345, dated 30 July 1943, Document no. 66 in Mansergh (1973), p. 134).

[40] Document no. 330 in Mansergh (1971), p. 476.

[41] See, for example, Document no. 102 in Mansergh (1973); see also Famine Inquiry Commission, India (1945a), pp. 59–62.

[42] See the Secretary of State's telegram to the Viceroy on 16 January 1943, Document no. 350 in Mansergh (1971), pp. 514–15. London continued to turn down requests by the government of India for shipping allocations throughout 1943; see Documents nos. 59, 71, 72, 74, 98, 139, 157, 207, and 219 in Mansergh (1973), and also Wavell (1973), Chapters 2 and 3).

[43] Mansergh (1971), p. 541.

Premier of Bengal] that he simply *must* produce some more rice out of Bengal for Ceylon even if Bengal itself went short! He was by no means unsympathetic, and it is possible that I may in the result screw a little out of them'.[44] The estimates of 'shortage' based on production figures (including that of the 'indifferent' winter crop) did not make such a suggestion look preposterous, even though—as we have seen—the forces leading to the famine were already in full swing.

Later in the spring, when the famine was about to reveal itself fully, the Viceroy sent, on 18 March, the cheerful news to the Secretary of State that 'the food situation in India generally is at present much improved'. While 'the situation in Bengal at present is disquieting', the food situation could be 'treated with guarded optimism, with special reference to the recent improvement of ths situation in India generally and the excellent prospects of the *rabi* harvest'.[45]

The severity of the famine when it did surface caused much official surprise; the Viceroy came to the conclusion that the 'chief factor' was 'morale'.[46] But the adherence to the FAD approach was not abandoned; the values of 'shortages' were recalculated specifically for Bengal for the period until the next crop. In a report transmitted to London by the Viceroy, the Governor of Bengal, Sir T. Rutherford, presented on 2 October 1943 a detailed account of the 'present food situation', including a lament about 'the dubiety of all available statistics and therefore lack of accurate knowledge of what the *real shortage* is',[47] without questioning the wisdom of the approach itself. 'Allowing 1 lb. a day' to those above fifteen years and '½ lb. a day to those below 15', and taking note of traders' stocks and estimates of 'carryover from 1941–42', it was now calculated that for the period until the next harvest 'the shortage was in the neighbourhood of 655,000 tons'.[48] This figure had to be revised upwards by the Viceroy within eight days, since an expert 'says my estimate of 655,000 tons as shortage is too low and suggests one million tons'.[49]

[44] Document no. 362 in Mansergh (1971), p. 544.

[45] Document no. 599 in Mansergh (1971), pp. 825–6.

[46] Wavell quoting Linlithgow, in Wavell (1973), p. 34.

[47] Document no. 158 in Mansergh (1973), p. 361; italics added.

[48] ibid., p. 362.

[49] Document no. 174 in Mansergh (1973), p. 390; the expert quoted was A.M.A.H. Ispahani, a businessman much involved in rice trading.

While practical considerations outside the FAD approach were often introduced in an *ad hoc* way in government notes on the food problem,[50] especially after the famine had broken out, the FAD view continued to occupy a pre-eminent position in the government's theory of the food crisis. By January 1944, the government appeared to have worked out a complicated FAD explanation of the famine: 'The experience of the past years has convinced the authorities in India that the loss of imports since 1942 has meant the consumption of the carry-over, and now, reserves having been consumed, is a major cause of shortage, and that, though the exhaustion of a concealed reserve has not been evident till now, its results will persist'.[51] As was noted earlier, not a single piece of serious statistics exists on the 'carry-over', and a study of the moving averages of availability taking note of production and net imports suggests no reason for presuming a sharp decline of carry-over (see Section 6.2).

Finally, when the time came to report on the famine and assess what had happened, the Famine Inquiry Commission also adopted FAD as its main approach—as we have already seen. The occurence of the famine was squared with production and trade figures by assuming a sharp decline of that mysterious— and unobserved—'carry-over from previous years'. Like the Phoenix, the FAD theory arose rejuvenated from the ashes, and it can be found today chirping in the current literature on the food crisis of the world, even making occasional references to the Bengal famine, 'when floods destroyed the rice crop, costing some 2 million to 4 million lives'.[52]

---

[50] See Mansergh (1971), Chapter 10, and Mansergh (1973), Chapter 4.

[51] Memorandum by the Secretary of State for India, War Cabinet Paper WP (44) 63, Document no. 347 in Mansergh (1973), p. 680.

[52] Brown and Eckholm (1974), p. 27. See also Masefield (1963), p. 14; quoted also in Aziz (1975), p. 27.

TABLE 6.9

Occupational Transition Matrix in Rural Bengal in the Pre-famine Period: January 1939–January 1943

1939	Peasant cultivation or share-cropping %	Part-time agricultural labour %	Agricultural labour %	Non-cultivating owner %	Fishing %	Craft %	Husking paddy %	Transport %	Trade %	Profession and service %	Non-agricultural labour %	Other productive occupations %	Destitute %
Peasant cultivation and share-cropping	91.8	3.3	1.9	0.9	0.0	0.2	0.2	0.1	0.4	0.3	0.1	0.1	0.7
Part-time agricultural labour	1.7	90.3	3.9	0.4	0.1	1.3	0.2	0.0	0.3	0.5	0.1	0.4	0.9
Agricultural labour	2.6	4.3	87.1	1.0	0.0	0.5	0.8	0.0	0.3	1.0	0.2	0.6	1.7
Non-cultivating owner	3.7	0.7	1.2	90.5	0.0	0.2	0.6	0.0	0.4	1.3	0.3	0.4	0.7
Fishing	3.8	2.8	1.3	0.3	68.3	21.0	0.0	0.0	0.3	0.0	0.3	0.3	1.6
Craft	8.0	0.7	1.6	2.7	0.0	81.1	0.1	0.1	0.6	1.0	0.3	0.7	3.0
Husking paddy	8.8	1.0	2.6	4.1	0.0	1.6	73.7	0.5	0.5	1.0	1.6	1.0	3.6
Transport	5.3	2.9	2.4	4.9	0.0	0.0	28.2	51.0	1.9	0.0	0.5	0.5	2.4
Trade	11.9	1.8	1.9	2.5	0.0	0.7	0.4	0.1	77.1	1.6	0.7	0.3	1.1
Profession and service	7.3	1.6	2.2	5.8	0.0	0.9	0.5	0.0	1.5	77.6	0.7	0.5	1.4
Non-agricultural labour	9.9	1.8	0.0	4.5	0.0	0.9	0.0	0.0	0.9	0.9	79.3	0.0	1.8
Other productive occupations	3.7	1.9	1.5	4.3	0.0	0.3	0.3	0.0	0.9	0.9	0.3	84.0	1.9
Destitute	0.4	0.0	2.2	0.0	0.0	0.4	2.2	0.0	2.9	1.8	1.5	1.1	87.6

TABLE 6.10

Occupational Transition Matrix in Rural Bengal in the Famine Period; January 1943–May 1944

1943	Peasant cultivation or share cropping %	Part-time agricultural labour %	Agricultural labour %	Non-cultivating owner %	Fishing %	Craft %	Husking paddy %	Transport %	Trade %	Profession and services %	Non-agricultural labour %	Other productive occupations %	Destitute %
Peasant cultivation or share-cropping	91.6	1.9	2.4	1.3	0.1	0.4	0.2	0.1	0.4	0.2	0.0	0.3	1.3
Part-time agricultural labour	2.6	86.9	6.8	0.5	0.0	0.2	0.6	0.1	0.3	0.3	0.2	0.2	1.4
Agricultural labour	0.9	1.5	88.2	0.0	0.1	0.5	1.5	0.2	0.3	1.2	0.2	0.8	4.6
Non-cultivating owner	0.6	0.1	0.8	92.6	0.0	1.1	0.8	0.1	0.5	1.2	0.2	0.5	1.6
Fishing	0.5	0.0	2.3	0.5	78.6	0.5	0.9	0.5	4.6	0.0	0.9	1.4	9.6
Craft	1.8	0.5	2.9	1.1	0.1	87.4	0.5	0.3	0.3	0.9	0.5	0.1	3.8
Husking paddy	0.0	0.4	0.8	0.0	0.4	0.8	90.6	0.4	0.8	0.0	0.4	0.8	4.7
Transport	0.9	1.7	7.8	0.0	0.0	3.5	0.9	78.5	0.0	0.9	0.0	0.0	6.0
Trade	1.8	0.6	2.8	1.1	0.1	0.6	0.4	17.5	69.6	2.0	0.5	0.8	2.2
Profession and services	1.4	0.4	0.9	1.2	0.0	0.6	0.5	0.3	0.9	91.5	0.1	0.1	2.1
Non-agricultural labour	3.7	2.2	5.2	0.0	0.0	0.0	0.8	0.0	0.0	0.0	82.8	1.5	3.7
Other productive occupations	0.6	1.8	1.5	0.6	0.0	0.6	0.0	0.3	0.3	1.5	0.0	88.4	4.6
Destitute	0.2	0.7	2.8	1.9	0.0	1.9	1.7	0.2	1.4	0.5	1.2	2.1	85.4

Chapter 7

The Ethiopian Famine

7.1 THE FAMINE 1972–4

The first recorded famine in Ethiopia goes back to the ninth
century. Between 1540 and 1742 there were, apparently, more
than ten major famines.[1] The so-called 'great Ethiopian famine'
hit the country during 1888–92, killing off possibly a third of the
total population,[2] and it is still remembered as *kifu qan* (evil
days). In comparison with the great Ethiopian famine, the
famine that Ethiopia experienced in 1972–4 might appear to be a
moderate affair, with mortality estimates varying between
50,000 and 200,000, in a population of about 27 million.[3] But as
Aykroyd (1974) puts it, 'a death toll of perhaps over 100,000' is
'inexcusable at this stage in the history of famine' (p. 203).

The province that was hit hardest by the famine was Wollo in
the north-east of Ethiopia, but it also affected the province of
Tigrai, further north, and some of the rest of the country, e.g.
Harerghe.[4] For Wollo the famine reached its peak in 1973, and
recovery was well under way by the end of that year. The same is
true of Tigrai, the other northern province affected by the famine
(though much less affected). But for Harerghe the famine came
into its own only in 1974. In a sense, there were really two
Ethiopian famines during this period: the first in 1972–3 with its
focus on north-east, especially Wollo, and the second in 1973–4
affecting mainly some provinces further south, particularly

---

[1] Zewde (1976), p. 52. See also Pankhurst (1961).

[2] See Pankhurst (1966).

[3] The lower of the two limits, viz. 40,000, comes from the estimate of 'total deaths due
to famine between 40,000 and 80,000', suggested by Miller and Holt (1975), p. 171, but
refers primarily to the first phase of the famine. The higher of the two limits, viz. 200,000,
represents mortality estimates presented in Shepherd (1975), which Gebre-Medhin and
Vahlquist (1977) suggest 'is hardly an exaggeration' (p. 197). For the total period 1972–5,
Rivers, Holt, Seaman, and Bowden (1976) estimate 'an excess of at least 100,000 deaths
due to starvation and associated diseases' (p. 355).

[4] According to the figures given by the Ethiopian Relief and Rehabilitation
Commission (1975), the proportion of 'affected' population in late 1973 was 41 per cent
for Wollo, 17 per cent for Tigrai, 8 per cent for Harerghe, 2.6 per cent for Shewa, 0.8 per
cent for Gemu Gofa, and negligible for the other provinces. See Hussein (1976), p. 45.

Harerghe. The biggest part of the mortality owing to starvation occurred in 1973, much of it in Wollo.

The 1971–2 rains were rather erratic, but the big drought that affected north-east Ethiopia, particularly Wollo, was largely the result of the failure of the main—*kremt*—rains in mid-1972, followed by the near-total failure of the spring—*belg*—rains in early 1973. The former had particularly disastrous effects on the lowlands, and the latter mainly on the highlands. The drought in Wollo and the north-east broke with the *kremt* rains in mid-1973, but a new drought situation developed further south.[5] Since the bulk of the crop is dependent on the main rains, the big decline in terms of food output in the north-east took place quite early, i.e. with the failure of the main rains of 1972 and the short-fall of the December 1972 harvest.

There is little doubt that by late 1972 there were many early signs of developing distress. In December 1972 the Ethiopian Red Cross was already trying to help over a thousand refugees from Wollo who had arrived outside Addis Ababa, the Ethiopian capital. By early 1973 crowds were lining parts of the north–south highway through Wollo, stopping buses and cars to ask for food (Holt and Seaman, 1976). A march by one and a half thousand agriculturists to Addis Ababa in March 1973 was apparently turned back by the police (Wiseberg, 1976). Official recognition of the developing famine came, however, very slowly, even though a study done by the Ministry of Agriculture in November 1972 had sounded a note of grim warning. In fact, the seriousness of the famine seems to have been systematically minimized by the government at the early stages. The international organizations were also rather slow in recognizing the situation as what it was—a severe famine—even though the local UNICEF area office and the Swedish-financed Ethiopian Nutrition Institute played an important part in the early stages of counter-famine initiatives.

The relief camps that were set up were, to start with, mainly the result of local initiative, often organized by local town committees, and relying heavily on the selfless efforts of a handful of local community development officers and public health workers. Reports of extraordinary overcrowding, sanitary

[5] See Hussein (1976), Seaman, Holt, and Rivers (1974) and Gebre-Medhin, Hay, Licke, and Maffi (1977).

failures, and grossly inadequate medical attention in the relief camps were rather horrifying, but not surprising given the limitation of the resources available in comparison with the gigantic size of the problem. When the starvation crisis was reaching its peak, in August 1973, 'over 60,000 people were crowded in relief camps which could not deal with a third of their number, and many more flooded into the towns'.[6] By the time foreign relief started arriving in a large scale two months later, the peak of the starvation crisis was already over, and the camp population had dwindled to 15,000.

A major international rescue operation eventually went into action. While the famine in Wollo and Tigrai had by then ebbed, there were plenty of poor people seeking relief. And fresh destitutes were being created elsewhere in the country as the focus of drought moved south and further east, for example to the Ogaden region of Harerghe. The Relief and Rehabilitation Commission's estimate of 'affected populatiom' went on *increasing* well into 1975, but there is little doubt that the severity of the distress was never as great as in 1973. In fact, the worst period of the famine went virtually unnoticed by the international community and only half acknowledged by the Ethiopian government, and the relief activity peaked well after the famine had ebbed.[7]

Even in terms of regional distribution of food aid, there were some curious mismatching of aid with distress:

The contrast between the chronology of the famine and that of bulk of food aid is startling. Government statistics . . . indicate that up to November 1973 only 12,000 tonnes of grain were distributed to all areas by the government. . . . Some 6,500 tonnes only went to Wollo. . . . In contrast between November 1973 and December 1974 Ethiopia received foreign relief grain donations of 126,000 tonnes, together with 11,000 tonnes of 'rehabitable foods'. Wollo and Tigrai received 70 per cent of this, despite the fact that their problems were nearly over. Harerghe, where famine was at its height, received only 8 per cent.[8]

7.2 FOOD AVAILABILITY

Since the Ethiopian famine clearly was initiated by a drought, and since drought causes crop failures (and, indeed, did so in this

---

[6] Holt and Seaman (1976), p. 4.
[7] See Wiseberg (1976).
[8] Rivers, Holt, Seaman, and Bowden (1976), p. 352.

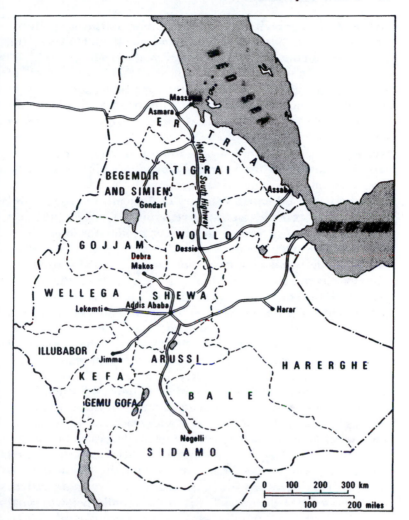

FIG. 7.1 Map of Ethiopia

case), it is easy to be predisposed towards accepting an explanation of the famine in terms of food availability decline (FAD).
But a drought causing an agricultural or pastoral crisis not only

reduces food supply; it also cuts the earnings of the agriculturist or the pastoralist, affecting his command over food. However, the first question concerns the volume of food output.

Those who have argued in favour of a FAD interpretation of the famine have very often quoted the 1972 November Survey of agricultural production done by the Ministry of Agriculture after the failure of the main rains. That a food shortage famine *should* have been predicted has also been frequently stated. The survey was indeed a very detailed one, done just before the famine erupted, and must be taken seriously. But does a picture of drastic food availability decline, in fact, emerge from this survey?

The report—Ethiopian Ministry of Agriculture (1973)—did not actually provide quantitative estimates of output, but classified districts according to whether production was 'above normal', 'normal', 'below normal', or 'substantially below normal'. This was done not only for each of the main crops, but also for 'aggregate production' for 1972–3, and the last is reproduced in Table 7.1. It appears that, while 65 per cent of the districts had normal output, 21 per cent had below-normal production and 14 per cent above-normal. The below-normal category is further split into those district that produced 'substantially below normal' and those below normal but not substantially so. The 'above-normal' category is not similarly split up into substantial above-normal output and others.

To give our analysis of output availability a downward bias, it may be assumed that none of the 'above-normal' districts was substantially so. Attaching the same importance to all the districts, the 14 per cent above-normal districts can be 'cancelled out' against the 14 per cent non-substantially below-normal districts. This leaves us with 65 per cent normal output districts, and 7 per cent of the districts with substantially below-normal output. Even if 'substantially below-normal output' is taken to be no output at all, which is clearly an underestimate, this indicates a displacement from normal output of 7 per cent. A 7 per cent decline in the output of food crops is hardly a devastating food availability decline (especially in an economy with primarily rain-dependent agriculture).

It is possible to use some other data, also provided by the same report, to arrive at an estimate of output decline. The report provides aggregates for each crop separately, noting which

TABLE 7.1
1972–3 Crop Production in Ethiopia: Provincial Evaluations

Region	Number of districts reporting	Percentage of districts in various categories				
		Normal	Above normal	Below normal	Net below normal	Substantially below normal
	(1)	(2)	(3)	(4)	(5) = (4) − (3)	(6), included in (4)
1. Wello	21	10	0	90	90	52
2. Arussi	20	70	5	25	20	10
3. Harerghe	22	39	23	39	16	9
4. Eritrea	23	78	4	18	14	9
5. Shewa	72	54	17	29	12	8
6. Tigrai	42	84	6	10	4	8
7. Wellega	35	86	0	14	14	0
8. Gemu Gofa	17	82	6	12	6	0
9. Illubabor	14	64	22	14	−8	0
10. Gojjam	22	82	14	4	−10	0
11. Kefa	9	45	33	22	−11	0
12. Begemdir and Simien	29	72	21	7	−14	0
13. Sidamo	23	78	22	0	−22	0
14. Bale	11	9	82	9	−73	0
Total	360	65	14	21	7	7

Source: Based on data presented in Ethiopian Ministry of Agriculture (1973) and Hussein (1976), Table 10.

districts were below normal, which above normal, etc. These are presented in Table 7.2. The relative weights to be attached to different crops have been calculated from their respective importance in terms of physical weight in the pre-famine year 1971–2 (using data presented in Hussein, 1976, Appendix 5).

The weighted deficit works out as a decline corresponding to below-normal production in 5.74 districts in *net*. Again, biasing the estimate towards the FAD view, it may be assumed that in these 5.74 districts nothing at all was produced, which will amount to an over-all reduction of under 6 per cent compared with normal production.

There is, thus, very little evidence of a dramatic decline in food availability in Ethiopia coinciding with the famine. Indeed, a modest increase in agricultural output for Ethiopia as a whole is recorded by the National Bank of Ethiopia (1976) for the famine year *vis-à-vis* the preceding years (Table 21, p. 79). The food output estimate given by the Food and Agriculture Organization of the United Nations for 1973 seems to vary (contrast the figures for this year in the *FAO Production Yearbooks* for 1974, 1975, and 1976 respectively), but the calorie consumption estimate indicated no significant diminution and possibly a sizeable rise over the preceding years. Table 7.3 presents the per head calorie consumption figures for 1973 and 1974 compared with 1961–5, 1964–6, 1967–9, 1970, and 1972, obtained from the *FAO*

TABLE 7.2
1972–3 Crop Production in Ethiopia: Crop Evaluations

Crop	Percentage of districts in various categories			Relative weight *1971–2*	Weighted net below normal districts (%)
	Above normal	Below normal	Net below normal		
	(1)	(2)	(3) = (2) − (1)	(4)	(5) = (4) × (3)
Barley	21	15	−6	0.259	− 1.55
Teff	18	25	7	0.228	1.60
Sorghum	16	33	17	0.182	3.09
Maize	17	28	11	0.160	1.76
Wheat	18	22	4	0.145	0.58
Others	14	24	10	0.026	0.26
Total				1.000	5.74

Source: Based on data presented in Ethiopian Ministry of Agriculture (1973) and Hussein (1976).

TABLE 7.3

Food Availability in Ethiopia: Calories per head, 1961–74

Period	Calories	Index value of calories per capita with row period = 100	
		1973	*1974*
1961–5	2,092	99	91
1964–6	1,910	109	100
1967–9	1,950	107	98
1970	1,980	105	97
1972	2,152	97	89
1973	2,081	100	92
1974	1,912	109	100

Source: The data for 1961–5, 1972, 1973, and 1974 are taken from *FAO Production Yearbook 1976*, vol. 30; and for 1964–6, 1967–9, and 1970 from *FAO Production Yearbook 1971*, vol. 25. Information for 1971 could not be obtained, which reflects a remaining gap in the published FAO series which was discontinued for the Production Yearbooks for 1972–5. There is probably some difference between the 1971 and 1976 Yearbooks for the early 1960s data, since the averages for 1961–3 and 1964–6 given in the 1971 Yearbook are *both* lower than the average for 1961–5 given in the 1976 Yearbook, though obviously this is not *necessarily* inconsistent since the year 1966 does not figure in the last average.

Production Yearbook for 1971 and 1976. (The food consumption series had been discontinued in the Yearbooks for 1972 to 1975, and the remaining gap is that for the year 1971, since the 1976 Yearbook provides data from 1972 onwards.) It appears from this that, while the 1973 availability figure is just a bit lower than that in 1972, it is hardly lower than the 1961–5, average, and a good deal higher than the averages for 1964–6, 1967–9, and 1970. Indeed, no picture of a sharp fall in food consumption per head in the famine year 1973 emerges from any of these data. There is, however, more evidence of a fall in the following year, 1974.

7.3 WOLLO: TRANSPORT CONSTRAINT OR ENTITLEMENT CONSTRAINT?

While there was no noticeable food availability decline for Ethiopia as a whole in the famine year of 1973, there was clearly a shortage of food in the province of Wollo. This shortage could in principle be explained in at least two quite different ways. One is to take the entitlement approach, and argue that the fall in food output in Wollo resulted in a *direct entitlement failure* on the part of

Wollo farmers and a *trade entitlement failure* for other classes in
Wollo, e.g. labourers and providers of services. There was not
merely a decline in the food to which the Wollo population was
directly entitled out of its own production, but also a collapse of
income and purchasing power and of the ability of the Wollo
population to attract food from elsewhere in Ethiopia. The
alternative explanation is to attribute the food shortage in Wollo
to transport difficulties in moving food to the province from
elsewhere in Ethiopia. According to this view, while there was no
food shortage in Ethiopia, food could not be moved into Wollo
because of a transport bottleneck. Indeed, transport limitation
has been much discussed in explaining the food shortage in
Wollo.

Roads are indeed quite underdeveloped *within* Wollo, and
problems of moving food deep into rural areas of Wollo must not
be underestimated. Nevertheless, I would like to argue that the
transport limitation explanation cannot explain the Wollo
famine, and the explanation has to be sought in entitlement
failures.

First, while roads are few and bad in much of Wollo, two
highways run through it, and the main north–south Ethiopian
highway linking Addis Ababa and Asmera runs right through the
area most affected by the famine.[9] Indeed, much of the early
information about the famine came from travellers being stopped
on the highway and asked for food (see Holt and Seaman, 1976).
Nearly all the relief camps that were eventually set up were
located near the highway, not merely because of easy access for
supplies coming in, but also because of the high intensity of
destitution in that region.[10] Underdeveloped roads would not
explain the starvation in these famine-affected regions.

Second, there were reports of movements of food *out of* Wollo
through the famine period. Food from Wollo went to Addis
Ababa and to Asmera.[11] This probably was not very large in
volume, but it provides some support for the market entitlement
view rather than the transport limitation view of food shortage in
Wollo.

Third, despite the disastrous failure of food output, food prices

[9] See Holt and Seaman (1976) and Belete *et al.* (1977).
[10] See Belete *et al.* (1977).
[11] See Holt and Seaman (1976), p. 5.

did not go up very much and for long in Wollo. When in October 1973 Holt and Seaman started their collection of food prices in the hardest hit district of Raya and Kobo, which had more than a tenth of its population in relief camps by May–June 1974,[12] they found that food prices were within 15 per cent of the pre-drought levels.[13]

Food prices in Dessie—the main grain market in Wollo—are given in Table 7.4.[14] Taking the average prices of 1970–2 as the 'pre-famine' levels, prices in the famine year 1973 were, on the whole, remarkably close to pre-famine levels: somewhat higher

TABLE 7.4
Wholesale Prices of Food Crops in Dessie, Wollo Province: 1970–3

Food crop	1970	1971	1972	1973	Percentage excess of 1973 price over 1970–2 average
White wheat	36	34	27	28	−13
Milling wheat	22	30	23	25	0
White sorghum	27	28	23	26	0
Other sorghum and zengada	23	24	19	21	−5
White teff	37	35	33	36	+3
Seregenga teff	33	31	29	34	+10
Red and abolse teff	31	29	27	30	+3
White barley	28	27	19	24	−3
Other barley	24	23	15	20	−3
Maize	21	20	23	21	−2
Millet (*dagussa*)	20	21	24	22	+2
Mixed peas	21	24	17	21	+2
Niger seed	37	32	24	25	−19
Rape seed	26	31	22	26	−1
Lin seed	40	42	25	30	−16

Source: National Bank of Ethiopia (for 1970 and 1971 data) and Ethiopian Grain Agency (for 1972 and 1973 data). I am most grateful to Julius Holt for making these unpublished figures available to me.
Note
Unit = Ethiopian Birr per quintal.

[12] Belete *et al.* (1977), Tables I and II.
[13] Holt and Seaman (1976). There were, however, reports of an earlier short period rise; see Seaman and Holt (1980).
[14] These prices collected by the Ethiopian Grain Agency relate to the Ethiopian calendar. So 1973 corresponds to September 1972–September 1973. While it begins a bit early (and no time breakdown could be obtained), it avoids the period of very late 1973 in which relief supplies started coming into Wollo in some volume. Also, the main crop failure was clear by September 1972, the *kremt* rains having already failed.

for some and somewhat lower for others. People starved to death without there being a substantial rise in food prices. In terms of the entitlement approach, there is, of course, no puzzle in this. Since the farmers' food entitlement is a direct entitlement (without going through the market), a collapse of it can operate without a rise in market prices. On the other hand, the transport limitation view would have suggested a substantial increase in prices because of the excess demand arising from supply limitation.

The transport limitation view is, therefore, not easy to defend. In so far as the starving people in Wollo could draw on food from the rest of Ethiopia *if* they had the market power to pull food into Wollo, the appropriate unit for a FAD analysis has to be Ethiopia rather than Wollo. Food didn't move into Wollo in sufficient amount (and some moved out), not so much because the roads didn't permit such movement, but because the Wollo residents lacked the market command.[15]

7.4 THE ECONOMIC BACKGROUND OF THE DESTITUTES

Who were the famine victims? What economic background did they come from? While no systematic survey of the occupational background of famine victims was undertaken,[16] there are several sources of information on this subject. Putting them together, something of a clear picture does emerge about the groups involved, even though the quantitative importance of different groups is difficult to establish.

It is quite clear that one group that was severely affected was the Afar community of nomadic pastoralists. They were among the group of refugees seeking help in Addis Ababa in December 1972, and they figured most prominently in the crowds lining in the north–south highway through Wollo in early 1973, stopping cars and buses asking for food. There is, in fact, overwhelming evidence that 'Afar pastoralists were amongst the first to face the acute problems after the rain failure of 1972'.[17]

In a study carried out in May–June 1974 of the inmates in the thirteen shelters in Wollo province, it was found that the different

[15] According to Ethiopian Grain Agency data, the Wollo grain prices in 1973 remained in the neighbourhood of—typically only a little higher than—those ruling in Addis Ababa, despite the starvation in Wollo.

[16] There is here a sharp contrast with the availability of occupational statistics for the Bengal famine of 1943, to a great extent because of the broad-based sample survey carried out by Mahalanobis, Mukherjea, and Ghosh (1946).

[17] Holt and Seaman (1976), p. 3.

regions of Wollo were remarkably differently represented in these relief camps. Table 7.5 presents the number of households from different *awrajas* (subregions) in Wollo, and it is clear that three of the *awrajas* stand out as having very much higher incidence of destitution: Raya and Kobo, Yeju, and Ambassel. Even in absolute numbers they provided more than three-quarters of all the destitutes in the relief camps. As it happens, all three of these subregions are mostly in the eastern lowlands of Wollo, and this is where the nomadic herdsmen primarily live. While community-specific incidence rates cannot be calculated from the data, it is quite clear that nomadic herdsmen were hit hard, and 'in the Wollo famine of 1973, the pastoral population hardest hit were the Afar'.[18]

But while the nomads may have been hit relatively hardest, in absolute numbers the destitutes were dominated by

TABLE 7.5

Subregional Variation of Relief Seeking in Wollo

Subregion (awraja)	Population (thousands)	Household numbers from the subregion in the relief camps	Number in relief camp per thousand from the subregion	Relative destitution index
(1)	(2)	(3)	(4)	(5)
1. Raya and Kobo	54	1,350	112.5	100
2. Yeju	159	1,994	56.4	50
3. Ambassel	261	1,639	28.3	25
4. Kalu	126	515	18.4	16
5. Awsa	73	184	11.3	10
6. Wag	142	169	5.4	5
7. Lasta	292	182	2.8	2
8. Dessie Zuria	179	110	2.8	2
9. Wadla Delanta	147	18	0.6	0.5
10. Wore Himenu	225	22	0.4	0.4
11. Borena	265	15	0.3	0.3
12. Were Ilu	137	0	0.0	0.0

Source: Columns (1), (2), and (3) are taken from Tables I and II in Belete *et al.* (1977). Column (4) is calculated from them, taking a household size of 4.5 persons, and agrees with the figures given in Table II of Belete *et al.* (1977) except for the elimination of what appears to be a computational slip there regarding the subregion Wag. Column (5) converts the figures in column (4) into a 0–100 linear index.

[18] Hussein (1976), p. 19.

agriculturists, since the latter is a very much larger group. In terms of numbers, the 'relief-centre populations were mainly made up of members of the farming peoples of principally low-land area which are many times more densely populated than the Afar region'.[19] In fact, even in the subregions of Raya and Kobo, Yeju, and Ambassel, the bulk of the destitutes came from the agricultural communities.

The agriculturists came to distress quite early as well. The 1,500 Wollo people who marched to Addis Ababa to beg for help in March 1973 were reported to be 'peasants'.[20] While it is always problematic to judge distress from protest movements, since it may reflect better organization and militancy rather than greater distress, there is little doubt that Wollo agriculturists were widely suffering from destitution very early in the 1973 famine.[21]

Among the population of the relief camps, the following groups seem to have predominated:

(1) women and children 'drawn from the surrounding agricultural land', who formed a majority of the relief camp population;

(2) a large number of men who had migrated to the more southerly camps, particularly in Dessie and Kombolcha 'from more northerly districts in search of work';

(3) people from roadside towns and their peripheries, consisting of 'professional beggars', 'male daily labourers who could no longer find sufficient work', and 'women in service occupations who were not wanted in these hard economic times: household servants of the less wealthy, water carriers whose work was taken over by members of clients' families, beer-sellers and prostitutes'.[22]

Interviews with the relief camp inhabitants also threw much light on the sequence of destitution in the settled farming communities.[23] With reduced crops and grazing as the crisis deepened, servants and dependants of farmers were evicted, and they were among the first to move to look for work elsewhere.

[19] Holt and Seaman (1976), p. 3.
[20] See Wiseberg (1976), p. 108, on contemporary records on this and other aspects of the early stages of the famine.
[21] See Hussein (1976) and Gebre-Medhin and Vahlquist (1977).
[22] Holt and Seaman (1976), pp. 3-5.
[23] See Gebre-Medhin *et al.* (1974); Holt and Seaman (1976); and Belete, Gebre-Medhin, Hailemariam, Maffi, Vahlquist, and Wolde-Gabriel (1977).

There followed a good deal of eviction of tenants from the land, and they too were set on the move. Both tenants as well as small-scale family-land (*rist*) holders were gradually led to sell livestock, in addition to losing a great many owing to the drought, and many seem to have run out of seeds when a second planting became necessary after a false start to the rains. While movement in search of work elsewhere is by no means uncommon in this part of Ethiopia, there was now an unusually large movement in search of employment for daily labour or harvest work. Among the places to which the migrants went were local towns within the Wollo region, the Setit-Humera cash cropping region near the border with Sudan, and the cotton plantations on the Awash River in the southern parts of the province. The wives and children of the migrating men either stayed with relatives, or came to town to beg for a living, or sought shelter in the relief camps.

There are also other sources of information on migration, including a study of ninety-two Muslim families from Koreb and Gayint, two villages near the border of Wollo and Begemdir-Simien (A. P. Wood, 1976). The vast majority of the migrants, in this case, earned their livelihood by cultivation. Other occupations mentioned were weaving, domestic service, and the sale of alcoholic drinks. In terms of propensity to move, it appears that neither those who owned much land nor the very poor moved easily, and 'those who moved were the wealthier tenants, and the small landowners' (p. 71). The explanation offered by Adrian Wood is as follows:

The poorer tenants had, as a result of seven years of drought, already exhausted their meagre resources and either left the area, become deeply indebted and hence tied to their benefactor, or died. The wealthier tenants, having more resources in terms of livestock and land under cultivation, had until this stage been able to survive independently but many were finding this increasingly difficult. Landowners, not having to pay rent, which most tenants appear to have paid throughout the drought, were less affected by the reduced yields. However, many of those with only small areas under cultivation and few livestock had exhausted their reserves after seven years of drought.[24]

Piecing together the available information, the destitution groups in the 1973–4 famine in Wollo would seem to include at

[24] A. P. Wood (1976), p. 71.

least the following occupation categories (and their dependants):
(1) pastoralists, particularly from the Afar community;
(2) evicted farm servants and dependants of farmers, and rural labourers;
(3) tenant cultivators, sometimes evicted, but often simply squeezed by economic circumstances;
(4) small land-owning cultivators;
(5) daily male labourers in urban areas;
(6) women in service occupations;
(7) weavers and other craftsmen;
(8) occupational beggars.

In contrast with the famine in Wollo and the north-east of Ethiopia, the later 'southern' famine was relatively small, in terms of both mortality and economic destitution. It affected principally Harerghe, the country's largest province, and to a lesser extent Bale and Sidamo. There is a good deal of mortality data from Harerghe,[25] and it would appear that the hardest-hit group were the pastoralists who were Ogaden Somalis and Issa Somalis. While a substantial majority of the population even of the Harerghe province are agriculturists, the famine victims were very largely the pastoralists from these nomadic groups. Because of the differences in normal nutritional levels of the different communities, this contrast is not easy to detect on the basis of the standard anthropometric measures, but descriptive accounts of the famine as well as survey of the relief camp inmates bring out the contrast sharply.[26] The differences are apparent also in the mortality statistics. This is especially clear from the data on mortality of children under five.[27] It appears, on the basis of a survey in 1974, that 'during the previous year this mortality rate of the under-five was virtually unchanged for agricultural peoples, but increased by about three-fold amongst pastoralists'.[28] Thus, in understanding the 'southern famine' in Harerghe, it is appropriate to concentrate on the pastoralists and

[25] See Seaman, Holt, and Rivers (1974; 1978) and Gebre-Medhin, Hay, Licke, and Maffi (1977).
[26] See Seaman, Holt, and Rivers (1974; 1978), Gebre-Medhin and Vahlquist (1977), p. 198; and Gebre-Medhin, Hay, Licke, and Maffi (1977), pp. 29–34.
[27] In Ethiopian famines a high mortality level of under-five children seems to be a common characteristic. In the 'north-eastern famine' also the children under five were especially affected. See Belete, Gebre-Medhin, Hailemariam, Maffi, Vahlquist, and Wolde-Gabriel (1977), pp. 18–19.
[28] Rivers, Holt, Seaman, and Bowden (1976), p. 352.

on the particular areas in which they lived, namely the northern and southern Ogaden regions and the Issa Desert.

7.5 AGRICULTURAL DESTITUTION AND ENTITLEMENTS

As was mentioned earlier, the biggest group of destitutes in the Wollo famine came from the agricultural background, and indeed were farmers—both tenants and small land-owning cultivators. The entitlement decline here took the form of *direct entitlement failure* (see Chapter 5) without involving the market in the immediate context. The output—typically of foodgrains—was severely reduced, and this led to starvation in a direct way. In so far as the Ethiopian farmer eats the food grown by the family without becoming involved in exchange to acquire food, the immediate influence affecting starvation is the decline of the food grown and owned by the family, rather than the fall in the total food output in the region as a whole.[29] The distinction is important, since the FAD approach would focus on the latter variable. The hunger of the Wollo peasant had a more direct origin.

But, of course, once his own crop had failed, the Wollo peasant would have tried to get hold of food through the market *in so far as* he could have exercised market command. But since the agricultural failure also amounts to a collapse of his *source* of market command (namely his income), he was not in a position to supplement his reduced food output by market purchase. As discussed in Section 7.3, the Wollo agriculturist could not provide much effective demand for food in the market, and despite widespread starvation the food prices in Dessie and elsewhere recorded very little increase.

The effective demand of the agriculturist was further restrained by three subsidiary factors in addition to the fall in agricultural output: (1) a fall in the market price of land,[30] (2) loss of livestock,[31] and (3) a fall in the market price of livestock.[32]

[29] So far as the *tenant* farmers are concerned, they also suffered from the inflexibility of rents and feudal dues, on which there was little relief (see Cliffe, 1974, and Hussein, 1976). There was also some rearrangement of rental agreements unfavourable to the tenants (see Hussein, 1976, and also Cohen and Weintraub, 1975).

[30] See A. P. Wood (1976) and Belete *et al.* (1977).

[31] See Miller and Holt (1975) and Hussein (1976).

[32] This was pointed out already in March 1973 by the Ethiopian Ministry of Agriculture (1973), while reporting on the November 1972 survey of crop losses: 'depressed prices for livestock in most deficient areas' were 'making losses high in

The decline in land and livestock prices is a common phenomenon in famine situations affecting agriculturists, since they
represent assets that the agriculturist tries to sell to acquire food
when all else fails; and the sudden increase in supply of these
assets in the market causes a price decline. The livestock *quantity*
declined largely as a result of the drought, and the interesting
point is that, despite this quantity reduction, the *prices* of farm
animals also fell. This too is a common combination in pastoral
famines, and will be taken up for a fuller discussion in the next
section.

Turning now to agricultural labour, the eviction of farm
servants was very widespread in Wollo during the famine. This
was a natural economy measure on the part of farmers faced with
an economic crisis of gigantic proportion, and fits into the general
pattern of 'derived destitution' also observed elsewhere (see
Chapter 6 and Appendix B). The resource ownership of the farm
servants is confined, for all practical purposes, to own labour-
power, and as unemployment develops the exchange entitlement
of the group collapses radically. Migration in search of work
elsewhere may or may not provide any substantial remedy, and
for those who died or ended up in relief camps it presumably did
not. Even for those who were successful in finding employment
elsewhere, the wives and children often died meanwhile, or had
to live in camps, since the process typically involved travelling
over distance and spending substantial amounts of time there to
earn enough to save something and return. In the mean time,
many of their dependants perished, especially children under
five.[33] Also, a great many families became permanently split as a
consequence of the prolonged separation.

The eviction of farmers' dependants reflected partly just hard-
headedness in hard times, but also the fact that many dependants
play a role not altogether dissimilar to servants—being given
'food and shelter in return for farm labour'.[34] They were turned
away for much the same reasons as farm servants were, and once
evicted they typically shared the same fate as the farm servants.

---

transactions involving livestock sales to supplement grain supplies' (pp. 8–9). See also
A. P. Wood (1976), pp. 72–3.

[33] See Belete, Gebre-Medhin, Hailemariam, Maffi, Vahlquist, and Wolde-Gabriel
(1977), pp. 18–9.

[34] Holt and Seaman (1976), p. 4.

Other occupational categories, e.g. weavers, craftsman, service sellers, urban labourers, and beggars, suffered mostly from straightforward 'derived destitution'. The economic decline of a large section of the community leads to a shrinkage of demand for commodities sold by other groups, in this case clothing, craft products, services, and even general labour power. Also, of course, living on charity is made that much more difficult. One decline leads to another, and so on, through the multiplier effect. Some of these occupations also became more competitive, with the influx of displaced rural men and women seeking work for survival, after migration into urban areas (see Hussein, 1976). These trade entitlement failures are the indirect results of agricultural decline in Wollo.

Two questions can be asked here. Since the destitution of the Wollo farmer was seen in terms of a *direct* entitlement failure, isn't there some inconsistency in assuming that the farmers cut down their demand for other products, since direct entitlements are calculated on the assumption of the whole of the own produce being used for consumption within the family (see Chapter 5)? The answer is no. While food entitlement reflects the *maximum* amount of food a person or a family can command, actual consumption can be less than that, and there is no inconsistency in taking a farmer (whose direct entitlement is calculated as his whole produce) to be selling a part of that produce to buy other goods and services. It might be quite natural in a famine situation to assume that the whole of the food entitlement will be consumed, but not so in non-famine situations. There is, thus, no inconsistency in assuming that the farmer in the famine year will *reduce* his consumption of non-food commodities and will consume more—perhaps all—of his food entitlement.

Second, this reduced demand for non-food commodities and the related reduced supply of food to the market can be seen as exerting an upward pressure on the prices of food. Isn't this inconsistent with the observed largely stationary prices of foodgrains at Dessie and elsewhere? The answer again is no. The reduced supply of foodgrains to the market will go hand in hand with a reduced demand for non-food commodities and a consequent reduced demand for food by the producers and sellers of these non-food commodities. The food demand will thus also go down with food supply in these markets, and it is not clear that food prices would have risen much in these markets even if they had been cut off from the foodgrains supply in the rest of Ethiopia. There is, of course, the additional fact that these markets were not thus cut off, and any big rise in food prices in Dessie would have led to an increased food movement into Dessie.

So far, little has been said about the destitution of the pastoralist. To this group I now turn.

7.6 PASTORAL ENTITLEMENTS AND THE NOMADIC HERDSMAN

As was noted earlier, in the 'north-eastern famine', especially in Wollo, the pastoralist—particularly of the Afar community— was hit very hard, and in the later 'southern famine' the most affected group in Hererghe were the pastoral nomads from the Ogaden Somali and the Issa Somali communities. It might appear that, while their sufferings were severe, the explanation would be simple enough: the drought killed animals and the nomads, not being able to eat animals, died of starvation. But the picture is a good deal more complex than this.

First, the pastoralists, particularly of the Afar community, were affected not merely by the drought in north-eastern Ethiopia, but also by the loss of grazing land owing to the expansion of commercial agriculture. About 50,000 hectares of good land in the Awash Valley were 'developed' during 1970–1 for growing commercial crops, particularly cotton and sugar, by a few big companies—mostly foreign-owned[35]—and this growth of commercial agriculture continued through the early 1970s. The land thus developed had been among the best of the grazing land available to the Afar pastoralist during the long dry season lasting from September to May, and this land alienation led to severe economic problems of its own for the Afar.[36] As Glynn Flood (1975) noted, 'if they are to be able to exploit the vast areas into which they move during the wet season, Afar pastoralists must have access to adequate dry season grazing near the river', and 'when a small area close to the river is made unavailable for dry season grazing, a much larger area away from the river is

---

[35] This development can be viewed, more generally, as part of the negative influence of international capitalist expansion. On that more general question, see the analyses of Baran (1962), Furtado (1964), Baran and Sweezy (1966), Magdoff (1968), Frank (1969), and Amin (1974), among other contributions.

[36] Bondestam (1974), Gebre-Medhin (1974), Flood (1975), and Hussein (1976).

rendered useless' (p. 65). The land that was 'developed' was particularly valuable to the Afar, being mostly in an area that 'flooded easily and took a long time to drain'—'land which gave good grazing during the hottest and driest part of the year from February to June' (p. 64).

It was in this situation that the drought of 1972–3 in north-eastern Ethiopia came. The wet season was late and short and not particularly wet, while the refuge of the dry weather had been already crucially curtailed by the alienation of land for commercial agriculture. Thus the impact of the drought was a great deal magnified by this structural change in the economy of the Awash Valley.[37]

Second, the economic distress of the pastoralist during the Ethiopian famine was not confined only to the loss of animals, whether this was due to drought or to displacement from traditional grazing grounds. The exchange entitlement associated with any given stock of animals *vis-à-vis* grains also fell sharply. It is sometimes overlooked that a pastoralist does not live only by eating animals or consuming animal products like milk. He also exchanges animals for other means of sustenance, chiefly grains. Indeed, given the 'normal' market prices prevailing in Ethiopia, animal calories cost about twice as much as grain calories,[38] and therefore a pastoral family can survive on a much lower holding of animals if they sell animals to buy grains for eating. Indeed, the typical pastoralist in these regions tends to meet about half of his calorie requirements through agricultural rather than pastoral products.[39]

While in the north-eastern famine in Wollo and elsewhere the exchange rates between animals and grains did fall, in the southern famine in Harerghe they collapsed in a totally dramatic manner. From a detailed survey of market prices conducted by Seaman, Holt, and Rivers (1974) covering different regions of Harerghe in May–June 1974, contemporary prices are available as well as the recollection of previous year's prices and the level of

[37] The Afar mainly use the middle and lower Awash Valley. The development of commercial agriculture was not, however, confined only to these parts of the Awash Valley. The growth of commercial agriculture in the upper valley of Awash led to the displacement of Kerega Oromo communities to find new pastures and also to the displacement of some peasant cultivation (see Bondestam, 1974, p. 480, and Hussein 1976, pp. 19–20).

[38] See Seaman, Holt, and Rivers (1978), pp. 38–9; also Hay (1975).

[39] See Rivers, Holt, Seaman, and Bowden (1976), p. 354.

'normal' prices. While the recall method is somewhat defective, especially in the context of prices,[40] the exchange rates between animals and grains calculated from these data are nevertheless of interest. Table 7.6 presents these derived exchange rates.[41]

It is clear that the exchange rate declines for animals against grains are very substantial, especially in pastoral (rather than agricultural) areas. Nevertheless, they may in fact *understate* the unfavourable exchange position of the pastoralists during the famine, since the animal prices had relatively recovered when the observations were made. Those who conducted the survey noted that 'it was stated by respondents in pastoral areas that livestock prices, and especially cattle prices, had fluctuated considerably within the last year, and that they were remarkably low in many localities at the time six to nine months before this survey, when the effects of drought were most severe' (Seaman, Holt and Rivers, 1974, p. 64; see also Seaman, Holt and Rivers, 1978, p. 39).

This decline in the exchange position was coupled with the loss of animals during the drought. The two effects are put together in Table 7.7. The value weights on the different types of animals have been calculated from their relative shares in the 'normal' pre-drought market value of the estimated 'average' stock of animals owned by a pastoral family in each region. The 'normal' pre-drought prices are taken from Table XVII of Seaman, Holt, and Rivers (1974), p. 62, and are the same as given in Table 7.6 above. The average animal holdings in the pre-drought situation are calculated from the observed average in June 1974 (given by Table X of Seaman, Holt, and Rivers, 1974, p. 45), and the relation between this observed herd and 'last year's herd' as estimated by these authors from the ratios of sale and death of animals (1974, Tables XII and XIII, pp. 46–7). Percentage of animal lost by death, presented in the next row of our Table 7.7, are also obtained from Table XII of Seaman, Holt, and Rivers (1974). The percentage losses of grain entitlement owing to

---

[40] The notion of 'normal' prices is particularly problematic, and earlier reports give somewhat different figures. See Seaman, Holt, and Rivers (1974), pp. 66–73, dealing with price levels given by two unpublished reports prepared respectively by the Ministry of Water Resources and the Ministry of Agriculture of the Imperial Ethiopian Government. However, the dramatic decline of the exchange rates of animals for grains follow from these figures as well.

[41] See also Gebre-Medhin, Hay, Licke, and Maffi (1977).

TABLE 7.6
Animal–Grain Exchange Rates in Different Strata in Hararghe

	Southern Ogaden stratum (pastoral)			Northern Ogaden stratum (pastoral)			Issa stratum (pastoral)			Strata in Hararghe strata (agricultural)		
	'Normal'	1973	1974	'Normal'	1973	1974	'Normal'	1973	1974	'Normal'	1973	1974
A Prices (Ethiopian dollars per quintal)												
Sorghum	16	37	51	17	27	42	16	24	32	15	25	31
Maize	14	34	48	14	24	36	15	21	27	14	20	27
Cattle	86	83	77	87	85	61	132	74	101	87	109	125
Sheep and goats	18	16	19	21	18	18	24	14	18	15	19	25
Camels	222	216	223	238	219	193	234	151	166	158	147	159
B Exchange rates (Index)												
Sorghum–Cattle	100	42	28	100	62	28	100	37	38	100	75	70
Maize–cattle	100	40	26	100	57	27	100	40	43	100	88	74
Sorghum–sheep	100	38	33	100	54	35	100	39	38	100	76	81
Maize–sheep	100	37	31	100	50	33	100	42	42	100	89	86
Sorghum–camel	100	42	32	100	58	33	100	43	35	100	56	49
Maize–camel	100	40	29	100	54	32	100	46	39	100	65	52

Source: Calculated from Seaman, Holt, and Rivers (1974), Tables XVI and XVII.

Table 7.7
Grain Entitlement Loss due to Animal Loss and Exchange Rate Change

	Southern Ogaden stratum				Northern Ogaden stratum				Issa stratum			
	Cattle	Goats and sheep	Camels	Average stock	Cattle	Goats and sheep	Camels	Average stock	Cattle	Goats and sheep	Camels	Average stock
Value weights in pre-drought holdings	0.571	0.157	0.271	1.000	0.295	0.276	0.429	1.000	0.396	0.425	0.179	1.000
Percentage animal loss owing to death (q)	47	45	52	48	56	61	55	57	88	74	69	79
Percentage grain entitlement loss owing to exchange rate change (p)	72	67	68	70	72	65	67	68	62	62	65	62
Percentage total grain entitlement loss ($p+q-pq$)	85	82	85	84	88	86	85	86	95	90	89	92
Ratio of exchange rate loss to animal ownership loss (p/q)	1.53	1.49	1.31	1.46	1.29	1.07	1.22	1.19	0.70	0.84	0.94	0.78

Source: see text.

exchange rate change *vis-à-vis* the predrought 'normal' levels are simply taken from the calculations presented in Table 7.6 above, taking sorghum as the grain in question for the purpose of these calculations. The percentage losses of grain entitlement from animal holdings as a combined result of animal loss and exchange rate deterioration are given in the next row, and these could be seen to be astonishingly large for all the pastoral areas, viz., 84 per cent for southern Ogaden, 86 per cent for northern Ogaden, and as much as 92 per cent for Issa desert.[42]

Another remarkable feature of these results concerns the relative contribution of animal loss and exchange rate deterioration on the total loss of entitlement to grains of the average pastoralist. In both southern Ogaden and northern Ogaden the contribution of the exchange rate seems substantially larger than that of animal loss as such. This is not so only in the Issa Desert, which was estimated to contain less than a third of the Ogaden population.

In fact, the relative contribution of the exchange rate change must be recognized to be even larger, when it is taken into account that (1) taking maize rather than sorghum as the index grain would increase the force of the exchange rate revision, and (2) the effect of animal loss is very considerably exaggerated in these calculations because of ignoring normal mortality in animals, which even in the absence of the drought conditions are typically quite large.[43] If the figures are revised to reflect these corrections, the relative contribution of exchange rate deterioration *vis-à-vis* animal mortality in the loss of grain entitlement would be even larger in all the areas under study. The *total* loss of grain entitlement, however, would be reduced, because more than half the recorded mortality in southern and northern Ogaden could be then attributed to normal death balanced by births.[44]

The grain entitlements are worth calculating, not because the pastoralist is likely to sell all his animals and buy grains, but—as

---

[42] Data presented by Gebre-Medhin, Hay, Licke and Maffi (1977) suggest a further deterioration in the year following, but they also note some doubts about the animal holding figures (p. 32). See also Hay (1975).

[43] See Seaman, Holt, and Rivers (1978), pp. 48, 56–7.

[44] For the same reason one can dispute the method of estimating 'last year's herd' used by Seaman, Holt, and Rivers (1974), which provides the basis for the weights used in Table 7.7 here. Summing 'the observed herd plus the number of animals reported to have

noted before—the pastoralist can normally acquire calories a good deal more cheaply through exchanging animals for grains. The typical pastoralist does depend on this, and in a situation of economic difficulty arising from loss of herd he is pushed to be even more dependent on grains. This is one reason why a drought that reduces both the animal stock and the grain output[45] very often leads to a reduction in animal price compared with grains. The proportionate reduction of animal offered in the market is typically a good deal less than the proportionate reduction in animal holdings, and can easily be a lot less than the proportionate reduction in the grain offered in the market.

There are three features in this that are worth distinguishing. First, grains at normal prices are cheaper sources of nutrition, and in a situation of economic decline demand tends to shift in that direction. Animals are 'superior' goods, and suffer in times of income collapse. When animal prices fall *vis-à-vis* grain this situation may change, but the emaciation of the animals in a drought situation also tends to lower the break-even exchange rate.

Second, for the pastoralist savings for the future takes the form of storing animals 'on the hoof', and in times of difficulty he may have to 'dissave' out of that stock by selling animals. For the peasant the saving is partly in the form of livestock, which he may also have to fling, and partly in the form of land. An unusual increase in land offer in a situation of economic decline is common, often leading to a fall in the relative price of land. Saving in the form of grain-stock is much less common, because of storage cost and perishability and also because the stock has no concurrent use value. Thus animals for the pastoralist serve both as output (like grains for the agriculturist) and as stored savings (like land—and animals—for the agriculturist). This too puts a bigger burden of adjustment on animal supply to the market in

---

died plus the number of animals reported to have been sold in the past year' (p.46) ignores new births and thus overestimates last year's real stock. In using these figures for weighting it would have to be assumed that *relative* weights are not much changed by the exclusion of birth data.

[45] While the animal stock holding in the different strata in Harerghe fell between 20 and 50 per cent in terms of average stock between June 1973 and June 1974 (see Table 7.7 above), the foodgrains output of Harerghe fell by about 30 per cent between 1972 and 1973 including the respective December harvests supplying food for the following year (see Ethiopian Ministry of Agriculture, 1974, p. 321).

times of distress, to meet the herdsmen's grain demand as well as his other needs for cash.

Finally, the consumption profile of a grain-stock is much more adjustable and amenable to control than that of livestock. Grain is divisible in a way that animals are not. Furthermore, whatever can be got out of a grain-stock can be got out immediately, in a manner that is impossible for the flow of animal products like milk. Thus, in terms of adjustability of the time pattern of food supply, animals are worse than grains when flexibility of the time pattern of consumption is important. This puts a further premium on grains *vis-à-vis* animals in situations of emergency compared with their normal price ratios, and the break-even exchange rate in terms of over-all calorie-value becomes a deceptive basis of comparison. This is one reason why the demand for grains as a source of food stays up even when animal prices drop sharply and grains become relatively much dearer than in the pre-crisis situation.

7.7. CONCLUDING REMARKS

The famine of 1972-74 in Ethiopia had two rather distinct parts: one affecting the north-east—especially the Wollo province—in 1972-73, and the other happening in the more southern provinces—especially Harerghe—in 1973-74. Total famine mortality seems to have been much higher in the north-eastern famine, for which relief came much too late. While in the north-eastern famine the relative incidence of starvation was probably greatest for the pastoral people, a majority of the famine victims in absolute numbers seem to have come from the agricultural community. In the southern famine—especially in Harerghe— the pastoral population has been the main group to suffer from the famine.

The Ethiopian famine took place with no abnormal reduction in food output, and consumption of food per head at the height of the famine in 1973 was fairly normal for Ethiopia as a whole. While the food output in Wollo was substantially reduced in 1973, the inability of Wollo to command food from outside was the result of the low purchasing power in that province. A remarkable feature of the Wollo famine is that food prices in general rose very little, and people were dying of starvation even when food was selling at prices not very different from pre-drought levels. The phenomenon can be understood in terms of extensive entitlement failures of various sections of the Wollo population.

The pastoral population—severely affected in both the north-eastern and southern parts of the famine—belonged to nomadic and semi-nomadic groups. They were affected not merely by the drought but also by the growth of commercial agriculture, displacing some of these communities from their traditional dry-weather grazing land, thereby vastly heightening the impact of the drought. The effect of the loss of animal stock was also compounded by a severe worsening of terms of trade of animals for grain, disrupting the pastoralist's normal method of meeting his food requirements. The characteristics of exchange relations between the pastoral and the agricultural economies thus contributed to the starvation of the herdsmen by making price movements reinforce—rather than counteract—the decline in the livestock quantity. The pastoralist, hit by the drought, was decimated by the market mechanism.

Chapter 8

Drought and Famine in the Sahel

8.1 THE SAHEL, THE DROUGHT, AND THE FAMINE

The name Sahel is derived from an Arabic word meaning 'shore' or 'border'. The Sahel refers to the border of the world's largest tropical desert: the Sahara. It is, in fact, the fringe of the desert, lying between the desert and the tropical rain forests of Africa. But within this general conception of the Sahel, a great many alternative specifications of it can be found in the vast literature on the Sahel produced by geographers and climatologists. It is useful to begin by sorting out the different approaches, if only to avoid possible confusion later in the analysis of the Sahelian drought.

(1) *The ecological definitions* The Sahel can be defined as the 'dry zone', comprising the 'arid' zone (with average rainfall per year less than 100 mm, or 4 in.) and the 'semi-arid' zone (with rainfall between 100 and 500 mm, or between 4 and 20 in.), on the southern fringe of the Sahara, and this coincides with a 'tropical steppe vegetation belt'.[1] It runs across the broadest part of Africa from the Atlantic to the Red Sea. The Sahel is sometimes defined not as the entire dry zone immediately south of the Sahara, but as only the semi-arid zone there. While covering less than the whole dry zone in this part of the world, it too runs from the Atlantic to the Red Sea.[2]

(2) *The politico-ecological definitions* On this view, the Sahel is defined as the 'semi-arid vegetation belt' in six West African countries, viz. Mauritania, Senegal, Mali, Upper Volta, Niger, and Chad.[3] Alternatively, and more broadly, the Sahel could refer to the 'dry zone' in these six countries.

---

[1] Harrison Church (1973), p. 62; see also Harrison Church (1961).

[2] See Winstanley (1976), p. 189. Winstanley's specification of rainfall for the semi-arid region is also on the *higher* side, viz. 'between 200 and 600 mm', so that not merely the arid zone but also regions at the northern end of the semi-arid zone as defined by Harrison Church (1973) is excluded in this view of the Sahel.

[3] See Matlock and Cockrum (1976) and Swift (1977b). Sometimes Gambia and Cape Verde are added to this list of six countries.

(3) *The political definitions* The word Sahel could be used, as it has been by the international news media, simply to refer to these six *countries* in West Africa (Mauritania, Senegal, Mali, Upper Volta, Niger, and Chad), affected by the recent drought.[4]

There is no point in spilling blood over the choice of the definition that should be used, but one must be careful to distinguish between the different senses of the word Sahel to be found in the literature, since not a little confusion has arisen from vagueness owing to this plethora of definitions—sometimes used implicitly rather than explicitly.

In this work the Sahel in the purely political characterization will be called 'Sahelian countries', covering Mauritania, Senegal, Mali, Upper Volta, Niger, and Chad. The politico-ecological definition will be used in the form of calling the dry Sahel region in the Sahelian countries as 'the dry Sahel region'. Finally, the purely ecological definition applied to the whole of Africa (without noting political divisions) will be captured by the expression 'the Sahel belt of Africa'.

I turn now to the drought in question. The reference is to the period of low rainfall during 1968–73. There is some controversy as to whether 1968 or even 1969 were, in fact, years of drought. It has been argued that 'the 1968–69 rains were more or less normal; they only appeared low by comparison with the pluvian 1960s, which detracted attention from the cyclical nature of rainfall in that area'.[5] It appears that 'the Sahel and Sudan zones probably received more rain between 1956 and 1965 than at any time in this century', and, it has been argued, after that 'just less than average rainfall' appeared as 'drought'.[6] But there can be little doubt that the drought period involved a very considerable shift in the rainfall isohyets in a southerly direction, making an arid zone out of parts of semi-arid regions and turning non-dry regions into semi-arid ones. And this is so not only in contrast with the immediate pluvial past, but also compared with earlier record.[7] While it is certainly not correct to say that 'the Sahel has never had a drought like this one',[8] the shift in the rainfall pattern

---

[4] See the map of Sahel countries on p. 130.

[5] Wiseberg (1976), p. 122, quoting the views of an MIT group of climatologists.

[6] Matlock and Cockrum (1976), p. 238.

[7] See Winstanley (1976), Bradley (1977), Schove (1977).

[8] Brown and Anderson (1976), p. 162; it must, however, be said in fairness to the authors that the drought *was* very unusual in terms of its *impact*, though not as a drought as

was very substantial, and the contrast with the rainy 1960s was particularly sharp.

The problem applied not merely to the dry Sahel region in the Sahelian countries, but to the whole of the Sahel belt of Africa, covering also parts of Sudan and Ethiopia. Indeed, there were clear links in the drought pattern associated with the Ethiopian famine studied in the last chapter and the drought affecting the Sahelian countries.

It is also worth noting that the short-fall of rain compared with normal was more severe further north within the Sahelian region; i.e., areas that normally receive less rainfall anyway suffered a bigger relative short-fall as well.[9] This is not altogether unusual, since there is some evidence that as we move north in this part of Africa not only does the mean rainfall level fall, but the coefficient of variation rises substantially.[10]

The pastoral and agricultural economy of the Sahel region was severely affected by the drought.[11] While, as we shall presently see, there were factors other than the drought in the causation of the famine, it would be stupid to pretend that the drought was not seriously destructive. The peak year of suffering seems to have been 1973, and the drought waned only with the good rains of 1974. The animal loss altogether was estimated, according to some calculations, to be as high as 'some 40 percent to 60 percent',[12] but there is a good deal of disputation on these quantitative magnitudes, and much variation from region to region. There is, however, very little scope for doubting the severity of the suffering that accompanied the drought, and the famine conditions that developed during this period. Of the six countries, Mauritania, Mali, and Niger seem to have been hit harder than the other countries.

Already by 1969 there were reports of 'prolonged drought across West Africa'.[13] The situation got worse as the drought progressed, and by the spring of 1972 the United Nations World

such. On the comparative evidence from earlier periods, see the technical papers cited above, and also Dalby and Harrison Church (1973), pp. 13–16, 29–45.

[9] See Bradley (1977), p. 50, Figure 2.

[10] See Winstanley (1976), p. 197, Figure 8.6.

[11] See Shear and Stacy (1976), Winstanley (1976), and Matlock and Cockrum (1976). In Section 8.2 of this chapter the output situation is reviewed.

[12] El-Khawas (1976), p. 77. See also Winstanley (1976) and Matlock and Cockrum (1976).

[13] See Sheets and Morris (1976), p. 36.

Food Programme noted that drought in the Sahelian countries had become 'endemic', requiring that 'special treatment' be given to the region in providing emergency food aid. By September that year the FAO had identified a coming 'disaster', with 'an acute emergency situation developing in large areas due to exceptionally poor harvests in the Sahel'. The level of starvation was by then, it appears, much greater than in the preceding four years of drought, and 'children and the elderly had already begun to succumb'.[14]

The peak year of the famine in the Sahelian countries was 1973, the starvation having by then gathered momentum in a cumulative process of destitution and deprivation.[15] The number of famine deaths during that year was estimated to be around 100,000.[16] But there is a good deal of disputation about the mortality estimates,[17] and rather little direct evidence on which a firm estimate can be based. There is also much debate on the extent to which the famine unleashed the forces of epidemic in the Sahelian countries. The threat of epidemics was widely noted, and reports of flaring up of diseases like measles did come through, but it has been argued that the epidemics were rather mild and to a great extent were confined to the relief camps where infections could spread fast.[18] Certainly, the epidemic flare-up was nothing in comparison with what was observed in some earlier famines, e.g. the Bengal famine of 1943 (see Appendix D below).

The relief operations, though slow to start with, were on quite a massive scale, and the provision of food, medicine, and shelter was helped by a good deal of international co-operation. The efficiency of the relief operations remains a highly disputed topic. Some have seen in such operations the clue to 'how disaster was avoided',[19] and have assigned a good deal of credit to international efforts as well as to efforts within the countries

[14] Sheets and Morris (1976), p. 38. The authors provide a blow-by-blow account of the international recognition of the Sahelian disaster and a sharp critique of the delay in responding to it.

[15] See Newman (1975).

[16] Center for Disease Control (1973), and Kloth (1974). See also Imperato (1976).

[17] See Seaman, Holt, Rivers, and Murlis (1973), Imperato (1976), and Caldwell (1977), pp. 94–5.

[18] See Imperato (1976), pp. 295–7, Sheets and Morris (1976), pp. 61–3, and Seaman, Holt, Rivers, and Murlis (1973), p. 7.

[19] See Imperato (1976) and Caldwell (1977).

themselves. Others have emphasized the sluggishness, the chaos, and the discrimination between different communities of victims as evidence of unpardonable mismanagement.[20]

8.2 FAD VIS-À-VIS ENTITLEMENTS

Was the Sahelian famine caused by a decline in food availability? The *per capita* food output did go down quite substantially. The figures of food availability per head in the six Sahelian countries as presented by the FAO are given in Table 8.1. There is much less of a decline in the food consumption per head judging by the FAO figures on calorie and protein consumption per head, as presented in Table 8.2. But, apart from Senegal, the other countries had a decline in food consumption per head as well, so that the FAD hypothesis does not stand rejected on the basis of these data.

TABLE 8.1
Net Food Output per Head (Index)

	1961–5	1968	1969	1970	1971	1972	1973	1974	1975
Chad	100	90	87	84	84	69	63	69	71
Mali	100	93	99	97	90	73	61	65	80
Mauritania	100	98	100	98	92	80	67	68	68
Niger	100	92	99	88	88	81	57	65	60
Senegal	100	81	87	66	89	56	67	88	107
Upper Volta	100	106	103	102	93	85	76	84	90

Source: FAO Production Yearbook *1976*, Table 6.

TABLE 8.2
Calorie Consumption per head in Sahel countries

	1961–5	1972	1973	1974
Chad	100	76	73	76
Mali	100	86	86	88
Mauritania	100	91	94	95
Niger	100	86	89	85
Senegal	100	93	104	107
Upper Volta	100	86	85	96

Source: Calculated from data given in Table 97 of *FAO Production Yearbook 1976*.

[20] See Sheets and Morris (1976), El-Khawas (1976) and Wiseberg (1976).

It is also worth emphasizing that the FAD view is not rejected even by the otherwise important observation that nearly all the Sahelian countries had enough food within their borders to prevent starvation had the food been divided equally, and that 'throughout the whole Sahel [the Sahelian countries] in every year from 1968 to 1972 the per caput supply [of cereals] exceeded this figure [FAO/WHO recommended food-intake per person] comfortably'.[21] It appears that an FAO survey 'documented that every Sahelian country, with the possible exception of mineral-rich Mauritania, actually produced enough grain to feed its total population even during the worst drought year'.[22] This is obviously relevant in emphasizing the importance of unequal distribution in starvation as well as giving us an insight into the type of information that FAO looked into in understanding the famine, but it does not, of course, have any bearing on the correctness of the FAD view of famines. The FAD approach is concerned primarily not with the *adequacy* of over-all food supply, but with its *decline* compared with past experience. In particular, the FAD claim is not that famines occur if and only if the average food supply per head is insufficient compared with some nutritional norm, but that famines occur if and only if there is a sharp *decline* in the average food availability per head. And, it could be argued, such a decline did take place for the Sahelian countries as a group during the drought of 1969–73. If the FAD approach to famines were to seek refuge in some comforting bosom, it probably couldn't do better in the modern world than choose the Sahelian famine: the food availability did go down, and—yes—there was a famine!

Despite this, I would argue that, even for the Sahelian famine, the FAD approach delivers rather little. First, in the peak year of famine, 1973, the decline in food availability per head was rather small even in comparison with the pluvial early 1960s for Mali, Mauritania, Niger, and Upper Volta (less than a 15 per cent decline of calorie availability per head), and none at all for Senegal. While the decline was much sharper for Chad (27 per cent), Chad was one of the less affected countries in the region,

[21] Marnham (1977), p. 17. See also Lappé and Collins (1977, 1978), and Lofchie (1975).

[22] Lappé and Collins (1977), p. 2, and footnote 6, quoting a letter from Dr. M. Ganzin, Director, Food Policy and Nutrition Division, FAO, Rome, a major authority on the Sahelian economy.

the famine having been most severe in Mauritania, Mali, and Niger, and possibly Upper Volta.[23] But none of these latter countries had a very sharp decline in food availability per head (Table 8.2). It could, however, be argued that in terms of food *output* per head (Table 8.1), Niger and Mali did have the biggest decline in the famine year of 1973, with the indices standing respectively at 57 and 61. But Senegal, which was less affected, had an index value of 56 for 1972, the lowest index value for any country for any year. As we move away from the gross factual statements to a bit more detailed information, the FAD analysis starts limping straightway.

Second, the rationale of the FAD approach, concentrating as it does on aggregate supply, rests in ignoring distributional changes. But there is clear evidence that dramatic shifts in the distribution of purchasing power were taking place in the drought years in the Sahelian countries, mainly between the dry Sahel regions in these countries and the rest of the regions. The drought affected the Sahel area rather than the savanna, in which the vast majority of the population of Sahelian countries live. The relief camps even in the south were full of people who had migrated from the Sahelian north into less dry areas in the south. The famine victims were almost exclusively the nomadic pastoral population from the Sahel region (including nomads, semi-nomads, and transhumants) and the sedentary population living in the Sahel region (agriculturists, fishermen, etc.).[24] Rather than looking at aggregate statistics like those of food availability per head, it would clearly make much more sense to look at the economic conditions of these groups of people in understanding the Sahelian famine.

Third, we indeed have direct evidence of the decline in income and purchasing power of pastoralists and agriculturists living in the Sahelian region. The destruction of crops and the death of animals in these parts of the Sahelian countries were very substantial.[25] While the crops affected were often of foodgrains and the animals do supply edible products, most sections of the Sahelian population rely also on trade for food.[26] The severe

[23] See Center for Disease Control (1973) and Kloth (1974).
[24] See Sheets and Morris (1976), Kloth (1974), Copans *et al.* (1975), Lofchie (1975), and Imperato (1976).
[25] See Winstanley (1976) and Matlock and Cockrum (1976).
[26] The role of the commercialization in heightening the impact of the drought on the

decline in agricultural and pastoral output in these particular regions thus meant a sharp reduction in the ability of the affected people to command food, whether from one's own output or through exchange. The situation is somewhat comparable to the picture we already found in Ethiopia during the drought and famine there (see Chapter 7 above), which could be seen as a related phenomenon in another part of the Sahel belt of Africa.

It is worth mentioning in this context that, from the point of view of the suffering of the individual agriculturist, it matters rather little whether the crop destroyed happens to be a food crop which is consumed directly, or a cash crop which is sold to buy food. In either case the person's entitlement to food collapses. It is this collapse that directly relates to his starvation (and that of his family) rather than some remote aggregate statistics about food supply per head. The same applies to the pastoralist who lives by selling animals and animal products; and, like the Afar or Somali pastoralists in Ethiopia, the Sahel pastoralists also rely substantially on trading animals and animal products for other goods, including grains, which provide cheaper calories.[27]

Thus, despite superficial plausibility, the FAD approach throws rather little light on the Sahelian famine. It is not my contention that the FAD *always* makes wrong predictions. (If it did, then the FAD approach could have provided a good basis of prediction, *applied in reverse!*) Predictions based on FAD may sometimes prove right (as in gross statements about the over-all Sahelian famine), sometimes wrong (as in the Bengal famine or in the Ethiopian famine). So the first point is that it isn't much of a predictor to rely on. But the more important point is that, even when its prediction happens to come out right about the existence of a famine in a broad area, it provides little guidance about the character of the famine—*who* died, *where*, and *why?*

8.3 DESTITUTION AND ENTITLEMENT

Of the total population of some 25 million in the Sahelian countries in 1974, about 10 per cent can be described as nomadic.[28] The definition includes semi-nomads and transhum-

---

Sahelian economy has been particularly emphasized by Comité Information Sahel (1974). See also Meillassoux (1974), Raynaut (1977), and Berry, Campbell and Emker (1977). Also Imperato (1976), pp. 285–6.

[27] See, among others, Seaman, Holt, Rivers, and Murlis (1973), and Haaland (1977).
[28] See Caldwell (1975).

ants in addition to pure nomads. At the time the drought hit, the population of the dry Sahel region in these countries was roughly 5 to 6 million.[29] So the nomads were no more than half the population of the dry Sahel region itself, and quite a small proportion of the total population of the Sahelian countries. But the share of the nomads in the mortality induced by the famine and in nutritional deficiency were both remarkably high,[30] and even among the victims of the famine there is some evidence of 'a shocking contrast between the nutritional state of sedentary victims of the drought and the deep starvation of the nomads'.[31]

The destitution of the nomadic pastoralist seems to have followed a process not dissimilar to the fate of the Ethiopian herdsmen of the Afar or Somali communities, studied in the last chapter. The animal loss in the dry Sahel area varied between 20 to 100 per cent depending on the region,[32] and this was compounded, as in Ethiopia, by the 'rapid destocking of animals in the Sahel' coinciding with 'a sharp drop in prices'.[33] The reasons for the fall in price seem to have been similar to those encountered in analysing the Ethiopian famine (see Chapter 7). A pastoralist depends on consuming cereals part of the year as a cheaper source of calories,[34] and may become more—and not less—dependent on exchanging animals for cereals in the straitened circumstances caused by the loss of animals.[35] The fixed money obligations arising from taxes, etc., that have to be met makes the pastoralist inclined to sell more rather than less, when the relative prices of animals fall.[36] The emaciation of animals would provide a more direct explanation of the sharp fall in prices. Whatever the cause, the statistics of the loss of animals understate the magnitude of the economic decline sustained by the pastoralist.

[29] See Imperato (1976), p. 285, and Marnham (1977), p. 7.

[30] See Kloth (1974), Sheets and Morris (1976), and Imperato (1976).

[31] Sheets and Morris (1976), p. 53.

[32] See Glantz (1976), pp. 77–8, 199–200, and FAO *Production Yearbook*, 1974, Tables 107–10.

[33] Club du Sahel (1977), p. 55.

[34] See Chapter 7 and also the references cited in note 27 in this chapter.

[35] The sale of 'an unusual proportion of their animals' was thus 'one of the pastoralists' means of defence' (Caldwell, 1977, p. 96).

[36] This notion leads naturally to the possibility of a backward-bending supply curve, which has been frequently mentioned. But since this is only one factor among many, such a backward bend may not occur in the *total* supply curve. The position also depends on the precise circumstances facing the pastoralist (see Haaland, 1977), and there is some empirical evidence against the backward bend (see Khalifa and Simpson, 1972).

The pastoralists migrated down south in quite large numbers during the Sahelian famine, and this movement of people and animals was one way of reducing the impact of the famine—indeed, according to one view was this group's 'chief defence'.[37] Better feeding conditions for the animals as well as opportunities for wage labour in the south permitted some relief, and the relief camps set up there also took a good many of the pastoralists from the north. There is some evidence, however, of discriminating treatment against the pastoral nomadic people in the relief camps, and a firm suggestion that the Sahelian governments were closely tied to (and more responsive to the needs of) the majority sedentary communities.[38]

Another group severely affected by the famine was the sedentary agriculturists from the dry Sahel region. While the position of the dry Sahel pastoralist was rather similar to that of the Afar and Somali nomads in the Ethiopian famine, that of the dry Sahel agriculturist could be compared with the predicament of the Wollo cultivator. His output was down, and whether he lived by eating his own product or by selling it in the market, his entitlement to food underwent a severe decline. For many cash crops, e.g. groundnuts, the impact of the drought seems to have been no less than on the total quantity of food output as such (see Table 8.3). The food output in the country in which he lived might have gone down by a moderate ratio, but his command over the food that was there slipped drastically. The extent of the decline varied depending on the precise region in question since the drought was far from uniform,[39] but for some of the dry Sahel agriculturists it was a case of straightforward ruin. The problem was made more difficult by the monetary obligations of taxation,[40] which had to be paid despite the drought, and by the loss of job opportunity arising from what we have been calling 'derived deprivation'.[41]

[37] Caldwell (1977), p. 96.

[38] See Sheets and Morris (1976).

[39] See Bradley (1977), pp. 39–40.

[40] It has been argued that the obligation to pay taxes in monetary terms has been an important reason for Sahelian farmers for moving from food crops to cash crops (see Berry, Campbell and Emker, 1977, p. 86). See also Comité Information Sahel (1974).

[41] See Chapters 1, 6, and 7. In the drought year the Sahelian labourer sought employment further away from home than normal. See, for example, Faulkingham (1977), Tables 17.7 and 17.8; there is a remarkable increase in the number of labourers from this Hausa village in Niger going to distant Kano (360 km), Lagos (910 km) and Abidjan (1,420 km) for wage employment in such occupations as being 'water career'.

TABLE 8.3
Food Output Compared with Output of Groundnuts in shell

	1966–8	1969	1970	1971	1972	1973	1974
Senegal							
Food	100	101	78	108	70	84	94
Groundnut	100	88	65	110	65	85	95
Niger							
Food	100	99	97	89	88	64	80
Groundnut	100	92	79	82	93	29	64
Mali							
Food	100	107	101	108	86	68	88
Groundnut	100	97	125	121	119	79	151
Chad							
Food	100	104	103	102	80	72	76
Groundnut	100	119	119	78	47	52	52

Source: Calculated from Tables 7 and 43 in *FAO Production Yearbook 1975*, changing the base of the index to the average for 1966, 1967, and 1968, with unchanged weights.

8.4 SOME POLICY ISSUES

Droughts may not be avoidable, but their effects can be. 'The weather and climate modification schemes proposed since 1900 for the regions in West and Central Africa surrounding and including the Sahara Desert'[42] are worthy fields of investigation. I expect some day one might indeed grow rice or catch fish in the Sahara. But while science marches on slowly, some means have to be found for freeing the Sahelian population from vulnerability to droughts and the prospect of famines. I end this chapter with brief comments on this issue.

One approach is to argue that the problem is not as bad as it might look from the perspective of the recent drought. One could say that droughts come and go, and they don't come all that frequently either: in this century the serious ones for the Sahel countries have been 1910–14, 1941–2, 1969–73. Is there a real need for special action? While smugness—like virtue—is its own reward, it is not a reward on which the Sahelian population can bank. Periodic famines may not be as bad as perpetual starvation, but one can scarcely find that situation acceptable.

Another approach is to argue that there is no real need to make the dry Sahel region economically non-vulnerable, since people

[42] Glantz and Parton (1976). See also Franke and Chasin (1979).

can emigrate. It has been argued that 'the inevitably limited funds available for development can be more effectively employed' in the moister area south of the dry Sahelian region, and that 'relevant governments should consider the feasibility of a strategic withdrawal from areas of very low and unreliable rainfall'.[43] This approach is further supported by the observation that many nomads interviewed in the south during and immediately after the drought years indicated a willingness to stay on in the south.

Depopulation as a solution to the problem of the Sahelian region overlooks a number of important factors. First, it seems that the bulk of the population from the Sahelian north who migrated south have, in fact, returned north again. Even if many had stayed on, that would have still left the Sahelian countries with the problem of what to do with the remaining dry Sahel population. It is not easy to change the way of life of a large community, nor is there any reason to suppose that the Sahelian northerner typically finds the economic opportunities in the south to be superior to those ruling in the north in the normal years. The problem is one of fluctuation of economic circumstances between wet and dry years rather than of a collapse of the economic potential of the north in general.

Second, it does seem economically most wasteful to give up the use of the resources available for agriculture, pastoralism, and fishing in the north and to crowd the southern savanna even more than it is already crowded. The southerner typically did not welcome the northern invasion, and there is good reason to think that large-scale permanent immigration would indeed worsen the economic conditions of the southern population.

Finally, the Sahelian countries do get many things from the economic production in the north, both of pastoral products as well as of cash crops. The Sahelian north is no 'basket case', and while a severe drought may make the northerner dependent on the southerner for his survival, the southerner normally gets various commodities and foreign exchange from the production taking place in the north.

It is necessary, therefore, to think of solutions of the Sahelian problem without choosing the drastic simplicity of depopulating

[43] This view is attributed to 'Professor Hodder of the School of Oriental and African Studies and others' by David Dalby in Dalby and Harrison Church (1973), p. 21.

the Sahel region. Since the source of the problem is variability rather than a secular decline, it is tempting to think in terms of insurance arrangements. The first question then is: what is to be insured? If FAD had been a good theory of famines and total food availability a good guide to starvation, then the thing to insure would have been the over-all supply of food in these countries. Some system of international insurance could be used to make resources available for import of food from abroad when domestic production of food fails and when the earnings of foreign exchange go down, making it difficult to import food by using currently earned exchange. While the Sahelian countries have had a declining trend of food output per head over the last decade or so, the trend rates have been much influenced by the sequence of drought years. Also, there have been some substantial shifts from food crops to cash crops, which reduce the food output per head but not necessarily the country's ability to buy food, since cash crops can be sold and exchanged for food in the international market. On the FAD approach, therefore, the problem may look simple enough: it is a case of occasional fall in food supply per head, which could be made good by an international insurance mechanism, so that enough food is available within the country.

But FAD isn't a very reliable guide. Despite its superficial plausibility in explaining the Sahelian famine, it delivers rather little even in this case, as we saw in the last section. There is need for concern not merely with how to get food into the country, but also with the way it could be commanded by the affected population. It is necessary to devise ways by which the population most affected by drought and economic difficulty can have the ability to obtain food through economic mechanisms. This contrast is particularly important in the context of recent developments such as growth of cash cropping, which have added to the country's over-all earning power but seem to have led to a decline of the exchange entitlement of particular sections of the population.

Thus, the insurance arrangements have to deal with command over food at the family level, and not merely at the national level. Private insurance of families of nomadic pastoralists and other groups in the dry Sahel region isn't an easy task, and indeed, such insurance rarely exists in any poor and backward country. Thus, the public sector would have to play a major role in the task of guaranteeing food to the vulnerable sections. Famine relief operations are, of course, insurance systems in some sense, but if a long-run solution to the problem of vulnerability has to be found, then clearly a less *ad hoc* system would have to be devised. Various alternative ways of doing this, varying from guaranteed social security benefits in the form of income supplementation to employment guarantee schemes, can be considered in this context.

But social security is not the only aspect of the problem. It is important to recognize the long-run changes in the Sahelian economy that have made the population of the dry Sahel region more vulnerable to droughts. One factor that has been noted is the increased vulnerability arising from the growing commericialization of the Sahelian economy.[44] As the Sahelian population has become more dependent on cash crops, there has been an increased dependence on markets for meeting its food requirements, and this has tended to supplement the variability arising from climatic fluctuations.[45] In the light of the analysis of variation of entitlement relations with which this book has been much concerned (see Chapters 1, 5, 6, and 7), this point may not need very much elaboration here. Compared with the farmer or the pastoralist who lives on what he grows and is thus vulnerable only to variations of his own output (arising from climatic considerations and other influences), the grower of cash crops, or the pastoralist heavily dependent on selling animal products, is vulnerable both to output fluctuations and to shifts in marketability of commodities and in exchange rates.[46] The worker employed in wage-based farms or other occupations is, of course, particularly vulnerable, since employment fluctuations owing to climatic shifts, or to other factors such as 'derived deprivation', can be very sharp indeed. While commercialization may have

[44] See Comité Information Sahel (1974).

[45] See Meillassoux (1974) and Comité Information Sahel (1974). See also Ball (1976) and Berry, Campbell, and Emker (1977).

[46] While price and quantity fluctuations can operate in opposite directions, thereby tempering the effects of each other, this is far from guaranteed. Indeed, as was seen in the last chapter and also in Section 8.3 above, the pastoralists often have to face a price decline along with a reduction in quantities. Similarly, a decline in agricultural output could lead to a reduction of wage employment, thereby leading to a collapse of the 'effective price' of labour power for those who are fired.

opened up new economic opportunities, it has also tended to increase the vulnerability of the Sahel population.

Commercialization has also had other worrying effects. The 'traditional symbiotic relationship between nomadic livestock and the crops' may have been disrupted in some regions by the growth of cash crops with a different seasonal rhythm (e.g., cotton being harvested later than the traditional food crops).[47] The livestock eating the post-harvest stubs from the agricultural fields, and in its turn fertilizing the fields by providing dung, may have fitted in nicely with traditional agriculture, but have often not co-ordinated at all well with cash crops. Furthermore, when traditional grazing land has been taken over for commercial farming, the pastoral population has, of course, directly suffered from a decline of resources.

Another long-run trend that seems to have been important is the partial breakdown of the traditional methods of insurance.[48] The political division of the dry Sahel region has put arbitary constraints on pastoral movements, reducing the scope for anti-drought responses. The practice of storing animals on the hoof as insurance seems to have become more expensive because of taxes. 'Fall-back hunting' has become almost impossible because of reduction of wild animals in the region.[49] The collapse of the traditional methods of fighting economic problems arising from periodical droughts may have played an important part in making the dry Sahel region more vulnerable to draught in recent years than it need have been. On some of these changes corrective policy actions are worth considering, but many of these developments are difficult to reverse.

Additional vulnerability has also arisen from over-grazing and an increase in the size of livestock population in the dry Sahelian region. To some extent, this was the result of the pluvial 1960s, preceding the drought,[50] and the problem would be different for

[47] See Norton (1976), pp. 260–1. Also Swift (1977b), pp. 171–3.

[48] See Swift (1977a, 1977b). See also Copans *et al.* (1975), Haaland (1977), and Caldwell (1977).

[49] Another long-run factor working in the same direction is the decline of trading possibilities across the Sahara, especially the disruption of the traditional Tuareg caravan trade, first by French interference and then by competition from traders with motorized transport (Baier, 1974; cited by Berry, Campbell and Emker, 1977, pp. 87–8).

[50] See Norton (1976), p. 261.

quite some time after the drought. But the nature of the nomadic economy has built-in forces operating in that direction. Since the pastures are held communally and animals owned privately, there is a conflict of economic rationale in the package, which becomes relevant when pasture land gets short in supply. Having additional animals for grazing adds to families' incomes, and while this might lead to loss of grass cover and erosion, and thus to reduced productivity for the pastoralists as a group, the loss to the individual family from the latter may be a good deal less than its gain from having additional animals. Thus a conflict of the type of the so-called 'prisoners' dilemma'[51] is inherent in the situation.

The problem is further compounded by the fact that the animals, aside from adding to the family's usual income, also serve as insurance, as was noted before, so that the tendency to enlarge one's herd, causing over-grazing, tends to be stimulated as uncertainty grows. And the over-grazing, in its turn, adds to the uncertainty, by denuding the grass cover and helping desert formation.

Contrary to what is sometimes said, the tendency of the pastoralist to have a large stock, contributing to over-grazing, does not indicate anything in the least foolish or shortsighted from his personal point of view. Policy formulation can hardly be helped by the failure to recognize this important fact.

The complexity of the problem was recently suggested by an official from a major donor country who had interviewed a Fulani herder in northern Upper Volta in the spring of 1973. He reported that the farmer, asked how he had been affected by the recent drought, said he had 100 head of cattle and had lost 50. The farmer continued, 'Next time I will have 200,' implying that by starting with twice as many he would save the 100 cattle he wants. Yet the land's carrying capacity is such that he will still have only 50 cattle, but his loss will have been much greater.[52]

As a piece of economic reasoning, this is, of course, sheer rubbish, as the Fulani herder must have seen straightaway, unless mesmerized by respect for the 'major donor country'. If the Fulani herder had begun with 200 rather than 100 animals, he would not have ended up with the same 50, and in fact in large

---

[51] For the basic Prisoners' Dilemma model, see Luce and Raiffa (1958), and conflicts of this kind can be found in many economic situations (see Sen, 1967a).

[52] Glantz (1976), p. 7.

pastoral communities he would have a good chance of retaining the same proportion, viz. 50 per cent, thereby ending up with the planned 100. The proportion of herd loss does depend on the *total* stock of animals, given the availability of grazing land, but the influence of one herder's individual herd size on the total animal stock will be very small indeed. So it isn't that he himself loses by starting off with 200 rather than 100 head of cattle, but that he thus contributes a little bit to the general reduction of survival possibility of animals in the whole region, and if many herders do the same then the survival ratio will indeed come down significantly. But the individual herder can hardly undo this general problem by keeping his own herd small unilaterally. The herder is sensible enough within his sphere of control, which is his own stock, but the totality of these individually sensible actions produces a social crisis.

In tackling this aspect of the problem, several alternative approaches are possible, varying from incentive schemes using taxes and subsidies, or regulations governing the size of the herds, to the formation of pastoral co-operatives.[53] The problem arises from private entitlement being positively responsive to one's private ownership of animals while being negatively responsive to ownership by others, and from each herder having direct control only over his own stock. The object of institutional change will be to eliminate the conflicts that arise from this dichotomy.

The food problem of the population in the dry Sahel region depends crucially on this set of institutional factors affecting food entitlement through production and exchange, and there is scope for action here. As discussed earlier, there is also need for a mechanism for directly tackling the problem of vulnerability through public institutions guaranteeing food entitlement. The last category includes not merely distribution of food when the problem becomes acute, but also more permanent arrangements for entitlement through social security and employment protection. What is needed is not ensuring food availability, but guaranteeing food entitlement.

---

[53] Various institutional reforms have been discussed in recent years. See Comité Information Sahel (1974), Copans *et al.* (1975), Widstrand (1975), Dahl and Hjort (1976, 1979), Glantz (1976), Norton (1976), Rapp, Le Houérou, and Lundholm (1976), Swift (1977a, 1977b), and Toupet (1977), among many other important contributions.

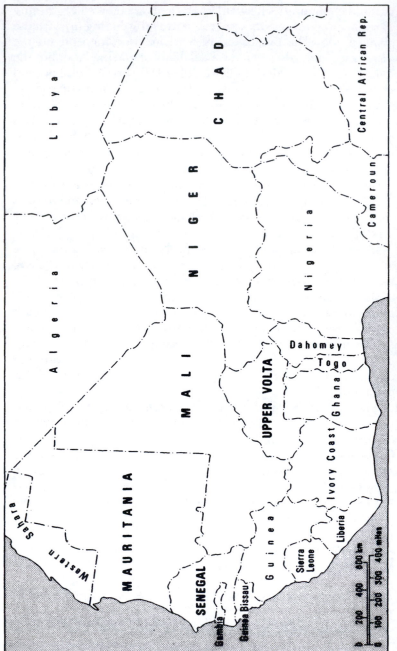

Fig. 8.1 Map of Sahel Countries

Chapter 9

Famine in Bangladesh

9.1 FLOODS AND FAMINE

First the floods; then the famine. So runs the capsule story of the Bangladesh famine of 1974. Gilbert Etienne describes the 1974 floods thus:

The floods of 1974 caused severe damage in the Northern districts. In normal years, the Brahmaputra encroaches on its Western bank by 30–60 m during peak floods. In 1974, over a distance of 100 km, it flooded land on a strip 300 m wide in areas having a density of 800 per sq. km. 24,000 people suffered heavy losses. Moreover alluvial deposits, while fertile in some areas, have such a high sand content in others that they are sterile. . . . Severe floods occurred at the end of June, taking away part of the *aus* [rice crop harvested in July–August]. A fortnight later the Brahmaputra again crossed the danger level just at the time of *aus* harvesting. After another fortnight the level of river rose again and seedlings of *aman* [rice crop transplanted in July–September and harvested in November–January] in their nurseries were in danger. Then, by the middle of August, floods reached their maximum for the year, affecting recently transplanted *aman*. It was not the end. At the begining of September the Brahmaputra again crossed the danger line, hitting once more what was left of paddy which has been transplanted after the previous floods.[1]

The price of rice rocketed during and immediately after the floods, as Table 9.1 shows. In some of the most affected districts, the rice price doubled in the three months between July and October. Reports of starvation could be heard immediately following the flood, and grew in severity. The government of Bangladesh officially declared famine in late September. Some *langarkhanas*, providing modest amounts of free cooked food to destitutes, were opened under private initiative early in September, and government-sponsored *langarkhanas* went into full operation in early October. At one stage nearly six thousand *langarkhanas* were providing cooked food relief to 4.35 million people—more than 6 per cent of the total population of the

[1] Etienne (1977a), pp. 113–4.

country. By November rice prices were begining to come down, and the need for relief seemed less intense. By the end of the month the *langarkhanas* were closed down.

TABLE 9.1
Rise in the Price of Rice in Bangladesh following the 1974 Floods

| Month in 1974 | Bangladesh average | Index of retail price of coarse rice | | |
		Mymensingh	Rangpur	Sylhet
July	100	100	100	100
August	121	130	116	129
September	150	169	184	160
October	178	202	183	204
November	151	162	113	167
December	133	132	85	155

Source: Calculated from Table 3.3 of Alamgir *et al.* (1977), p. 58.

TABLE 9.2
Number Obtaining Food Relief in Langarkhanas:
Bangladesh Famine, 1974

District	Number of persons fed daily (thousands)	Number fed as proportion of total population (%)
Rangpur	935.6	17.18
Mymensingh	899.0	11.88
Dinajpur	221.0	8.60
Sylhet	362.7	7.62
Barisal	281.0	7.15
Khulna	245.7	6.91
Bogra	123.0	5.51
Noakhali	178.4	5.50
Patuakhali	65.8	4.39
Jessore	128.5	3.86
Faridpur	148.2	3.65
Comilla	205.1	3.52
Rajshahi	147.5	3.46
Kushtia	64.9	3.45
Tangail	70.5	3.39
Pabna	57.9	2.06
Dacca	155.7	2.05
Chittagong	54.7	1.27
Chittagong Hill Tracts	0	0

Source: Data provided by Alamgir (1979).

The severity of the famine varied from region to region. Table 9.2 presents the proportion of a district's population that

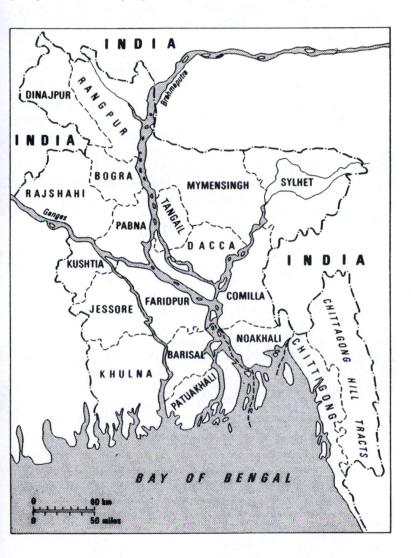

FIG. 9.1 Map of Bangladesh

obtained relief from the *langarkhanas*, varying from 17 per cent in Rangpur to none in Chittagong Hill Tracts. Judged by this criterion, the five most affected districts were Rangpur, Mymensingh, Dinajpur, Sylhet, and Barisal, in that order. In the famine survey carried out by the Bangladesh Institute of Development Studies[2] in November 1974, Mymensingh, Rangpur, and Sylhet were selected as the 'famine districts'. The choice was based on the 'maximum depth of inundation' being '6 feet and above in a period of 3 months and above', along with 'the proportion of population seeking relief in *langarkhanas* being 5 per cent and above'.[3] Dinajpur, which is some distance from the raging Brahmaputra and other rivers (see the map of Bangladesh, Fig. 8.1), did not figure in this list despite having a higher percentage seeking relief than Sylhet, but it appears that 'a considerable proportion of *langarkhana* inmates in this district came from the adjoining district of Rangpur.'

Mortality estimates vary widely. The official figure of death due to the famine is 26,000.[4] Other estimates indicate much higher mortality, including the estimation that in Rangpur district alone '80 to 100 thousand persons died of starvation and malnutrition in 2–3 months'.[5] There is little doubt that the mortality figure would have been a good deal higher but for the massive relief operation, inadequate as it was. In addition to government-sponsored relief, voluntary organizations played an important part, both in providing relief outside the distressed villages and in the form of movements of self-reliance within many of the villages.[6]

9.2 FOOD IMPORTS AND GOVERNMENT STOCKS

There is little doubt that the government of Bangladesh found itself severely constrained by the lack of an adequate food stock, and that this prevented running a larger operation at the height of the famine.[7] By 1974 Bangladesh was already chronically

---

[2] See Alamgir *et al.* (1977), and Alamgir (1980). As will be clear, this chapter draws heavily on the information provided by this survey, and on other data, analyses, and insights provided by Alamgir (1978a, 1980).

[3] Alamgir (1980).

[4] Alamgir (1978a, p. 2).

[5] Haque, Mehta, Rahman and Wignaraja (1975), p. 43. Alamgir (1980) suggests an excess-death figure around one million between August 1974 and January 1975, and a further half a million in the year following (pp. 142–3).

[6] See Rahman (1974a, 1974b).

[7] See N. Islam (1977).

dependent on import of food from abroad, and despite the famine conditions the government succeeded in importing less foodgrains in 1974 than in 1973 (see Table 9.3). In fact, in the crucial months of September and October the imports fell to a trickle, and the amount of foodgrains imported during these two months, rather than being larger, was less than one-fifth of the imports in those months in the preceding year. In constraining the operations of the Bangladesh government, the shortage of food stock clearly did play an important negative part.

TABLE 9.3

Import of Foodgrains into Bangladesh, 1973 and 1974

Month	1973	1974
January	228	38
February	194	90
March	467	99
April	212	147
May	179	224
June	126	135
July	83	291
August	159	225
September	263	29
October	287	76
November	59	190
December	83	149
Total	2,340	1,693

Source: Table 6.18 in Alamgir (1980).
Note
Unit = 1,000 tons

It is worth mentioning in this context that Bangladesh, like many other countries in the world, had been receiving regular food aid from the United States. But the US food aid came under severe threat precisely at this point of time, since the United States decided to seek stoppage of Bangladesh's trade with Cuba. This apparently came shortly after a desperately dollar-short Bangladesh government had to cancel two purchase orders from American grain companies for delivery in autumn.

The U.S. threatened to cut off food aid in September 1974. At that time the American ambassador called upon Dr. Nurul Islam, Chairman of Bangladesh's Planning Commission, under instructions from the State

Department, to formally request that Bangladesh cease exporting jute to Cuba. Under PL480, a recipient country cannot trade with blacklisted countries such as Cuba. Islam retorted by expressing surprise and shock that the United States would actually insist that a destitute Bangladesh should restrict its exports. The government of Bangladesh cancelled further exports of jute to Cuba at a time when competition from Indian jute and low world market prices had substantially eroded its foreign exchange earnings.[8]

Only after Bangladesh gave in and sacrificed its trade with Cuba was the flow of American food resumed. By then the autumn famine was largely over.[9]

The problem of import planning had been compounded by rise of international prices of grains and shortage of credit. The government's expectation of a much larger food output in 1974 also led to disappointment. It can be seen that the import of food in the early months of 1974 was also substantially short of the corresponding figures for the year before. Furthermore, internal procurement had been less successful than planned; and, with a total foodgrains production of 11.8 million tons in 1974, the government stock varied from month to month between 347 thousand and 130 thousand over the year.[10] This affected the scale of relief operations not merely in terms of the number that could be covered, but also—and more importantly—in terms of the amount of food that could be given to each destitute.[11]

That food availability served as a constraint in government relief operations is not in dispute. But this would establish nothing about the causation of the famine itself. Was the famine caused by a decline of food availability resulting from the floods? Was there a general shortage of food? Does the FAD explantaion hold? I take up these questions next.

[8] McHenry and Bird (1977), p. 82.
[9] For further details of this episode, see McHenry and Bird (1977); also Sobhan (1979). For more general discussions of negative features of food aid, see George (1976) and Lappé and Collins (1977, 1978).
[10] Table 6.2 of Alamgir (1980). However, Alamgir argues that even with the import problems the government was unduly conservative in its relief operations, with the disbursement of food in the crucial famine months being a small proportion of the government stock. See also Rahman (1974a, 1974b) for a critique of the scale and organization of government relief operations.
[11] See Table 5.15 of Alamgir (1979).

9.3 FOOD AVAILABILITY DECLINE?

As was mentioned in Chapter 6 when analysing the great Bengal famine of 1943, there are three main rice crops in Bengal: *aman*, *aus*, and *boro*. The relative importance of these crops in Bangladesh now as well as their exact timing, are not however quite the same as in Bengal 1943, partly because of the fact that Bangladesh does not cover the whole of undivided Bengal, but also because of changes in the types of seeds and cropping methods over the years since 1943. In Bangladesh for the period 1971–6, the relative shares were the following: *aman* (harvested in November–January), 56 per cent; *aus* (harvested in July–August), 25 per cent; and *boro* (harvested in April–June), 19 per cent.

Like the Bengal famine of 1943, the peak of the Bangladesh famine of 1974 coincided with the *aus* harvesting time and preceded the time of *aman* harvesting. It is thus best to define the production-based supply of 1974 by adding the *aman* crop of 1973–4 (November–January) to the *boro* and *aus* crops of 1974. Indeed, as in Chapter 6, that is how the production of a particular year will be defined, i.e. including the *aman* crop harvested during the *preceding* November to January of that year. Table 9.4 presents the yearly rice output from 1971 to 1975. It also presents the index of *per capita* rice output. It can be seen that 1974 was a local peak year in terms of both total output and *per capita* output of rice.[12]

TABLE 9.4
Rice Output of Bangladesh, 1971–5

Year	Production of rice (thousand tons)	Index of rice production	Per capita rice output (tons)	Index of per capita rice output
1971	10,445	100	0.133	100
1972	9,706	93	0.120	90
1973	10,459	100	0.126	95
1974	11,778	113	0.139	105
1975	11,480	110	0.132	99

Basis: Data taken from Table 6.4 of Alamgir (1980).

[12] It is, however, worth remarking that, as far as *per capita* output is concerned, this is a local peak, and the highest levels achieved in the 1960s were not quite matched in these

In moving from rice production to foodgrains availability, wheat output, though tiny, has to be added and international trade must be taken into account. This is done in Table 9.5. It is found, once again, that 1974 was a local peak.[13] If one went by over-all food availability, one would expect a famine less in 1974 than in *any* of the other years. And yet the famine did occur precisely in 1974.

TABLE 9.5

Foodgrains Availability in Bangladesh, 1971–5

Year	Total available foodgrains for consumption (million tons)	Population (millions)	Per capita availability (oz./day)	Index of per capita availability
1971	10.740	70.679	14.9	100
1972	11.271	72.535	15.3	103
1973	11.572	74.441	15.3	103
1974	12.355	76.398	15.9	107
1975	12.022	78.405	14.9	100

Source: Data taken from Table 6.23 of Alamgir (1980).

It is, however, necessary to consider the possibility that the decline in food availability was a regional one, and that it could not get sorted out within Bangladesh because of problems of food movement including the inter-district barriers imposed officially (mainly to help procurement). Was there an exceptional decline in the districts most affected by the famine?

Table 9.6 presents the amounts of rice produced in the different districts, and also the percentage change in output between 1973 and 1974. It appears from it that output declined only in two districts, whereas the famine was much more widespread. It also appears that the most famine-affected

years in the 1970s. Nevertheless, two-year and three-year moving averages also rise rather than dip as we take up periods ending in 1974 (following one method used, among others, in Chapter 6), and it is difficult to deny that the output picture improved rather than worsened as the 'famine year' 1974 came.

[13] One area of some uncertainty is the extent of smuggling of foodgrains into India from Bangladesh. Some accounts suggest that this would have been very small indeed (see Reddaway and Rahman, 1975), while others suggest the possibility of the figures being substantially higher. Whatever the truth about these absolute magnitudes, there is no reason to expect that the smuggling of rice out of Bangladesh would have *increased* in the famine year when the relative price of rice in Bangladesh *vis-à-vis* that in India rose sharply.

TABLE 9.6

Production of Rice in Bangladesh Districts, 1973 and 1974

District	1974	1973	Change from 1973 to 1974 (%)
Khulna	462	325	+42.2
Chittagong Hill Tracts	93	67	+38.8
Dinajpur	666	504	+32.1
Bogra	478	380	+25.8
Jessore	531	426	+24.6
Kushtia	221	180	+22.8
Mymensingh	1,065	871	+22.3
Tangail	322	264	+22.0
Faridpur	484	403	+20.1
Rangpur	1,122	958	+17.1
Chittagong	725	644	+12.6
Pabna	282	251	+12.4
Sylhet	1,068	968	+10.3
Dacca	675	625	+8.0
Noakhali	538	505	+6.5
Rajshahi	679	638	+6.4
Comilla	836	805	+3.9
Barisal	600	664	−9.6
Patuakhali	229	342	−33.0

Source: Data taken from Table 6.28 of Alamgir (1980); the percentage change figure for Dinajpur is corrected.

Note

Unit = 1,000 tons

districts, namely Mymensingh, Rangpur, Sylhet, had substantial *increases* in output (22, 17, and 10 per cent respectively). Looking instead at the three top-ranked districts in terms of lowness of output growth, we obtain Patuakhali, Barisal, and Comilla, which together account for only 12.7 per cent of the destitutes receiving relief in *langarkhanas*. In general, the ranking of inter-district indicators of famine intensity (Table 9.2) and the ranking of lowness of output growth (Table 9.6) hardly relate to each other, and the rank correlation coefficient between the two is *minus* .5.

The corresponding availability estimates of foodgrains *per capita* are presented in Table 9.7. The three so-called famine districts typically had comfortable *rises* in availability per head: 3 per cent in Sylhet, 10 per cent in Rangpur, and 11 per cent in Mymensingh. If, on the other hand, we look at the three top-

TABLE 9.7

Per capita Availability of Foodgrains in Bangladesh Districts,
1973 and 1974

(oz./day)

District	1974	1973	Change (%)
Dinajpur	25.1	20.4	+23.0
Mymensingh	22.8	20.6	+10.7
Sylhet	22.1	21.4	+3.3
Bogra	20.8	19.3	+7.8
Rangpur	20.1	18.3	+9.8
Chittagong	19.7	18.4	+7.1
Noakhali	16.7	17.8	−6.2
Jessore	16.3	14.6	+11.6
Khulna	16.2	13.8	+17.4
Barisal	16.0	18.6	−14.0
Rajshahi	15.8	15.6	+1.3
Patuakhali	15.7	24.1	−34.9
Tangail	15.3	14.7	+4.1
Comilla	14.9	16.1	−7.5
Chittagong Hill Tracts	14.4	14.8	−2.7
Dacca	13.8	14.5	−4.6
Faridpur	13.5	12.0	+12.5
Kushtia	12.8	12.0	+6.7
Pabna	10.8	10.4	+3.8

Source: Table 6.29, Alamgir (1980) based on figures of the Directorate of Procurement,
Distribution, and Rationing of the Government of Bangladesh.

ranked districts in terms of lowness of availability change
(Patuakhali, Barisal, and Comilla), this again would account for
only about 13 per cent of the destitutes in the *langarkhanas*. The
rank correlation coefficient between inter-district famine intensity and the lowness of availability change is *minus* .33,
hardly an encouraging piece of statistics.

  If, instead of looking at the *change* of availability, the districts
are ranked according to the lowness of *absolute* availability *per
capita*, again the explanation of famine conditions is not
enhanced. The so-called famine districts come at the *other* end—
the ranks of Rangpur, Sylhet, and Mymensingh being respectively 15, 17 and 18 out of nineteen states—each with relatively
high availability of foodgrains per head.[14] The top-ranked low-
availability districts (Pabna, Kushtia, and Faridpur) account for

  [14] Even the estimates of July–October availability put these three states among the
relatively better supplied; see Table 6.37 of Alamgir (1980).

only about 6 per cent of the *langarkhana* destitutes. Finally, the rank correlation coefficient of inter-district famine intensity and lowness of availability is *minus* .73, which does little in favour of the FAD view.

Undoubtedly, these high and significant negative rank correlations may be partly influenced by the fact that the famine-stricken districts received preferential treatment in the governmental allocation of foodgrains, but that would have hardly transformed shortages into relative opulence. Indeed, as was shown already, the output figures also give no comfort to the FAD view. The relief-oriented distributions were a relatively small part of total food consumption, and furthermore the amount of food given per destitute was—as noted before—*lower* in the more severely stricken districts.[15]

The food availability approach offers very little in the way of explanation of the Bangladesh famine of 1974. The total output, as well as availability figures for Bangladesh as a whole, point precisely in the opposite direction, as do the inter-district figures of production as well as availability. Whatever the Bangladesh famine of 1974 might have been, it wasn't a FAD famine.

9.4 OCCUPATIONAL DISTRIBUTION AND INTENSITY
      OF DESTITUTION

Who were the famine victims? Thanks to the survey of *langarkhana* inmates conducted by the Bangladesh Institute of Development Studies in November 1974, it is possible to give some kind of an answer to this question (even though the sample was not quite randomly chosen). Table 9.8 presents a broad occupational breakdown according to the major source of income. The largest group of destitutes in the *langarkhanas* were labourers (45 per cent), followed closely by farmers (39 per cent). If the labourers are split into agricultural and non-agricultural workers, the groups of farmers would appear to be the single largest category. This fact has been widely noted, and rightly so. On the other hand, it must not be forgotten that farmers as defined for the surveys were also the largest single group of rural households.

To get an idea of the relative intensity of destitution, the

---

[15] See Table 5.15 of Alamgir (1980). The calorie equivalent of daily wheat ration in October 1974 varied between 452 in *langarkhanas* in the famine districts of Mymensingh and Rangpur to 2,069 the non-famine district of Pabna.

TABLE 9.8

Occupational Distribution of Destitution in Bangladesh 1974

Occupation	Number of langarkhana inmates	Percentage of total langarkhana inmates
Labourers	351	44.5
of whom:		
(1) agricultural labourers	190	24.1
(2) other labourers	161	20.4
Farmers	305	38.7
Others	132	16.8
Total	788	100.0

Source: Table 5.3 of Alamgir (1980).

occupational distribution of destitutes has to be compared with the occupational distribution of the population from which the destitutes were drawn. This isn't easy to do since there is no survey that covers exactly the population from which the destitutes came. However, to get some idea it is possible to use Mia's (1976) study of the occupational distribution of rural heads of households and also the study by the Bangladesh Institute of occupational distribution of rural households by major sources of income. These are used in Table 9.9 to calculate two indices of intensity of destitution.

According to both indices, labourers do stand out as the most affected group by substantial margins. While it will be a mistake to attach too much importance to the exact values of these indices, the relative ordering of labourers *vis-à-vis* others including farmers is clear enough.

A similar conclusion emerges from the estimates of occupation-specific death rates during the famine months as obtained by the survey of selected villages by the Bangladesh Institute. These are presented in Table 9.10. While the small group of transport workers had a higher mortality rate than general wage labourers, the latter came close to the top and exceeded considerably the mortality rate of other groups—including farmers.

The land ownership statistics of *langarkhana* inmates are also worth noting. Table 9.11 presents the available information on

TABLE 9.9

Intensity of Destitution by Occupation in Bangladesh, 1974

Occupation	Percentage of total langarkhana inmates	Percentage of heads of rural households in Bangladesh	Percentage of rural households by major sources of income in Bangladesh	Intensity index I	Intensity index II
	(1)	(2)	(3)	(4) = (1)/(2)	(5) = (1)/(3)
Labourers	44.5	27.9	23.4	1.59	1.90
Farmers	38.7	41.8	59.7	0.93	0.65
Others	16.8	30.3	17.0	0.55	0.99
All	100.0	100.0	100.0	1.00	1.00

Source: Column (1) from Table 9.8 above; Column (2) from Mia (1976) and Alamgir (1978a), Table XII; Column (3) from Alamgir (1980), Table 8.12.

TABLE 9.10

Occupation-specific Mortality Rates in Selected Bangladeshi Villages during August–October 1974

Occupation	Death rate per 1,000	Death rate among children 10 years and below per 1,000
Transport	100	286
Wage labour	88	128
Trade	53	80
Farming	38	64
'Others'	29	n.a.
Service	16	12
Total	47	74

Source: Table 5.5 of Alamgir (1980).

this from the *langarkhana* survey by the Bangladesh Institute. Of the inmate households, 32 per cent owned no land at all. Perhaps more importantly, 81 per cent owned less than half an acre of land *if* they owned any land at all. This compares with 33 per cent of rural households owning half an acre or less of land in the

TABLE 9.11

Land Ownership of Langarkhana Inmates, Bangladesh, 1974

Size group of land	Number of inmate households	Percentage of inmate households	Percentage of rural population households	Incidence of destitution
	(1)	(2)	(3)	(4) = (2)/(3)
Less than ½ acre	639	81.09	32.69	2.481
½ acre or more; less than 1 acre	57	7.23	13.13	0.551
1 acre or more; less than 2½ acres	81	10.28	28.80	0.357
2½ acres or more; less than 5 acres	10	1.27	16.74	0.076
5 acres or more	1	0.13	8.62	0.015
Total	788	100.0	100.0	1.000

Source: Calculated from Table 5.2 of Alamgir (1980), and Table 6.11 of Alamgir *et al.* (1977). The 'rural population' refers to the households sampled in eight villages in the latter work.

villages surveyed by the Bangladesh Institute. It is the landless end of the village spectrum that is caught firmly at the *langarkhanas*. The average chance of ending up in *langarkhanas* for those with less than half an acre of land was 4½ times that of those owning between half an acre and one acre of land, and 165 times that of those with five acres or more. This corroborates the picture based on occupational statistics, and asserts in addition that quite a few of the farmers who are distinguished from landless labourers among the *langarkhana* inmates are, in fact, very tiny farmers indeed.

9.5 EXCHANGE ENTITLEMENT OF LABOUR POWER

Since the typical destitutes had as their endowment only labour power with—at best—little bits of land, the most important part of the entitlement relation to look at is the entitlement based on labour power. In Table 9.12 the indices of rice-exchange for rural labour for each month in 1974 are presented with two alternative bases: (a) December 1973 as 100, and (b) the same month in 1973 as 100. The decline of the e_j indices in the months just preceding

TABLE 9.12

Indices of Rice-Exchange Rate e_j of Rural Labour during the Bangladesh Famine, 1974

Base: (*a*) December 1973 values;   (*b*) Same month 1973 values

Month	Rural wage rate 1973	1974	Price of rice 1973	1974	Index value of rice-exchange rate e_j for 1974 month (a)	(b)
January	4.78	6.22	72.37	92.11	86	102
February	4.91	6.36	76.68	98.93	82	100
March	5.14	7.17	83.84	117.33	78	100
April	5.35	8.22	96.49	136.98	77	108
May	5.47	8.72	96.29	135.68	82	113
June	5.83	8.26	91.11	139.04	76	93
July	6.02	8.61	87.06	141.78	78	88
August	5.81	8.82	85.92	171.25	66	76
September	5.72	8.80	89.47	212.80	53	65
October	5.85	8.64	94.11	251.78	44	55
November	6.00	8.39	89.65	213.73	50	59
December	6.32	8.70	80.90	188.98	59	59

Source: Calculations based on data compiled by the Bangladesh Institute of Development Studies, reported in Alamgir *et al.* (1977), Tables 3.3 and 4.3.

the famine and through the famine months is very sharp indeed. The fall is a bit less if we use the same-month–previous-year base, which does something to eliminate the seasonal drop, but even there the fall is large. At the peak of the famine the fall is 35 to 45 per cent compared with the same month in the previous year, for a group of people already close to subsistence.

The sharpest decline comes just after the floods started, and Table 9.13 presents the fall of the rice-exchange rate of rural labour from June to October. There was no such decline in the preceding year (see Table 9.12), and data for earlier years also show no substantial seasonal fall over these months.

Turning now to the inter-district picture, the three famine districts also turn out to be precisely the three top ranked districts in terms of decline in the rice-entitlement of wages (see Table

TABLE 9.13
Rice Entitlement of Wage Rate: Index Values for October 1974 with June 1974 as 100

	Wage rate index	Rice price index	Percentage decline of the exchange rate of wage labour with rice in rural Bangladesh
Bangladesh	104.6	181.1	42.2
Mymensingh	69.0	225.9	69.5
Rangpur	80.0	190.3	58.0
Sylhet	100.0	236.0	57.6
Noakhali	100.0	209.8	52.3
Barisal	87.0	177.3	50.9
Chittagong Hill Tracts	100.0	201.3	50.3
Tangail	106.3	211.4	49.7
Pabna	100.0	172.3	42.0
Chittagong	100.0	170.5	41.3
Patuakhali	100.0	167.9	40.4
Dacca	118.9	192.6	38.3
Khulna	96.2	153.9	37.5
Bogra	100.0	158.2	36.8
Dinajpur	114.3	179.1	36.2
Comilla	135.7	205.0	33.8
Jessore	108.3	155.0	30.1
Kushtia	112.0	151.4	26.0
Rajshahi	123.1	156.4	21.3
Faridpur	158.3	164.5	3.8

Source: Calculated from Tables 3.3 and 4.3 of Alamgir *et al.* (1977), pp. 57–8 and 92.

9.13). The entitlement ratio fell by 58 per cent in Rangpur and Sylhet and by 70 per cent in Mymensingh, and with that kind of decline in the entitlement to rice, labourers would be pushed firmly towards starvation and death. The over-all picture for *all* districts considered is a bit muddier, even though the rank correlation coefficient, while not high (.32), is positive and significant, and contrasts sharply with the significantly negative results we obtained with various versions of the FAD approach. The exchange entitlement approach—applied in the simple form of only looking at rice-entitlement of wages—already provides a good bit of the explanation of destitution, even though it leaves room for other factors to be brought in.[16].

Finally, the share of *langarkhana* destitutes accounted for by the three top-ranked states in terms of rice-entitlement decline is over 50 per cent. This contrasts with 6 to 13 per cent in the various versions of the food availability approach, as found in Section 9.3. The difference is partly a matter of district size, but also a matter of district identification. The percentages of destitution in the three 'worst affected' districts under the rice-entitlement approach are (18%, 12%, 8%) as opposed to (7%, 4%, 4%) and (4%, 3%, 2%) under different versions of the FAD approach.

The decline in terms of trade of labour power *vis-à-vis* rice was clearly reinforced by a decline in employment opportunities in the famine year.[17] Here the floods played a part. While the decline in the *aman* crop that got partly washed out in June–September 1974 did not reflect itself in the form of a lower output until after the famine, the decline in employment opportunities was immediate.[18] Table 9.14 presents the normal seasonal

[16] One such factor was the deterioration of the terms of trade of jute *vis-à-vis* rice, which has been commented on in other contexts, mainly the reduced incentive to grow raw jute (see Faaland and Parkinson, 1976, pp. 59–61, 135–6). In terms of entitlement rather than price incentive for production, this meant a drop in the rice-entitlement for jute growers, and would have added to the distress of the farmers producing raw jute. For famine conditions in neighbouring Assam in India in the same period, a sharp decline in the relative price of jute clearly played a major part (see Prabhakar, 1974, p. 1767). There was also a decline in acreage under jute during 1974 leading to some loss of employment (see Alamgir, 1980, p. 304, footnote 9), leading to some loss of employment.

[17] See Rahman (1974a, 1974b), Adnan and Rahman (1978), and Alamgir (1978a, 1980), among others.

[18] The 'derived destitution' in the form of reduced demand for rural services and crafts leading to reduction of exchange entitlements of the related occupations was also immediate.

TABLE 9.14
*Normal Seasonal Pattern of Employment in
Cultivation: Char Shamraj Village*
(days worked)

Month	Cultivation	Activity rank
Baisak (April–May)	1,872	9
Jaistha (May–June)	2,496	8
Ashar (June–July)	4,804	1
Sravan (July–August)	4,786	2
Bhadra (August–Sept.)	2,665	7
Aswin (Sept.–Oct.)	526	12
Kartik (Oct.–Nov.)	3,181	5
Agrahayan (Nov.–Dec.)	4,667	3
Poush (Dec.–Jan.)	3,239	4
Magh (Jan.–Feb.)	2,811	6
Falgoon (Feb.–March)	1,791	10
Chaitra (March–April)	1,243	11

Source: Fieldwork by Village Study Group in Char Samraj reported in Rushidan Islam (1977), p. 12.

rhythm of work, in terms of days worked, in cultivation in a Bengali village (in this case, Char Shamraj). It is seen that peak employment takes place in June–August, and this is of course precisely the time when the floods hit, drastically reducing the scope of employment in cultivation. The decline in the rice-entitlement of wage was thus compounded by the fall in the employment opportunity—a vital determinant of exchange entitlement of labour power.[19]

In understanding the causation of destitution, therefore, one has to go much beyond the statistics of food availability. The output and availability of foodgrains may have peaked in 1974, but the market forces determining the relative wage *vis-à-vis* rice was moving sharply against the former. While we haven't got the data that would permit a satisfactory causal analysis of the factors affecting the exchange rates, it is possible to make a few observations on its general nature.

First, even though the decline in the *aman* crop could not have affected the total amount of foodgrains in Bangladesh during the

[19] Recovery from the famine took place in November as the next season of busy activity began—mercifully free from natural calamities.

famine months (since that crop would not have been harvested until November–January *following* the famine), the expectation of the decline must have had some effect on the level of rice price.[20] In fact, the rumour of decline was rather stronger than the actual fall in *aman* output, but speculative withdrawals can feed comfortably on such rumours.

Second, the rise in rice price could not, however, have been the result of the flood only. Indeed, in the early months of 1974, long before the floods, rice prices were rising sharply—almost as fast as they did during the flood and immediately after. Table 9.15 presents the monthly rise in rice price through 1974, and it is seen that in Bangladesh as a whole, and specifically in the famine districts, there are sharp rises in the earlier part of the year, much before the floods hit. Thus the explanation of the rise in rice price must be sought partly in influences that have nothing to do with

TABLE 9.15

Rise in the Price of Rice in Bangladesh in 1974

Month in 1974	Bangladesh average	Percentage rise in the retail price of coarse rice in each month over the preceeding month		
		Mymensingh	Rangpur	Sylhet
January	+14	+14	+16	+6
February	+7	+11	+2	+22
March	+19	+27	+19	+15
April	+17	+16	+16	+19
May	−1	−16	+17	−17
June	+2	−2	0	−2
July	+2	+12	+4	+16
August	+21	+30	+16	+29
September	+24	+29	+58	+24
October	+18	+20	0	+28
November	−15	−20	−38	−18
December	−12	−19	−25	−7

Source: Calculated from Table 3.3 of Alamgir *et al.* (1977), pp. 57–8.

[20] If we replace the *aman* harvested in December 1973 by that harvested in December 1974 in the 1974 production figure in Table 9.4, the index value of 1974 falls from 103 to 97. Re-indexing all the years by replacing the preceding *aman* crop by the *aman* that comes at the end of the relevant year, the index values stand as follows: 1971, 100; 1972, 91; 1972, 107; 1973, 100; 1974, 99; 1975, 108. It has the effect of converting 1974 from a local peak to a local trough.

the floods. And this is where a macroeconomic study dealing with such factors as effective demand, money supply, etc., could contribute substantially.

Third, while the decline in the rice-entitlement of wage is to a great extent the result of the rise in rice price, there was also a decline in absolute money wage rate in a few districts, including the famine districts of Mymensingh and Rangpur, between June and October of 1974 (see Table 9.13). It is quite remarkable that, not merely did the money wage fail to stay in line with rice price; it actually fell in absolute terms in these districts. The weakening of the market strength of labour that this reflects may be partly traceable to the decline in employment opportunities as a result of the flood and related contraction of rural economic activities.

9.6 A QUESTION OF FOCUS

The enormity of economic problems facing Bangladesh has been widely observed. The fear of population running ahead of food production has been regularly voiced. It is not my intention to dismiss these problems and fears. But what emerges irresistably from the preceding analysis is the danger of concentrating only on the aggregative issues, overlooking the details of the entitlement system on which the survival of millions of Bangladeshi people crucially depends. The focus on population and food supply would have been innocuous but for what it does to hide the realities that determine who can command how much food.

Bangladesh remains a traditional rural economy in many significant respects. Nearly three-quarters of its population live on agriculture and about 90 per cent live in rural areas.[21] Yet the economic organization is not one of market-independent peasant agriculture. About a quarter of the rural population survive by exchanging labour at market wages and commanding food with what they earn. For them a variation of the exchange relationships can spell ruin. There is, in fact, some evidence that in recent years in Bangladesh the wage system itself has moved more towards money wages, away from payments in kind—chiefly food.[22] More modern, perhaps; more vulnerable, certainly.

The process of sale of land by small peasants cuts down not

[21] On the general nature of the Bangladesh economy and various aspects of its economic performance, see Faaland and Parkinson (1976); also Etienne (1977a).

[22] See Clay (1976).

only the peasant's normal income, but also the stability of his earnings—making him more vulnerable to exchange rate shifts. Table 9.16 presents this pattern of land sales in the villages studied by the Bangladesh Institute in the years leading up to the famine. One sees a clear bias towards land alienation on the part of the smaller landholders.[23] The development not merely generally impoverished the group of small peasants;[24] it also increased the ease with which members of the class could sink into starvation even in a year of relative plenty as a result of shifts of rice-entitlement of labour power.

TABLE 9.16

Proportion of Owned Land Sold According to Landholding of Sellers, 1972–4

| Landholding group | Percentage of owned land sold | | |
	1972	1973	1974
Less that 1 acre	39	29	54
1 to less than 2 acres	19	17	24
2 to less than 5 acres	12	18	12
5 acres and above	10	10	11

Source: Table XXVII of Alamgir (1978a).

Other occupation groups also depend on being able to command food by exchanging things that they produce and sell. Boatmen and transport workers had a high mortality in the Bengal famine in 1943; they had again exceptionally high mortality in the famine of 1974. Village craftsmen, producers of services, petty traders, and a whole host of other occupations live by exchange—and from time to time perish by exchange.

There has been a welcome tendency recently to move away from figures of national income per head (and other such national aggregates) to income distribution, in particular to poverty. But even the group of the poor is too broad a category, and it is possible for the proportion of population below the poverty line to fall while those who are in poverty experience a deepening of

[23] See also Rahman (1974a, 1974b), Khan (1977), Abdullah (1976a, 1976b), Adnan and Rahman (1978), and Hartmann and Boyce (1979).
[24] For a global analysis of the relation between rural poverty and land concentration, see Griffin (1976).

their deprivation. This was one of the reasons why it was argued that distribution below the poverty line has to be taken into account in arriving at a fuller picture of poverty (see Chapter 3 and Appendix C).

It seems that an example of a divergent development of this kind can be found in the recent experience of Bangladesh. Some calculations done by Azizur Rahman Khan are presented in Table 9.17. It would appear from this that, while the proportion of people below the poverty line (defined as the level of income at which people meet 90 per cent of the recommended calorie intake) *fell*, or at least rose little, between late 1960s and mid-1970s, the proportion in 'extreme poverty'—defined as having levels of income less than adequate to meet 80 per cent of the recommended calorie intake—*rose* sharply.[25] Thus a general intensification of starvation may have gone hand in hand with a reduction of the head-count measure of poverty for the defined 'poverty line'. Shocking disasters can lie deeply hidden in comforting aggregate magnitudes.

The analysis of exchange entitlements and the study of the

TABLE 9.17

Percentage of Rural Population in Poverty and in Extreme Poverty

	Poor	Extremely poor	Change of the percentage of the poor since 1968–9	Change of the percentage of the extremely poor since 1968–9
1968–9	76.0	25.1		
1973–4	78.5	42.1	+3.3	+67.7
1975 (first quarter)	61.8	41.1	−18.7	+63.7

Basis: Table 48 of Khan (1977). 'Poor' people are those with incomes less than adequate for meeting 90 per cent of recommended calorie intake, and 'extremely poor' are those with less than adequate incomes to meet 80 per cent of the recommended calorie intake.

[25] See also Osmani (1978).

famine presented here can be extended in many ways by taking a more detailed view of the relationships that govern people's ability to command food and other essential goods. But even this simple analysis has been sufficient to demonstrate that the FAD view provides no explanation of the Bangladesh famine, and that a better understanding of the famine can be found through the entitlement approach.

Chapter 10

Entitlements and Deprivation

The view that famines are caused by food availability decline—the FAD view—was questioned on grounds of cogency in the first chapter of this monograph. Empirical studies of some of the larger recent famines confirmed that famines could thrive even without a general decline in food availability (see Chapter 6, 7, and 9). Even in those cases in which a famine *is* accompanied by a reduction in the amount of food available per head, the causal mechanism precipitating starvation has to bring in many variables other than the general availability of food (see Chapter 8). The FAD approach gives little clue to the causal mechanism of starvation, since it does not go into the *relationship* of people to food. Whatever may be the oracular power of the FAD view, it is certainly Delphic in its reticence.

A food-centred view tells us rather little about starvation. It does not tell us how starvation can develop even without a decline in food availability. Nor does it tell us—even when starvation is accompanied by a fall in food supply—why some groups had to starve while others could feed themselves. The over-all food picture is too remote an economic variable to tell us much about starvation. On the other hand, if we look at the food going to *particular* groups, then of course we can say a good deal about starvation. But, then, one is not far from just describing the starvation itself, rather than explaining what happened. If some people had to starve, then clearly, they didn't have enough food, but the question is: *why* didn't they have food? What allows one group rather than another to get hold of the food that is there? These questions lead to the entitlement approach, which has been explored in this monograph, going from economic phenomena into social, political, and legal issues.

A person's ability to command food—indeed, to command any commodity he wishes to acquire or retain—depends on the entitlement relations that govern possession and use in that society. It depends on what he owns, what exchange possibilities are offered to him, what is given to him free, and what is taken away from him. For example, a barber owns his labour power and some specialized skill, neither of which he can eat, and he has to sell his hairdressing service to earn an income to buy food. His entitlement to food may collapse even without any change in food availability if for any reason the demand for hairdressing collapses and if he fails to find another job or any social security benefit. Similarly, a craftsman producing, say, sandals may have his food entitlement squashed if the demand for sandals falls sharply, or if the supply of leather becomes scarce, and starvation can occur with food availability in the economy unchanged. A general labourer has to earn his income by selling his labour power (or through social security benefit) before he can establish his command over food in a free-market economy; unemployment *without* public support will make him starve. A sharp change in the relative prices of sandals, or haircuts, or labour power (i.e. wages) *vis-à-vis* food can make the food entitlements of the respective group fall below the starvation level. It is the totality of entitlement relations that governs whether a person will have the ability to acquire enough food to avoid starvation, and food supply is only one influence among many affecting his entitlement relations.

It is sometimes said that starvation may be caused not by food shortage but by the shortage of income and purchasing power. This can be seen as a rudimentary way of trying to catch the essence of the entitlement approach, since income does give one entitlement to food in a market economy. While income may not always provide command in a fully planned economy, or in a 'shortage economy', in which a different system of entitlement might hold,[1] the income-centred view will be relevant in most circumstances in which famines have occurred.[2] But the inadequacy of the income-centred view arises from the fact that, even in those circumstances in which income does provide command, it offers only a partial picture of the entitlement pattern, and starting the story with the shortage of income is to

[1] See Kornai (1979a) for a far-reaching probe into economics of the 'shortage economy'. See also Kornai (1979b).

[2] A possible exception might conceivably be the Russian famines of 1932–4, but they have not been fully studied yet. See, however, Dalrymple (1964, 1965) and Brown and Anderson (1976, Chapter 6).

leave the tale half-told. People died because they didn't have the income to buy food, but how come they didn't have the income? What they can earn depends on what they can sell and at what price, and starting off with incomes leaves out that part of the entitlement picture. Futhermore, sometimes the income may be just 'notional', e.g. a peasant's possession of the foodgrains he has grown, and then the income-and-purchasing-power story is a bit oblique. To talk about his entitlement to the food he has grown is, of course, more direct. But the main advantage of the entitlement approach rests not in simplicity as such, but—as explained above—in providing a more comprehensive account of a person's ability to command commodities in general and food in particular.

10.2 THE POOR: A LEGITIMATE CATEGORY?

The entitlement approach requires the use of categories based on certain types of discrimination. A small peasant and a landless labourer may both be poor, but their fortunes are not tied together. In understanding the proneness to starvation of either we have to view them not as members of the huge army of 'the poor', but as members of particular classes, belonging to particular occupational groups, having different ownership endowments, and being governed by rather different entitlement relations. Classifying the population into the rich and the poor may serve some purpose in some context, but it is far too undiscriminating to be helpful in analysing starvation, famines, or even poverty.

The grossest category is, of course, the category of the entire population. It is on this that FAD concentrates, in checking food availability per head, and comes to grief (Chapters 6–9). The entitlement approach not merely rejects such grossness; it demands much greater refinement of categories to be able to characterize entitlements of different groups, with each group putting together different people who have similar endowments and entitlements. As a category for causal analysis, 'the poor' isn't a very helpful one, since different groups sharing the same predicament of poverty get there in widely different ways. The contrast between the performances of different occupation groups in famine situations, even between groups that are all typically poor, indicates the need for avoiding gross categories such as the poor and the rich.

So much for causal analysis. But it might be thought that, while the category of the poor isn't very helpful in such causal analysis, it is useful in the *evaluation* of the extent of poverty in the nation. Indeed, the poor are usually huddled together for a head count in quantifying poverty. There is clearly some legitimacy in the category of the poor in this evaluative context in so far as there is a clear break in our concern about people at the 'poverty line'. In Chapter 2 it was argued that the problem of poverty assessment is quite distinct from the issue of assessment of inequality and requires paying particular attention to the category of the poor. On the other hand, even for evaluative purposes there is need for discrimination *among* the poor according to the severity of deprivation. In the head-count measure, the starving wreck counts no more than the barely poor, and it is easy to construct examples in which in an obvious sense there is an intensification of poverty while the head-count measures is unchanged or records a diminution (see Chapter 3 and Appendix C). Thus, while the category of the poor has some legitimacy in the evaluative context, it is still far too gross a category and requires to be broken down.

The category of the poor is not merely inadequate for evaluative exercises and a nuisance for causal analysis, it can also have distorting effects on policy matters. On the causal side, the lack of discrimination between different circumstances leading to poverty gives rise to a lack of focus in policy choice. Evaluative grossness can also distort. With the use of the head-count measure of poverty, the best rewards to poverty-removal policies are almost always obtained by concentrating on the people who are *just* below the poverty line rather than on those suffering from deep poverty. There is indeed a certain amount of empirical evidence that gross characterizations of poverty do lead to distortions of public policy.[3]

10.3 WORLD FOOD AVAILABILITY AND STARVATION

The FAD approach applied to the food availability for the population of an entire country is a gross approach, lacking in

---

[3] See Sen (1975, Appendix A; 1976d).

relevant discrimination. What is a good deal more gross is the FAD approach applied to the population of the world as a whole. The balancing of world supply and world population has nevertheless received a lot of attention recently. While a fall in food availability per head for the world as a whole is neither a necessary nor a sufficient condition for intensification of hunger in the world, it has typically been assumed that the two *are* rather well correlated with each other. The evidence in favour of that assumption is not abundant, but it may be reasonable to suppose that, if the food availability per head were to go on persistently declining, starvation would be sooner or later accentuated. Different institutions and authors have provided estimates of 'short-falls' the 1980s and beyond, some more alarming than others.[4]

I have little to add to this exacting exercise, except to point out the sensitivity of the results to the assumptions chosen and the remarkable lack of uniformity in the methodologies that have been thought to be appropriate. As far as the present is concerned—rather than the future—there is no real evidence of food supply falling behind population growth for the world as a whole, even though this has been observed for a number of countries. There is no outstripping of food growth by population expansion even when we look at the global picturing leaving out the United States, which has been such a large supplier of food to other countries. The 'balance' in the future will depend on a variety of economic and political conditions,[5] but there is as yet no indication that world population expansion has started gaining on the growth of world food supply.

But if the analysis presented in the earlier chapters of this monograph is correct, it is quite possible that severe famine conditions can develop for reasons that are not directly connected with food production at all. The entitlement approach places food production within a network of relationships, and shifts in some of these relations can precipitate gigantic famines even without receiving any impulse from food production.

[4] See, for example, Borgstrom (1969), Ehrlich and Ehrlich (1972), Brown and Eckholm (1974), and Aziz (1975).

[5] See, among others, D. G. Johnson (1967, 1975), Borgstrom (1973), Aziz (1977), Taylor (1975), Sinha (1976a, 1976b, 1977), Barraclough (1977), Buringh (1977), Etienne (1977b), Lappé and Collins (1977), Poleman (1977), Rado and Sinha (1977), Harle (1978), Hay (1978a, 1978b), Sinha and Gordon Drabek (1978), and Interfutures (1979).

It is not my purpose to deny the importance of food production, or of some of the well-analysed issues in international food policy. It *is* rewarding to consider international insurance arrangements to reduce the food supply vulnerability of particular countries.[6] It *is* relevant to know how international food aid affects domestic production and distribution, and the world food prices.[7] It *is* also useful to do food balance sheets and integrate them into social account procedures, and to go into more elaborate analysis of 'food systems'.[8] The focus that emerges from this monograph looks at a different direction, namely the need to view the food problem as a relation between people and food in terms of a network of entitlement relations.

Some of the relations are simple (e.g. the peasant's entitlement to the food grown by him), while others are more complex (e.g. the nomad's entitlement to grain through exchange of animals, leading to a net gain in calories—see Chapters 7 and 8). Some involve the use of the market mechanism (e.g. selling craft products to buy food—see Chapter 6), while others depend on public policy (e.g. employment benefits, or relief in *langarkhanas* and destitution camps—see Chapters 6–9). Some are affected by macroeconomic developments (e.g. demand-pull inflation—see Chapters 6 and 9), while others deal with local calamities (e.g. regional slump—see Chapter 7), or with microeconomic failures (e.g. denial of fishing rights to a particular community in a particular region[9]). Some are much influenced by speculative activities, while others are not.[10]

It is the set of these diverse influences seen from the perspective of entitlement relations that received attention in this

[6] See, D. G. Johnson (1975, 1976), Kaldor (1976), Taylor and Sarris (1976), Aziz (1977), Josling (1977), Weckstein (1977), Reutlinger (1978), Konandreas, Huddleston and Ramangkura (1979), among others.

[7] See Mann (1968), Rogers, Srivastava and Heady (1972), Isenman and Singer (1977), Lappé and Collins (1977), Taylor (1977), and Svedberg (1978, 1979).

[8] See Joy and Payne (1975), Pyatt and Thorbecke (1976), Lörstad (1976), UNRISD (1976), Dickson (1977), Manetsch (1977), Hay (1978a, 1980), de Haen (1978), Chichilnisky (1979), and others, for pointers to different approaches.

[9] See Rangasami (1975), dealing with a local famine in the Goalpara district of Assam in India. See also Rangasami (1974a, 1974b).

[10] In the Bengal famine of 1943 professional speculators played an important part in the *second* phase of the famine (see Chapter 6, and Sen, 1977b). Holt and Seaman (1979) have argued for analysing this phase in terms of a 'catastrophe' pattern, and in this rapid change speculation was clearly important. On catastrophe theory, see Thom (1975) and Zeeman (1977).

monograph, through the analysis of actual famines which have taken place in recent years. In considering food policy, what emerges from this work is the importance of this angle of vision.

10.4 MARKET AND FOOD MOVEMENTS

Whether markets serve well the remedial function of curing famines by food movements has been the subject of a good deal of debating over centuries. Adam Smith (1776) took the view that it did, and that point of view was eloquently defended by Robert Malthus (1800) among others (see Appendix B). These arguments in political economy were widely used by policy-makers, not least in the British Empire.[11]

When a famine was developing in Gujerat in 1812, the Governor of Bombay turned down a proposal for moving food into an affected areas by asserting the advisability of leaving such matters to the market mechanism, quoting 'the celebrated author of the *Wealth of Nations*'.[12] Warren Hastings, who had tackled a famine in Bengal in 1783–4 by using public channels for moving food into the region, was rapped on the knuckles by Colonel Baird-Smith for not having understood his Adam Smith, adding that Hastings could 'scarcely have been expected' to have absorbed Adam Smith so soon (1783) after the publication (1776) of the *Wealth of Nations*.[13] The basically non-interventionist famine policy in India lasted late into the nineteenth century, changing only around the last quarter of it.

Firm believers in the market mechanism were often disappointed by the failure of the market to deliver much. During the Orissa famine of 1865–6, Ravenshaw the Commissioner of Cuttack Division, expressed disappointment that private trade did not bring much food from outside which should have happened since 'under all ordinary rules of political economy the urgent demand for grain in the Cuttack division *ought to have created* a supply from other and more favoured parts'.[14]

Rashid (1979) has argued that even a non-monopolized group of traders can act together in a monopolistic way to hinder

---

[11] See Bhatia (1767), Ambirajan (1978) and Rashid (1980).
[12] Quoted in Ambirajan (1978), p. 71. See also Aykroyd (1974).
[13] Quoted in Ambirajan (1978), p. 75.
[14] See Ambirajan (1980), p. 76; italics added.

movement of grains to relieve excess demand.[15] This could be so, but in a slump famine starvation and hunger can go hand in hand with little market pull, and even competitive traders may have little incentive to bring in foodgrain from elsewhere. Adam Smith's proposition is, in fact, concerned with efficiency in meeting a market demand, but it says nothing on meeting a need that has not been translated into effective demand because of lack of market-based entitlement and shortage of purchasing power.

Indeed, in many famines complaints have been heard that, while famine was raging, food was being *exported* from the famine-stricken country or region. This was, in fact, found to be the case in a relatively small scale in Wollo in 1973 (Chapter 7), and also in Bangladesh in 1974 (Chapter 9). It was a major political issue in the Irish famine of 1840s: 'In the long and troubled history of England and Ireland no issue provoked so much anger or so embittered relations between the two countries as the indisputable fact that huge quantities of food were exported from Ireland to England throughout the period when the people of Ireland were dying of starvation.'[16] Such movements out of famine-stricken areas have been observed in Indian famines as well.[17] In China, British refusal to ban rice exports from famine-affected Hunan was one of the causes of an uprising in 1906, and latter a similar issue was involved in the famous Changsha rice riot of 1910.[18]

Viewed from the entitlement angle, there is nothing extraordinary in the market mechanism taking food away from famine-stricken areas to elsewhere. Market demands are not reflections of biological needs or psychological desires, but choices based on exchange entitlement relations. If one doesn't have much to exchange, one can't demand very much, and may thus lose out in competition with others whose needs may be a good deal less acute, but whose entitlements are stronger.[19] In

[15] It is also possible to show how easily speculation can be destabilizing (see Hart, 1977).

[16] Woodham-Smith (1975), p. 70.

[17] See Ghosh (1979). Also Bhatia (1967) and Rashid (1980).

[18] Esherick (1976). Food movement from Bangladesh into India during the Bangladesh famine was also a politically explosive issue.

[19] This is one of the reasons why it is misleading to characterize a famine arising from a crop failure as being due to a fall in food availability. With crop failure people's incomes also collapse—and their ability to attract food from elsewhere—and the situation is best seen as a failure of entitlement and not as just a drop in food availability.

fact, in a slump famine such a tendency will be quite common, unless other regions have a more severe depression. Thus, food being *exported* from famine-stricken areas may be a 'natural' characteristic of the market which respects entitlement rather than needs.

10.5 FAMINES AS FAILURES OF ENTITLEMENT

The entitlement approach views famines as economic disasters, not as just food crises. The empirical studies brought out several distinct ways in which famines can develop—defying the stereotyped uniformity of food availability decline (FAD). While famine victims share a common predicament, the economic forces leading to that predicament can be most diverse.

A comparative picture of some aspects of four famines studied in Chapters 6, 7, and 9 is presented in Table 10.1, though it misses out many other contrasts discussed in detail in those chapters. (The famines in the six Sahel countries analysed in Chapter 8 have not been included in the table because of some lack of uniformity between the experiences of the different Sahel countries, but the over-all picture is rather similar to that of the Ethiopian famines.)

That famines can take place without a substantial food availability decline is of interest mainly because of the hold that the food availability approach has in the usual famine analysis.[20] It has also led to disastrous policy failure in the past.[21] The entitlement approach concentrates instead on the ability of different sections of the population to establish command over food, using the entitlement relations operating in that society depending on its legal, economic, political, and social characteristics.

I end with four general observations about the entitlement approach to famines. First, the entitlement approach provides a general framework for analysing famines rather than one particular hypothesis about their causation. There is, of course, a

---

[20] In addition to explicit use of the FAD approach, very often it is implicitly employed in separating out the total food supply per head as the strategic variable to look at.

[21] The failure to *anticipate* the Bengal famine, which killed about three million people, and indeed the inability even to *recognise* it when it came, can be traced largely to the government's overriding concern with aggregate food availability statistics (see Chapter 6 above, and Sen, 1977b).

TABLE 10.1

Comparative Analysis of Four Famines

Which famine?	Was there a food availability collapse?	Which occupation group provided the largest number of famine victims?	Did that group suffer substantial endowment loss?	Did that group suffer exchange entitlement shifts?	Did that group suffer direct entitlement failure?	Did that group suffer trade entitlement failure?	What was the general economist climate
Bengal famine 1943	No	Rural labour	No	Yes	No	Yes	Boom
Ethiopian famine (Wollo) 1973	No	Farmer	A little, Yes	Yes	Yes	No	Slump
Ethiopian famine (Harerghe) 1974	Yes	Pastoralist	Yes	Yes	Yes	Yes	Slump
Bangladesh famine 1974	No	Rural labour	Earlier, yes	Yes	No	Yes	Mixed

very *general* hypothesis underlying the approach, which is subject to empirical testing. It will be violated if starvation in famines is shown to arise not from entitlement failures but either from choice characteristics (e.g. people refusing to eat unfamiliar food which they are in a position to buy,[22] or people refusing to work[23]), or from non-entitlement transfers (e.g. looting [24]). But the main interest in the approach does not, I think, lie in checking *whether* most famines are related to entitlement failures, which I suspect would be found to be the case, but in characterizing the nature and *causes* of the entitlement failures where such failures occur. The contrast between different types of entitlement failures is important in understanding the precise causation of famines and in devising famine policies: anticipation, relief, and prevention.

Second, it is of interest that famines can arise in over-all *boom* conditions (as in Bengal in 1943) as well as in *slump* conditions (as in Ethiopia in 1974). Slump famines may appear to be less contrary to the 'common sense' about famines, even though it is, in fact, quite possible for such a slump to involve contraction of

---

[22] However, anecdotal accounts of dietary inflexibilities can be less flexible than the dietary habits themselves, as judged by the following interesting statement by Dom Moraes, the distinguished poet: '. . . in India in the 1940's there was a famine in Bengal and millions of people died. During the famine, the British brought in a large amount of wheat. Now, the people of Bengal are traditionally rice eaters and they would not change their eating habits; they literally starved to death in front of shops and mobile units where wheat was available. Education must reach such people' (Moraes, 1975, p. 40). Education must, of course, reach all, but there is, in fact, little evidence of the hungry refusing any edible commodities during the Bengal famine (see Famine Inquiry Commission, 1945a; also Ghosh, 1944 and Das 1949). The explanation of people dying in front of shops has to be sought elsewhere, in particular in the shortage of purchasing power and the minuteness of free distribution compared with the size of the hungry population queuing up for any food whatsoever (see Chapter 6 above).

[23] Haile Selassie, the Emperor of Ethiopia, apparently provided the following remarkable analysis of the famine in his country in June 1973: 'Rich and poor have always existed and always will. Why? Because there are those that work...and those that prefer to do nothing....We have said wealth has to be gained through hard work. We have said those who don't work starve.' (Interview report by Oriana Fallaci; quoted by Wiseberg, 1976, p. 108.) They have indeed 'said' that for many centuries, in different lands.

[24] Such non-entitlement transfers have played a part in some famines of the past. As an example, see Walter Mallory's (1926) account of the 1925 famine in Szechwan: 'The Kweichow troops invaded southern Szechwan and after some fighting were driven out. When they left they took with them all available beasts of burden, loaded with grain. The Szechwan troops who replaced them brought very little in the way of supplies and forthwith appropriated the remainder of the food reserves of the district—leaving the population, who had no interests in either side, to starve' (pp. 78–9).

outputs *other than* those of food (e.g. of cash crops). Boom famines might seem particularly counter-intuitive; but, as discussed, famines can take place with increased output in general and of food in particular if the command system (e.g. market pull) shifts against some particular group. In this relative shift the process of the boom itself may play a major part if the boom takes the form of uneven expansion (for example favouring the urban population and leaving the rural labourers relatively behind). In the fight for market command over food, one group can suffer precisely from another group's prosperity, with the Devil taking the hindmost.[25]

Third, it is important to distinguish between decline of food *availability* and that of *direct entitlement* to food. The former is concerned with how much food there is in the economy in question, while the latter deals with each food-grower's output of food which he is entitled to consume directly. In a peasant economy a crop failure would reduce both availability and the direct entitlement to food of the peasants. But in so far as the peasant typically lives on his own-grown food and has little ability to sell and buy additional food from the market anyway, the immediate reason for his starvation would be his direct entitlement failure rather than a decline in food availability in the market. Indeed, if his own crop fails while those of others do not, the total supply may be large while he starves. Similarly, if his crop is large while that of others go down, he may still be able to do quite well despite the fall in total supply. The analytical contrast is important even though the two phenomena may happen simultaneously in a general crop failure. While such a crop failure may superficially look like just a crisis of food availability, something more than availability is involved. This is important to recognize also from the policy point of view, since just moving food into such an area will not help the affected population when what is required is the generation of food entitlement.

Finally, the focus on entitlement has the effect of emphasizing

---

[25] When the fast progressing groups are themselves poor, the development of the famine may be accompanied by a reduction in the number of people below some general 'poverty line', leading to a recorded reduction of poverty as it is conventionally measured, i.e. in terms of head-count ratio. The problem is less acute with distribution-sensitive measures of poverty. See Appendix C.

legal rights. Other relevant factors, for example market forces, can be seen as operating *through* a system of legal relations (ownership rights, contractual obligations, legal exchanges, etc.). The law stands between food availability and food entitlement. Starvation deaths can reflect legality with a vengeance.

Appendix A

Exchange Entitlement

A.1 FIXED PRICE EXCHANGES

X is the non-negative orthant of n-dimensional real space, representing the amounts of n commodities; it is the set of all non-negative vectors of all commodities. Y is the power-set of X, i.e., the set of all subsets of X. Let $\mathbf{x}$ be the vector of commodities (including 'labour power') that the person owns, and $\mathbf{p}$ is the n-vector of prices faced by him.

Given his ownership vector $\mathbf{x}$, his exchange entitlement set $E(\mathbf{x})$ is the set of vectors any one of which he can acquire by exchanging $\mathbf{x}$.

(A1) $$E(\mathbf{x}) = \{\mathbf{y} \mid \mathbf{y} \in X \,\&\, \mathbf{p}\,\mathbf{y} \leqslant \mathbf{p}\,\mathbf{x}\}.$$

The function $E(.)$ from X to Y is his 'exchange entitlement mapping', or E-mapping, for short.

Two explanatory points. First, clearly $\mathbf{x} \in E(\mathbf{x})$. Second, the exchanges covered by (A1) are not, of course, confined to selling all of $\mathbf{x}$, and a part of it can be retained (since this will not affect the exchange-possibility of the remainder, as given by (A1)).

Let the set of commodity vectors that satisfy the specified minimum food requirement be given by $F \subseteq X$. Starvation must occur, in the absence of non-entitlement transfers (such as looting), if $E(\mathbf{x}) \cap F = \varnothing$. The 'starvation set' S of ownership vectors consists of those vectors $\mathbf{x}$ in X such that the exchange entitlement set $E(\mathbf{x})$ contains no vector satisfying the minimum food requirements. Obviously, S depends on F and the E-mapping.

(A2) $$S = \{\mathbf{x} \mid \mathbf{x} \in X \,\&\, E(\mathbf{x}) \cap F = \varnothing\}.$$

To illustrate consider a simple two-commodity case with commodity 1 standing for food, and let OA in Figure A1 represent the minimum food requirement. The price ratio is given by p. The starvation set S is given by the region OAB.

More generally, when food is not one commodity but many and the 'food requirements' can be met in many different ways, let the minimum cost of meeting the food requirements, i.e. for attaining any vector in F, be $m(\mathbf{p}, F)$.

(A3) $$m(\mathbf{p}, F) = \min_{\mathbf{x}} \mathbf{p}\,\mathbf{x} \mid \mathbf{x} \in F.$$

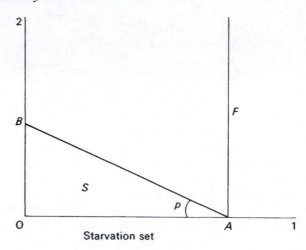

Fɪɢ. Aɪ Starvation set

The starvation set can be alternatively characterized for this case as:

(A4) $S = \{\mathbf{x}\,|\,\mathbf{x} \in X\,\&\,\mathbf{px} < m(\mathbf{p}, F)\}$.

Finally, it may be noted that it is possible to specify F taking into account taste constraints (see Chapter 2). In applying these concepts to the analysis of famines as opposed to regular poverty the taste constraints may, however, play a rather limited role. It is also possible to include essential non-food requirements in the specification of F.

A.2 VARIABLE PRICE EXCHANGES

If the person is not a price-taker, then the simple model outlined above will not work, in particular equations (A1), (A3), and (A4). In general, we can characterize the exchange possibilities in terms of a 'net cost function' $f(\mathbf{y}, \mathbf{z})$, representing the net cost of buying $\mathbf{y}$ and selling $\mathbf{z}$:

(A5) $f(\mathbf{y}, \mathbf{z})$ is a real-valued function, with $f(\mathbf{O}, \mathbf{O}) = \mathrm{O}$.

The E-mapping can now be redefined as:

(A6) $E(\mathbf{x}) = \{(\mathbf{x} - \mathbf{z} + \mathbf{y})\,|\,\mathbf{y}, \mathbf{z} \in X\,\&\,\mathbf{z} \leqslant \mathbf{x}\,\&\,f(\mathbf{y}, \mathbf{z}) \leqslant \mathrm{O}\}$.

The interpretation of $\mathbf{z}$ is, of course, that of the vector of sales by this person, while $\mathbf{y}$ stands for his purchases. Obviously, $\mathbf{x} \in E(\mathbf{x})$.

The starvation set S is still given by (A2), but now coupled with (A5) and (A6).

A.3 DIRECT PRODUCTION AND TRADE

The person can use his ownership vector not only for trade, or for his own consumption, but also for production. The production possibilities open to him can be characterized by another mapping $Q(.)$ from X to Y, representing, for any vector of inputs $\mathbf{s}$, the set $Q(\mathbf{s})$ of output vectors, any of which he can produce.

(A7) $\qquad\qquad Q(.)$ mapping from X to Y

with $Q(\mathbf{O}) = \{\mathbf{O}\}$, unit set consisting of the null vector.

Consider, now, the person owning $\mathbf{x}$, buying $\mathbf{r}$ to be used as inputs, buying $\mathbf{y}$ to be used for consumption, selling $\mathbf{z}$ to meet the cost of purchases, and producing $\mathbf{q}$ by using a part $\mathbf{s}$ of $\mathbf{x}$ *plus* purchased inputs $\mathbf{r}$. The exchange entitlement mapping is now given by:

(A8) $\quad E(\mathbf{x}) = \{(\mathbf{x}-\mathbf{s}+\mathbf{q}-\mathbf{z}+\mathbf{y}) | \mathbf{r}, \mathbf{s}, \mathbf{y}, \mathbf{z} \in X \,\&\, (\mathbf{s}+\mathbf{z})$
$\qquad\qquad \leqslant (\mathbf{x}+\mathbf{q}) \,\&\, \mathbf{q} \in Q(\mathbf{s}+\mathbf{r}) \,\&\, f(\mathbf{r}+\mathbf{y}, \mathbf{z}) \leqslant \mathbf{O}\}.$

The functions $f(.)$ and $Q(.)$ can be defined to take note of taxes, subsidies, social security benefits, etc.

The starvation set once again is given by (A2), combined with this.

A.4 SPECIAL CASES

We can now consider some special stipulations, taking (A2), (A5), (A7), and (A8) as the general structure.

Stipulation   (i): $\mathbf{r} = \mathbf{O}$.

Stipulation   (ii): $Q(\mathbf{s}) = \{\mathbf{s}\}$, unit set, keeping $\mathbf{s}$ unaffected.

Stipulation   (iii): $f(\mathbf{y}, \mathbf{z}) = \mathbf{p}(\mathbf{y}-\mathbf{z})$, where $\mathbf{p}$ is a non-negative n-vector.

If we stipulate (i), (ii), and (iii), we are back to the case covered in Section A.1, with exchange entitlement mapping characterized by (A1) and the starvation set by (A4). If only (i) and (ii) are stipulated but not (iii), then we have the case without direct production, but also without fixed prices for exchange, essentially the same[1] as the one discussed in Section A.2. If only stipulation (i) is imposed, direct production is permitted with owned resources only, without the person being able to set himself up at all as an 'entrepreneur', purchasing inputs for productive use. Combined with (iii) this provides an

---

[1] The only difference is a purely formal one, viz., that production being 'undertaken' with $\mathbf{s}$ yielding just $\mathbf{s}$ is not really a 'production' at all, though $Q(\mathbf{s}) = \{\mathbf{s}\}$ makes it look like that, formally.

analogue to the usual simple characterization of production and competitive trade, as in figure A2, with OAB standing for $E(\mathbf{x})$, given the production frontier CD and the inter-good exchange rate given by angle ABO.

A.5 ECONOMIC STATUS AND MODES OF PRODUCTION

The landless labourer, having nothing to sell other than his 'labour power' and not in a position to undertake production on his own, is covered by stipulations (i) and (ii), i.e. the case discussed in Section A.2. If the wage rate is fixed and so are the commodity prices, then this reduces to the simpler case covered in Section A.1, with stipulation (iii) being imposed as well.

The small peasant farmer, undertaking production with his own resources, including his labour power, land, etc., corresponds to the case with stipulation (i). Since typically small peasants, even in the poor developing countries, buy some inputs from outside, and sometimes even labour power (especially at the time of harvesting), it is perhaps best to think of stipulation (i) as being a bit of an exaggeration, with the true situation being captured accurately only in some model within the general framework of Section A.3.

The share-cropper also falls in this category, since he undertakes production, gets some part of the return (and $Q(.)$ must now be seen as his return function and not the function of total production), and buys some inputs (though typically not all). If the owner provides all the resources other than the share-cropper's labour power, then the case is one in which stipulation (i) does hold, interpreting $Q(.)$ as a function of his own labour.

The large farmer will clearly violate all the stipulations in question. But if he is an absentee landlord, then there will be a new stipulation that **s** will not contain any of one's own labour. If the absentee landlord rents out his land at a fixed rent then it will again be a case as in Section A.1 or A.2, without production being directly involved in the landlord's exchange entitlement. If he leases it out to a share-cropper, then whether the production circumstances are directly involved or not will depend on whether he plays an active part in the production decisions. If he does, then the choices introduced by $Q(.)$ are open to him; if not, he is just selling the services of his land for a reward, which, though variable, is not within his control once contracted out.

Similar contrasts can be drawn outside agriculture as well, e.g. the industrial proletariat living on selling his labour power, the capitalist industrialist producing mainly with purchased inputs, and so on.

When a labourer fails to find employment, the entitlement question depends on what arrangements for social security there happens to be.

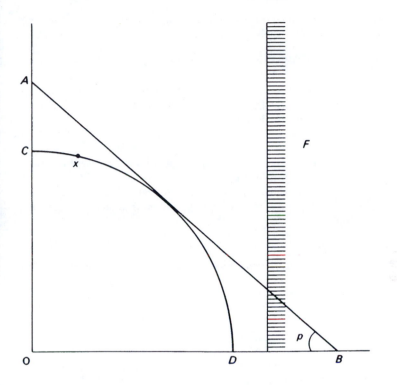

Fɪɢ. A2 Entitlement set with Own Production and Competitive Trade

If there are guaranteed unemployment benefits, then the entitlements arising therefrom can be characterized as a special case of entitlement related to labour power as such. This will require a dual set of prices for labour power, viz. a wage rate *w* if the person finds employment and a social insurance benefit *b* if he does not, with *w* > *b*. The entitlement is characterized not in terms of what he *expects*, but in terms of whether or not he can actually find employment. The focus is not on a person's subjective assessment, but on the real possibilities. This means that even in a given market situation there may be big differences between the positions of different workers in it, depending on whether the person's entitlement gets determined by his wage rate (or wage rates) or by social security benefits. In the absence of a social security system, the contrast is even sharper, since the entitlement of his labour power will be zero if he cannot obtain employment.[2]

A.6 OWN-PRODUCTION ENTITLEMENT

In Sections A.1 and A.2 a person's exchange entitlement was considered in terms of trade only. Later, production was incorporated into the general structure of exchange entitlement, treating production as a form of exchange (with 'nature'). But in some contexts, it is useful to distinguish between the entitlements arising purely from trade and those arising purely from production without any trade. The 'pure trade entitlement relation' $T(.)$ can be defined in exactly the same way as the exchange entitlement relation was defined in the absence of production possibilities—the only difference being that now production possibilities can exist without being taken into account in the T-mapping.

(A9) $T(\mathbf{x}) = \{(\mathbf{x} - \mathbf{z} + \mathbf{y}) | \mathbf{y}, \mathbf{z} \in X \ \& \ \mathbf{z} \leqslant \mathbf{x} \ \& \ f(\mathbf{y}, \mathbf{z}) \leqslant \mathrm{O}\}.$

The other pure case is production without any trade, and this leads to the 'own-production entitlement relation' $P(.)$, as defined below. In Chapter 5 $P(.)$ was also called the 'direct entitlement relation'.

(A10) $P(\mathbf{x}) = \{(\mathbf{x} - \mathbf{s} + \mathbf{q}) | \mathbf{s} \in X \ \& \ \mathbf{s} \leqslant \mathbf{x} \ \& \ \mathbf{q} \in Q(\mathbf{s})\}$

It is easily checked that $T(\mathbf{x}), P(\mathbf{x}) \subseteq E(\mathbf{x})$, but $E(\mathbf{x})$ is *not* in general $\subseteq T(\mathbf{x}) \cup P(\mathbf{x})$. Note also that $\mathbf{x}$ belongs to both $T(\mathbf{x})$ and $P(\mathbf{x})$.

The own-production entitlement relation gives an idea of what the person can secure independently of the working of the rest of the economy. If $P(\mathbf{x}) \cap F$ is non-empty, then the person can see to it that he does not starve, no matter how the rest of the economy operates. This consideration is of some importance when the trade relations are subject to sharp fluctuations owing to forces operating on the economy as a whole, as is frequently the case in times of famine. The case of $P(\mathbf{x}) \cap F \neq \varnothing$ will be called 'trade-independent security'.

In the literature of 'general equilibrium', it is typically assumed that every one has trade-independent security. As Tjalling Koopmans (1957) puts it, 'they assume that each consumer can, if necessary, survive on the basis of the resources he holds and the direct use of his own labor, without engaging in exchange, and still have something to spare of some type of labor which is sure to meet with a positive price in

---

[2] This is one reason why the concept of 'exchange entitlement' cannot be reduced to a derivative of '*terms* of trade', since the possibility of trade is itself a part of the picture captured by exchange entitlement, including non-trade (e.g. unemployment). Another reason is, of course, the fact that exchange entitlements include production possibilities as well.

any equilibrium' (p. 59).[3] But this is a very exacting assumption, and is violated by most of humanity in modern societies. While a peasant with his own land and other resources needed to grow food may indeed have trade-independent security,.an industrial worker with only his labour power to sell clearly does not. Nor would even the industrial capitalist, unless he happens to keep a large stock of food, since the strength of his position in terms of command over food arises from exchange and not from direct holding or of own-production entitlement.

Even within the rural economy, landless agricultural labourers have little chance of survival except through selling their labour power, and the position contrasts sharply with that of peasants. Indeed, the growth of a labouring class with nothing but labour power to sell (i.e., the emergence of labour power as a 'commodity' in the Marxian sense) has led to a very widespread absence of trade-independent security, and— as discussed in Chapter 5—the problem of vulnerability to famine situation has much to do with this development. The phase of economic development *after* the emergence of a large class of wage labourers but *before* the development of social security arrangements is potentially a deeply vulnerable one.[4]

Finally, even for landless rural population, the exchange entitlement can vary a great deal depending precisely on tenancy arrangements. Security of tenure gives an entitlement of a kind that, while formally involving trade, can be seen as something very like own-production entitlement. Even a share-cropper with security of tenure is, in this respect, in a much less vulnerable position than an agricultural labourer, who can be fired quite easily. Another advantage that the share-cropper has over agricultural labourer relates to the fact that his returns typically take the form of a part of the actual output. If the output happens to be foodgrains, this makes him a good deal less vulnerable to the vagaries of the market than the agricultural labourer employed at a monetary wage. This lower vulnerability can, of course, co-exist with vicious 'exploitation' of the share-cropper, viewed from a different perspective.

---

[3] See also Arrow and Hahn (1971), pp. 116–22.
[4] Some problems of this "pure exchange system transition"—PEST for short—are discussed in Sen (1980d).

Appendix B

Illustrative Models of Exchange Entitlement

B.1 INTRODUCTORY REMARKS

The determination of exchange entitlements in any real economy is a complex process, since a variety of influences—economic, social, *and* political—operate on the parameters in $f(.)$, $Q(.)$, etc., for each group. The process, as discussed in the text, will also vary substantially according to the precise institutional structure of the economy. While there is clearly little point in trying to develop a general theory of exchange entitlement determination (Appendix A was, of course, concerned exclusively with *characterization* rather than *determination* of exchange entitlements), there is perhaps some merit in illustrating the nature of the problem by considering some simple models. Two such models are presented in this Note, one based on Malthus's analysis in *An Investigation of the Cause of the Present High Price of Provisions* (1800), and the other trying to capture an important aspect of the causation of the Bengal famine in 1943, analysed in Chapter 6.

B.2 MALTHUS ON THE POOR LAWS AND THE PRICE OF CORN

There is little doubt that Malthus's analysis of food shortage in 1800 was a supplement to his theory of population presented two years earlier:

> To what then can we attribute the present inability in the country to support its inhabitants, but to the increase of population? I own that I cannot but consider the late severe pressures of distress on every deficiency in our crops, as a very strong exemplification of a principle which I endeavoured to explain in an essay published about two years ago, entitled, *An Essay on the Principle of Population, as it affects the future Improvement of Society*. It was considered by many who read it, merely as a specious argument, inapplicable to the present state of society; because it contradicted some preconceived opinions on these subjects. Two years' reflection have, however, served strongly to convince me of the truth of the principle there advanced, and of its being the real cause of the continued depression and poverty of the lower classes of society, of the total inadequacy of all the present establishments in their favour to relieve them, and of the periodical returns of such seasons of distress as we have of late experienced.[1]

But over and above claiming confirmation for his theory of food shortage arising from population expansion, Malthus also presented a theory linking food shortage to the behaviour of prices and

---

[1] Malthus (1880), p. 25.

distribution, and that theory was not essentially dependent on the *genesis* of the food shortage. It is that theory with which I am concerned in this Note, and not with Malthus's theory of population.

Malthus's analysis of adjustments of food prices had two notable features. First, prices had to rise to eliminate a sufficient number of demanders from the market to make the current supply last. The price rise was caused not by speculative activities but simply by the role of prices to adjust demand to supply.

It seems now to be universally agreed, that the stock of old corn remaining on hand at the beginning of the harvest this year was unusually small, notwithstanding that the harvest came on nearly a month sooner than could have been expected in the beginning of June. This is a clear, decided, and unanswerable proof that there had been no speculations in corn that were prejudicial to the country. All that the larger farmers and cornfactors had done, was to raise the corn to that price which excluded a sufficient number from their usual consumption, to enable the supply to last throughout the year.[2]

The second feature was the role attributed to the operation of the system of parish allowances in making it difficult to eliminate the demand for food by the poor, thereby leading to a much larger increase in prices.

This price, however, has been most essentially and powerfully affected by the ability that has been given to the labouring poor, by means of parish allowances, of continuing to purchase wheat notwithstanding its extraordinary rise.[3]

Malthus did not, of course, condemn the parish allowances for this reason, but regarded it as absurd that the poor should complain of the price rise.

I do not, however, by any means, intend to infer, from what I have said, that the parish allowances have been prejudicial to the state; or that, as far as the system has been hitherto pursued, or is likely to be pursued, in this country, that it is not one of the best modes of relief that the circumstances of the case will admit. The system of the poor laws, in general, I certainly do most heartily condemn, as I have expressed in another place, but I am inclined to think that their operation in the present scarcity has been advantageous to the country. The principal benefit which they have produced, is exactly that which is most bitterly complained of—the high price of all the necessaries of life. The poor cry out

---

[2] Malthus (1880), p. 16. It is worth remarking that Malthus's arguments in favour of the stabilizing role of speculation, on grounds that if the speculator 'be wrong in his speculation, he loses perhaps very considerably himself' (p. 15), is in line with the modern defence of speculation as a stabilizing activity. Indeed, Malthus anticipates by a good many years John Stuart Mill's similar argument, to which the ancestry of the defence of the stabilizing role of speculation is usually traced. (See Hart, 1977, for an illuminating analysis of the limitation of the argument.)

[3] Malthus (1880), p. 16.

loudly at this price; but, in so doing, they are very little aware of what they are about; for it has undoubtedly been owing to this price that a much greater number of them has not been starved.[4]

Indeed, in the system of parish allowances, Malthus saw a mechanism that would magnify the price rise owing to the food shortage in an almost unending price explosion.

The poor complained to the justices that their wages would not enable them to supply their families in the single article of bread. The justices very humanely, and I am far from saying improperly, listened to their complaints, inquired what was the smallest sum on which they could support their families, at the then price of wheat, and gave an order of relief on the parish accordingly. The poor were now enabled for a short time, to purchase nearly their usual quantity of flour; but the stock in the country was not sufficient, even with the prospect of importation, to allow of the usual distribution to all its members. The crop was consuming too fast. Every market day the demand exceeded the supply; and those whose business it was to judge on these subjects, felt convinced, that in a month or two the scarcity would be greater than it was at that time. Those who were able, therefore, kept back their corn. . . . The corn, therefore, naturally rose. The poor were again distressed. Fresh complaints were made to the justices, and a further relief granted; but, like the water from the mouth of Tantalus, the corn still slipped from the grasp of the poor; and rose again so as to disable them from purchasing a sufficiency to keep their families in health. The alarm now became still greater, and more general. . . . With further relief and additional command of money in the lower classes, and the consequent increased consumption, the number of purchasers at the then price would naturally exceed the supply. The corn would in consequence continue rising.[5]

Malthus was most critical of the proposal to insulate the poor against price rises by making the wages paid to the poor proportional to food prices. He saw in this the possibility of dragging the middle classes down to starvation also.

It has often been proposed, and more than once I believe, in the House of Commons, to proportion the price of labour exactly to the price of provisions. This, though it would be always a bad plan, might pass tolerably in years of moderate plenty, or in a country that was in the habit of considerable exportation of grain. But let us see what would be its operation in a real scarcity. We suppose, for the sake of the argument, that by law every kind of labour is to be paid accurately in proportion to the price of corn, and that the rich are to be assessed to the utmost to support those in the same manner who are thrown out of employment, and fall upon the parish. We allow the scarcity to be an irremediable deficiency of one-fourth of all the provisions of the country. . . . The middle classes of society would very soon be blended with the poor; and the largest fortunes could not long stand against the accumulated

[4] Malthus (1800), pp. 18–19.
[5] Malthus (1800), pp. 11–13.

pressure of the extraordinary price of provisions, on the one hand, and the still more extraordinary assessments for allowances to those who had no other means of support, on the other. The corn-factors and farmers would undoubtedly be the last that suffered, but, at the expiration of the three quarters of a year, what they received with one hand, they must give away with the other; and a most complete levelling of all property, would take place. All would have the same quantity of money. All the provisions of the country would be consumed; and all the people would starve together.[6]

Malthus hastened to reassure his readers, most of whom had—I take it—little to gain from 'a most complete levelling of all property' and from the food shortage being shared by all starving 'together', that 'there is no kind of fear, that any such tragic event should ever happen in any country' (p. 18).

Malthus's analysis can be captured in terms of a simple model, dealing both with the influence of poor laws on prices, and consequently on the exchange entitlement of the different classes, and with the 'tragic' possibility so feared by Malthus. Let the money incomes of the rich and poor be y_1 and y_2 per head respectively, and their respective numbers be n_1 and n_2. The income of the poor consists of their money earning w and receipt of transfer t from the rich arranged by the Poor Laws, while the income of the rich consists of their money earning u *minus* what they have to pay for the Poor Law transfers. The transfers are aimed at giving the poor the ability to buy a decent ration r of food grains at the prevailing price p, if that is possible. The 'tragic event' considered by Malthus refers to the hypothetical possibility that there are no limits to transfers as long as the rich are richer than the poor.

Considering the exchange entitlement of the rich and the poor only for the special case of command over corn, they are given respectively by e_1 and e_2:

(B1) $\qquad\qquad e_i = y_i/p,$ $\qquad\qquad$ with $i = 1, 2$

(B2) $\qquad\qquad y_1 = u - (tn_2/n_1),$ $\qquad$ subject to $y_1 \geqslant y_2$.

(B3) $\qquad\qquad y_2 = w + t.$

If the proposed Poor Law transfer t is inadequate to provide the poor with adequate exchange entitlement for them to enjoy the decent ration r, then the transfer t is to be revised upwards, as long as the income of the rich y_1 remains higher than y_2. So there are two alternative conditions of equilibrium, viz.:

(B4) $\qquad$ either $\qquad\qquad e_2 = r$

$\qquad\qquad$ or $\qquad\qquad\quad y_1 = y_2$.

[6] Malthus (1800), pp. 17–18.

As long as $e_2 < r$, and $y_2 < y_1$, the value of the transfer t is to be raised upwards.

Finally, the model of price determination that Malthus considers in this case is simply one of the price being high enough to meet the money demand for a given supply of corn. Assuming that the poor spend all their income on corn, while the rich spend a proportion $c \leqslant 1$ of their income on corn, the total money demand is given by:

(B5) $$D = cy_1 n_1 + y_2 n_2.$$

The price of corn for the given supply q is, then,

(B6) $$p = D/q.$$

The exchange entitlement of the poor can be shown, by combining (B1), (B5), and (B6), to equal the following:

(B7) $$e_2 = (y_2 q)/(cy_1 n_1 + y_2 n_2).$$

If e_2 is large enough to meet the ration requirement r, then an equilibrium is well established at that point without the rich being levelled down to the level of the poor. This is one case that Malthus considers, and he comments on the effect of Poor Law transfers on raising the price of corn. It is easily checked that the price of corn is indeed positively related to the transfer value t, given $c < 1$:

(B8) $$p = \{ cun_1 + wn_2 + tn_2(1-c) \}/q$$

It is the recognition of this relationship that prompts Malthus to express his ire that the poor, in crying out 'loudly at this high price', are 'very little aware of what they are about; for it has undoubtedly been owing to this price that a much greater number of them has not been starved'. Malthus also spells out the process of equilibriation in terms of a sequence of steps with the value of transfer t having to be raised to meet r, and then this rise in t causing the price of corn to rise, leading to the need for a fresh upward revision of the transfer value t. While the dynamic model is under-specified, it is easy to complete it, in more than one way.

The other case that Malthus considered is the 'tragic event' in which the equilibriation takes place with $y_1 = y_2$: 'all would have the same quantity of money'. The stage is set for this by combining the plan of making the income of the poor proportional to 'the price of provisions' for them to be able to meet food requirements in full, while there is 'an irremediable deficiency of one-fourth of all the provisions of the country'. Forgetting the arbitrary figure of one-fourth, the point is that the food supply q is being taken to be less than what will be needed to entitle everyone to the norm of the food ration of r. This amounts to the following:

(B9)
$$q < (n_1 + n_2)r.$$

Considering the inequality (B9) with the equation (B7), it is easily obtained:

(B10)
$$e_2 < \{y_2(n_1 + n_2)r\}/(cy_1 n_1 + y_2 n_2).$$

Assuming that, as long as the rich have an income at least as large as that of the poor, i.e. $y_1 \geqslant y_2$, the expenditure on food by the rich must also be at least as large as that of the poor, i.e. $cy_1 \geqslant y_2$, it follows from (B10) that $e_2 < r$. Thus, assuming that e goes to 1 as y_1 approaches y_2, the only possible equilibrium emerges when $c = 1$ at $y_1 = y_2$, that 'tragic event' when 'all the people would starve together', rather than the rich starving less than the poor.

In this formulation of Malthus's model the effect of price rise on the income of grain sellers has not been explicitly brought in. This is, of course, easy enough to do—most simply by making u and w rise with price p—and it will not affect either of the two propositions under discussion. It will introduce a 'money-expenditure multiplier effect' of a rise in t, reinforcing its direct price-raising effect. And it will leave the reasoning about the only possible equilibrium being one of $e_2 = r$, or of $y_1 = y_2$, quite unaffected.

B.3 A MODEL OF INTER-CLASS DISTRIBUTION AND EXCHANGE ENTITLEMENT

Malthus's model is one of short-run price determination with supply of foodgrains being given. This feature of it is not inappropriate for analysing a famine situation developing when the foodgrains output has already been fixed by the preceding crop for quite a few months. In providing a simple model of interdependence to capture one aspect of the Bengal famine of 1943, I shall retain this feature. But the classification of the population has to be different from that of Malthus to bring in different classes with different economic roles. And the 'circularity' of exchange has to be studied.

In what follows, a five-class economy will be considered, denoted by the indices 1, . . ., 5 respectively as:

1 agricultural capitalists and landlords;
2 peasants;
3 urban and semi-urban workers (urban industrial labour force, military construction workers, urban casual labourers, etc.);
4 rural workers (agricultural labourers);

5 rural household producers (rural service providers, craftsmen, etc.).[7]

This is, of course, quite a drastic simplification (contrast the class structure considered in Chapter 6), but it is adequate for the purpose of bringing out some of the more important contrasting movements of exchange entitlement.

The number of people in each group is denoted by n_i, with $i = 1, \ldots,$ 5, respectively. The foodgrains output in peasant farms is given by q_2 per peasant, and in non-peasant farms by q_1 per person of the landed class. The money wage rates of protected and unprotected workers are given respectively by w_3 and w_4. The money income of the rural household producers is denoted by v per person; the physical units of output is taken to be one unit per person (thus the price of the product per unit is also v).

The price of foodgrains is determined by the money demand D^f for the marketed supply of foodgrains and that supply is determined by proportions m_1 and m_2 marketed out of the non-peasant and peasant farming outputs respectively.

(B11)
$$p = D^f/(n_1 m_1 q_1 + n_2 m_2 q_2).$$

The money demand for the marketed supply of foodgrains comes from urban and semi-urban workers, rural workers and rural household producers, with the respective money demands being represented by D^f_i, with $i = 3, 4, 5$.

(B12)
$$D^f = \sum_{i=3}^{5} D^f_i.$$

The price of household products of group 5 are determined also by the money demand for it, D^v, and its supply, which is given by n_5, since the physical output is one per person. D^v is made up of demands from the various groups.

(B13)
$$v = D^v/n_5.$$

(B14)
$$D^v = \sum_{i=1}^{5} D^v_i.$$

Now the demand relations. Agricultural capitalists and landlords, and peasants, respectively spend proportions h_1 and h_2 of their money

---

[7] In this model, the industrial capitalists have not been explicitly considered. They are, of course, implicitly present in the determination of employment and wage rates to the urban and semi-urban labour force, and in the political economy underlying rationing of foodgrains. But as far as their own demands are concerned it is assumed that industrial capitalists' demand for foodgrains and rural household products is a negligible part of the total demand in the two respective markets.

incomes on rural household products. Urban and semi-urban workers are taken here to be protected by a wage policy—or rationing at controlled prices with government subsidizing real income by food subsidy (see Chapter 6)—in such a way that each of them can obtain r amount of foodgrains. They do not demand any rural household services or goods. Rural workers spend a proportions c_4 and h_4 on foodgrains and rural household products, respectively, and $c_4 + h_4 = 1$. Rural household producers spend proportions c_5 and h_5 on foodgrains and rural household products, respectively, and $c_5 + h_5 = 1$. (It is assumed that rural household producers also demand products of their sector in the market; this is to take note of the fact that there are many types of such products in reality.)

(B15) $$D_i^v = q_i n_i m_i p h_i, \qquad \text{with } i = 1, 2.$$

(B16) $$D_3^f = n_3 r p.$$

(B17) $$D_4^f = n_4 w_4 c_4.$$

(B18) $$D_4^v = n_4 w_4 h_4.$$

(B19) $$D_5^f = n_5 v c_5.$$

(B20) $$D_5^v = n_5 v h_5.$$

(B21) $$D_1^f = D_2^f = D_3^v = 0.$$

Piecing together (B13), (B14), (B15), (B18), (B20), and (B21), the price v of rural household products is seen to be given by the following:

(B22) $$v = [p(n_1 m_1 q_1 h_1 + n_2 m_2 q_2 h_2) + n_4 w_4 h_4]/n_5(1 - h_5)$$

Using (B11), (B12), (B16), (B17), (B19), (B21), and (B22), and noting that $c_i + h_i = 1$ for $i = 4, 5$, it can be shown that the price of foodgrains is given by the following:

(B23) $$p = n_4 w_4 /[n_1 m_1 q_1 (1 - h_1) + n_2 m_2 q_2 (1 - h_2) - n_3 r].$$

In this short-run model the following parameters are taken as fixed: the outputs q_i, the shares marketed m_i, the numbers involved n_i, and the consumption ratios h_i and c_i. The money wage w_4 of the rural workers is also taken as fixed, the payments being seasonal and having been made. The difference that is being considered arises from an expansion of the urban and semi-urban activities owing to military expenditure, defence-related industries, and construction, and related economic activities. The simplest characterization of that is in terms of a raising of r, the real ration guaranteed in the urban sector. (Much of the change in 1943 Bengal, which this model tries to imitate in general terms, took the form of drawing labour from ill-paid occupations or the pool of unemployment to a rather buoyant wage sector. The industrial labour force and the general residents of Calcutta were also guaranteed fairly substantial food rations through the state policy of procurement and subsidization of the retail price; see Chapter 6.)

It is easily checked, from (B22) and (B23), that

(B24) $$\frac{dp}{dr} > 0, \text{ and } \frac{dv}{dr} > 0.$$

This is straightforward enough, but the more interesting question concerns the effect of a higher r on the exchange entitlement of each class of people considered. While exchange entitlement $E(\mathbf{x})$ specifies a *set* of commodity vectors, any of which can be commanded by the person in question by using his ownership vector $\mathbf{x}$ (see Appendix A), I shall in this particular exercise confine the analysis to the total amount of foodgrains e_i that could be commanded by a typical member of each class i.

The entitlement per head e_3 of the protected urban labour force is, of course, given by r, and that of the peasants e_2 is simply given by the food produced per head in peasant farms. The entitlement e_4 of rural workers is given by the amount of food that the wage rate w_4 will buy, and the corresponding figure for rural household producers e_5 equals the food that v will buy. And the entitlement of agricultural capitalists and landed classes is determined by the output q_1 *minus* the amount of food that has to be sold to meet the wage bill per person in class 1, i.e. the wages of (n_4/n_1) rural workers.

(B25.1) $e_1 = q_1 - (n_4 w_4/n_1 p) = q_1 - e_4(n_4/n_1).$

(B25.2) $e_2 = q_2.$

(B25.3) $e_3 = r.$

(B25.4) $e_4 = (w_4/p)\,[n_4 h_4(w_4/p)]$

(B25.5) $e_5 = (v/p) = [n_1 m_1 q_1 h_1 + n_2 m_2 q_2 h_2 + n_4 h_4(w_4/p)]/n_5(1 - h_5).$

It follows from (B24) and (B25) that the effect of a higher value of r is to:

(1) *increase* the exchange entitlement e_1 of *agricultural capitalists*, etc.:
(2) keep *unaffected* the exchange entitlement e_2 of *peasants*;
(3) *increase* the exchange entitlement e_3 of the *protected urban labour force*;
(4) *reduce* the exchange entitlement e_4 of the *rural labour force*;
(5) *reduce* the exchange entitlement e_5 of the *rural household producers*.

In so far as this simple model catches an aspect of the Bengal famine of 1943, this is more obviously so for Phase I than for Phase II of the famine (see Chapter 6). Phase II of the famine was much dominated by speculative activities which have not been brought in at all in the model presented above.

A speculative reduction of the proportion of foodgrains marketed, i.e. lower values of m_1 and m_2, will have the consequence of *reinforcing* the effects noted above (see B25.1–B25.5). Such a reduction, compared with normal years, was observed in Phase I as well (see Chapter 6). But in Phase II the speculative activities of professional traders as well as the market movements reflecting a terrible panic would require the analysis presented above to be supplemented in a more radical way.

I end this Appendix with five remarks. First, in so far as the 1943 output (including the December 1942 harvest) was somewhat—though not severely—lower than average, the position of the peasants too would have been worse in 1943 compared with that in a typical year. The analysis presented above assumes everything else the same, and while it does capture the fact that the famine affected most the agricultural labour force and the providers of rural services and crafts, it does not bring out that other groups also suffered a certain amount. In the case of the peasants, there is also the further fact, which has been noted, that some peasants sold off their grains supply too early, egged on by traders dangling before them higher prices than usual, and then had to buy back grains later for their own consumption at a much higher price. This type of dynamic process must be an important feature of a more complete model, especially of Phase II.

Second, the distress of the rural labour force has been captured in the model presented here only in terms of a declining command over food given by the wages,[8] but another feature was a reduction of employment, on which there are few firm data but much informal evidence. This, of course, would have led to a dramatic decline of exchange entitlement for those thrown out of employment.

Third, while the urban labour force is characterized here as being fully cushioned against food price rise, this was not so for the whole period or for all the urban labour force. Again, the model has exaggerated a true feature into an over-simplified generalization. Perhaps it is also worth remarking that the protection enjoyed by the urban labour force in the Bengal famine of 1943 was also rather unusual, and in considering the relevance of the model presented here for other famines, the economic operations of the different classes will have to be differently delineated.

Fourth, the model presented here is one of single-period interdependence. It is possible to investigate the same interdependences in a multi-period context; and even to consider a cumulative buildup of these effects.

[8] In the model the money wages w_4 of agricultural workers have been taken to be given, but in reality w_4 typically went up with food prices but much less than proportionately (see Chapter 6).

Finally, in the model presented above the decline of the rural household producers is traceable ultimately to the distress of others, viz. the rural labourers. This interdependence could be heightened by incorporating the fact that destitution of rural labourers would also lead to their incomes being largely spent all on foodgrains, involving a dramatically lower h_4—the *proportion* of income spent on non-food household products—and thus even greater distress for rural household producers. The characterization of this interdependence presented in the model is, of course, an over-simplification; but—as discussed in Chapters 5–10—the general phenomenon of 'derived destitution' is one of the features of famines that requires a good deal more attention than it tends to get. This feature is among the consequences of interdependence analysed in this section.

Appendix C

Measurement of Poverty

C.1. POVERTY GAPS AND HEAD COUNTS

S is the set of people in a community of n people. Person i's income is y_i, and those whose incomes are no higher than π (the poverty line) are poor, making up the set $T \subseteq S$. The poor, q in number, are ranked according to income, and person i in T has the rank $r(i)$, being $r(i)$th richest among the poor. Equi-incomed persons are ranked in any arbitrary order, but once the ranking has been done, $r(i)$ is, in fact, a strict ordering.

The poverty gap of person i in T is g_i, given by:

(C1) $$g_i = \pi - y_i.$$

The total poverty gap of the poor is denoted g, and is given by:

(C2) $$g = \sum_{i \in T} g_i.$$

The two standard measures of poverty are the head-count ratio H and the income-gap ratio I, given respectively by:

(C3) $$H = q/n$$
(C4) $$I = g/q\pi.$$

Denote the mean income of the poor as y^* and their mean poverty gap as g^*:

(C5) $$y^* = \sum_{i \in T} y_i/q$$
(C6) $$g^* = \pi - y^* = g/q.$$

The income-gap ratio can also be expressed as:

(C4*) $$I = g^*/\pi.$$

Consider now the following axioms of legitimacy of poverty measures. Take $\mathbf{x}$ and $\mathbf{y}$ as two n-vectors of income with x_i and y_i the incomes of person i in the two cases, respectively, and let the poverty measures be such that $\mathbf{x}$ and $\mathbf{y}$ yield values $P(\mathbf{x})$ and $P(\mathbf{y})$ respectively (given π and S). In all the axioms proposed in this section the set S of people and π the poverty-line income are assumed to be given. $T(\mathbf{x})$ and $T(\mathbf{y})$ are the poor in S respectively for $\mathbf{x}$ and $\mathbf{y}$.

Monotonicity Axiom If for some $j \in T(\mathbf{x}) \cap T(\mathbf{y})$: $x_j > y_j$, and for all $i \in S$ such that $i \neq j$: $x_i = y_i$, then $P(\mathbf{x}) < P(\mathbf{y})$.

Weak Transfer Axiom If for some $j \in [\{T(\mathbf{x}) \cap T(\mathbf{y})\} \cup \{(S - T(\mathbf{x})) \cap (S - T(\mathbf{y}))\}]$ and $k \in T(\mathbf{x}) \cap T(\mathbf{y})$: $[(x_j > y_j \geqslant y_k > x_k)$ & $(x_j - y_j = y_k - x_k)]$, and for all $i \in S$ such that $i \neq j, k$: $x_i = y_i$, then $P(\mathbf{x}) > \mathbf{P}(\mathbf{y})$.

The monotonicity axiom says that, given other things, a reduction in income of someone below the poverty line must increase the poverty measure. The weak transfer axiom says that a pure transfer of income to a poor person below the poverty line from a richer person, without making either cross the poverty line, must reduce the poverty measure.[1]

It is easily checked that the head-count measures H violates both the monotonicity axiom and the weak transfer axiom. H is invariant with respect to both the fall of the income of a poor person, and to transfers of the kind envisaged in the weak transfer axiom.[2] In fact, a *reverse* transfer, i.e. from the poor to someone richer, will either leave H unchanged or make it go down, but will *never* make it go up. The income-gap ratio I satisfies the monotonicity axiom, but violates the weak transfer axiom when j is below the poverty line throughout, i.e. when $j \in T(\mathbf{x})$. It follows immediately that no function of H and I, $\psi(H, I)$, can satisfy the weak transfer axiom. Indeed, both H and I are blind to distribution among the poor.

However, both H and I satisfy one of the possible qualities of a poverty measure that was discussed in Chapter 2, to wit, independence of the income levels of those who are *above* the poverty line. One consequence of this is that no fall in the income of the poor can be *outweighed* by any rise—no matter how large—in the incomes of the rich.

Focus Axiom If $x_i = y_i$ for all $i \in T(\mathbf{x}) \cup T(\mathbf{y})$, then $P(\mathbf{x}) = P(\mathbf{y})$.

The focus axiom is motivated by the view that the poverty measure is a characteristic of the poor, and not of the general poverty of the nation. It does not, however, try to reflect the *relative* burden of poverty, viz. what proportion of income of the rich would be needed to wipe out the poverty gaps of the poor,[3] since that is clearly eased by the rich being

---

[1] In Sen (1976a) the 'transfer axiom' was more demanding in that the poverty measure was required to record a decline even if the transfer made the richer person fall below the poverty line, thus swelling the number of the poor. That version makes poverty measurement, in an important way, independent of the number below the poverty line, which raises other problems (see Section C.3 below).

[2] Contrast: 'Its [the new Poor Law's] only effect was that whereas previously three to four million half paupers had existed, a million total paupers now appeared, and the rest, still half paupers, merely went without relief. The poverty of agricultural districts has increased every year' (Engels, 1892, p. 288).

[3] See Anand (1977) and Beckerman (1979a, 1979b) for the relevance of that perspective for policy discussion.

richer, even when all the poor remain just as poor and miserable.

C.2 AXIOMATIC DERIVATION OF MEASURE P

The approach used in the derivation of measure P, which was informally discussed in Chapter 3, can be justified either by bringing in the notion of personal welfare conceived in ordinal terms (or—redundantly—in more demanding cardinal terms), or by directly axiomatizing on income distributions. In earlier contributions (Sen, 1973b, 1976a), the former, welfare-based, notion was used, but here the simpler and directly income-based format will be employed.

Poverty can be conceived of as a weighted sum of the poverty gaps of the poor:

$$(C7) \qquad P = A(n, q, \pi) \sum_{i \in T} v_i g_i$$

where v_i is the weight on the poverty gap g_i of person i, and $A(n,q,\pi)$ is a normalizing parameter dependent on the total number of people n, the number of poor people q, and the poverty line π. Note that it has *not* been specified that v_i must depend only on the size of person i's poverty gap g_i or income level y_i, so that—despite the superficially additive form—no separability requirement has been imposed by (C7).

In the light of the perspective of relative deprivation (see Chapter 3), it may be reasonable to think of the weight v_i of the poverty gap of i to be dependent on i's relative position *vis-à-vis* others in the same reference group. If the reference group is the group of the poor, this makes $r(i)$, i.e. the rank of the poor person i among the poor, a relevant determinant of v_i. Going one step further, v_i can be made an increasing function of $r(i)$, so that the weight depends on where i stands in the ranking *vis-à-vis* other poor people. The simplest case of such as increasing function is the identity mapping $m = f(m)$.

Ranked Relative Deprivation (Axiom R) Poverty is measured as in (C7) with the weight v_i on person i's poverty gap equalling i's income rank among the poor:

$$(C8) \qquad v_i = r(i).$$

The rule, as discussed in Chapter 3, is in the same spirit as Borda's (1781) use of rank-order weighting.[4]

The other axiom used at this stage is based on the idea that the inadequacy of the head-count ratio and the income-gap measure taken together arises from their inability to be sensitive to the distribution of

---

[4] See Sen (1976b) for the use of a similar axiom in making distribution-sensitive comparisons of real income. On that general problem, see also Graaff (1977), Hammond (1978), Osmani (1978), Sen (1979a), Marris (1980), and Broder and Morris (1980).

income among the poor, and when that distributional problem is eliminated, a combination of H and I should suffice. Thus, in dealing with alternative cases in *each* of which all the poor persons have the same income, H and I should be informationally adequate. One of the simplest ways of combining H and I in a function $\psi(H, I)$ is to take their product, which provides a convenient normalization.

Normalized Absolute Deprivation (Axiom A) If for all $i \in T$: $y_i = y^*$, then:

$$(C9) \qquad\qquad P = HI.$$

THEOREM C1 For large numbers of the poor, the only poverty measure satisfying Axioms R and A is given by:

$$(C10) \qquad\qquad P = H\{I + (1 - I)G\}$$

when G is the Gini coefficient of income distribution among the poor.

Proof. In (C7), putting $g^* = g_i$ for all i, we get:

$$(C11) \qquad\qquad P = \tfrac{1}{2}\{A(n,q,\pi)\, g^*\, q(q+1)\}.$$

This, combined with (C3), (C4*), and (C9), yields:

$$(C12) \qquad\qquad A(n,q,\pi) = 2/(q+1)n\pi.$$

Combining (C7), (C8), and (C12), we obtain:

$$(C13) \qquad P = \frac{2}{(q+1)n\pi} \sum_{r(i)=1}^{q} (\pi - y_i)\, r(i).$$

Noting that the Gini coefficient for any q-membered population with mean income y^* and income ranks $r(i) = 1, \ldots, q$ can be easily written as (see Sen, 1973a, p. 31):

$$(C14) \qquad G = 1 + \frac{1}{q} - \frac{2}{q^2 y^*} \sum_{r(i)=1}^{q} y_i r(i)$$

a little simplification yields:

$$(C15) \qquad P = H[1 - (1 - I)\{1 - Gq/(q+1)\}].$$

For large q, (C15) reduces to (C10), thereby establishing the theorem.[5]

An alternative expression of P can be obtained by eliminating I and

[5] This proof is essentially the same as in Sen (1976a), except for the somewhat remoter axiomatization used there, involving personal welfare levels. In fact, in Sen (1976a), the axioms are first used to translate the welfare-based requirements into corresponding income requirements, and then the proof goes through on the income space, in the same way as above. See also Osmani (1978).

replacing it by its equivalent $1 - (y^*/\pi)$, as seen from $(C4^*)$ and $(C6)$. This procedure, discussed by Anand (1977), yields:

$$(C16) \qquad P = H\{1 - y^*(1 - G)/\pi\}.$$

Note also that the measure P satisfies the monotonicity axiom, the weak transfer axiom, and the focus axiom.

C.3 ALTERNATIVES AND VARIATIONS

In this section some variations of the poverty measure P are considered. Axioms R and A can be varied in certain ways, yielding measures that differ from P in some specific respects. The concept of poverty has enough ambiguity to permit such alternative interpretations (see Chapters 2 and 3). But all these variations share with measure P a sensitivity to distributional considerations among the poor, in addition to the aspects of poverty captured by H and I.

One idea is to modify the income-gap element I in the measure of deprivation by taking the mean poverty gap not as a percentage of the poverty level income π but as a percentage of the mean income of the community, where μ is the mean income of the entire community.

$$(C17) \qquad I^* = g^*/\mu.$$

HI^* clearly equals the ratio of the aggregate poverty gap to total national income or GDP:[6]

$$(C18) \qquad HI^* = g/n\mu.$$

Alternative Normalized Absolute Deprivation (Axiom A^*) If for all $i \in T$: $y_i = y^*$, then:

$$(C19) \qquad P = HI^*.$$

It is easily checked that Axioms A^* and R lead to a modified poverty measure P_1, which has been proposed and extensively explored by Sudhir Anand (1977), and which differs from P by a multiplicative constant reflecting normalization per unit of national mean income rather than the poverty line income:

$$(C20) \qquad P_1 = P\pi/\mu.$$

P_1 has the feature of being sensitive to the income of the non-poor as well. A rise in the income of a non-poor person, given other things, will reduce I^* and obviously will also reduce the modified poverty measure P_1. If a rise in the income of *anyone* can be taken to be a reduction of the poverty of the nation, then P_1 is to be preferred over P, since P is

---

[*] Beckerman (1979a, 1979b) puts this measure to good use as an indicator of the relative burden of poverty, but also warns against reading too much into this ratio.

insensitive to income rises of the rich. It may also be noted that HI^* expresses the percentage of national income that would have to be devoted to transfers if poverty were to be wiped out by redistribution, and in this sense HI^* reflects the *relative* burden of poverty of the nation compared with its aggregate income.

On the other hand, it can be argued that the relative burden of poverty is really a different exercise from the description of poverty in terms of prevailing notions of deprivation. More importantly, P_1 has the characteristic that some increase in the income shortfall of the poor may be compensated by a sufficently high rise in the income of the non-poor. And this can be objected to on the ground that poverty is a characteristic of the poor, and a reduction of the incomes of the poor must increase the measure of poverty, no matter how much the incomes of the non-poor go up at the same time (see Chapter 2). P satisfies this condition, formalized as the focus axiom, but P_1 does not.

The choice of the index must ultimately depend on the purpose for which such a measure is sought. For descriptive excercises on 'the state of the poor' (to quote the title of the famous treatise of F. M. Eden (1797)), P would have an obvious advantage over P_1. But if, on the other hand, the intention is to check the country's *potential* ability to meet the challenge of poverty, P_1 has a clear advantage. The two versions, therefore, are concerned with two rather different things.

Variants of Axiom R may also be considered. Nanak Kakwani (1980a) has provided various alternatives to Axiom R yielding some measures closely related to the measure P. An especially interesting one—we may call it P_2—makes the weight v_i on the short-fall of person i depend not on the number of people among the poor *vis-à-vis* whom i is relatively deprived, but on the aggregate income of these people. P_2 has the merit of making i's extent of deprivation sensitive to the actual incomes enjoyed by those who are richer than him though lying below the poverty line. On the other hand, P_2 takes no note of how the aggregate income of these people is divided among them, and, more importantly, no note even of the number of persons among whom this aggregate income is divided. The sense of relative deprivation is made to depend on the sum-total of income of those who, while poor, are better off then the person in question, and no other information is used regarding the disposition of that sum-total.

In a different contribution, Kakwani (1980b) modifies Axiom R to provide a more general structure. Essentially, Kakwani's axiom makes the weight v_i the kth power of the income rank of person i among the poor.

Axiom R* Poverty is measured as in (C7) with the weights v_i given by:

$$(C21) \qquad\qquad v_i = [r(i)]^k.$$

For the poverty measure, call it P_3, derived from this, the sensitivity of between-poor income distribution will depend on the value of k. The poverty measure P obviously corresponding to $k = 1$, making it, as Kakwani (1980b) puts it, 'equally sensitive to a transfer of income at all positions'. The generalization involved in P_3 permits various alternative assumptions about transfer sensitivity, e.g. giving greater weight to transfers of income at the lower end of the distribution of income.

A different generalization based on a reinterpretation of the poverty index P has been proposed by Blackorby and Donaldson (1980a). They note that the measure P can be seen as the product of the head-count ratio H and the proportionate gap between the poverty-line income π and the Atkinson–Kolm 'equally distributed equivalent income' (e^g) of the incomes of the poor when the evaluation is done with the Gini social evaluation function.[7]

(C22) $$P = H\ (\pi - e^g)/\pi, \quad \text{with } e^g = y^*\ (1 - G).$$

If the social evaluation function is changed, a new poverty measure would emerge correspondingly, with the equally distributed equivalent income defined according to *that* social evaluation function.[8]

(C23) $$P_4 = H(\pi - e)/\pi.$$

Blackorby and Donaldson chose an ethical interpretation of the poverty measures. The value of e reflects that level of income which, if shared by all the poor, would be judged by the social evaluation function to be exactly as good as the actual distribution of income among the poor. But it is easily seen that the format permits a descriptive interpretation as well, viz. e standing for that level of income which, if shared by all the poor, will be regarded as displaying as much over-all poverty as the actual distribution of income among the poor. The issues involved in the choice between descriptive and ethical interpretations of poverty have been discussed in Chapters 2 and 3 and will not be pursued further.[9] The poverty measures can be mathematically interpreted in either way, and the real question is one of relevance

---

[7] For the concept of equally distributed equivalent income, see Kolm (1969) and Atkinson (1970). For the relation of the poverty measure P to the Gini evaluation function, see Sen (1973b, 1976a), and related matters in Sen (1974, 1976b). See also Graaff (1946), Sen (1973a), Pyatt (1976, 1980), Sastry (1977, 1980), Osmani (1978), Dorfman (1979), Kakwani (1980a), Yitzhaki (1979), Fields (1980), Donaldson and Weymark (1980a, 1980b), Radhakrishna and Sarma (1980), and Sastry and Suryanarayana (1980).

[8] Blackorby and Donaldson (1980a) point out the need for some assumptions about the general characteristics of such a social evaluation function, especially its homotheticity, and strict separability of a kind that permits one to rank the distribution of income among the poor independently of the incomes of those who are richer.

[9] See also Sen (1978b).

of the excercise to the motivation that leads to the search for a measure of poverty.

A particular descriptive characteristic of the poverty measure P has been the subject of some detailed investigation. While it is clear that the measure P of poverty must record a rise when there is a transfer of income from a poorer person to one who is richer provided that does not make the richer person cross the poverty line, exactly the opposite *can* happen—depending on the exact values—when such a crossing does take place (see Sen, 1977a, p. 77). It is arguable whether a poverty measure should not show increased poverty *whenever* some income is transferred from a poorer to a richer person, no matter whether this makes the richer person cease to be regarded as poor because of his crossing the poverty line. Thon (1979, 1980) has explored the analytical relations involved in such monotonic transfer sensitivity, and has proposed a variation of P that would ensure that the poverty measure records an increase whenever there is a transfer of income from a person who is poor to one who is richer. He modifies Axiom R to make the weight v_i on the poor i's income gap g_i equal his income rank $R(i)$ among *all* the people in the community, and not merely among the poor (as under Axiom R).

Axiom R^{**}   Poverty is measured as in (C7) with the weights v_i given by:

$$(C24) \qquad\qquad v_i = R(i).$$

Combined with the original structure with slight modifications, Axiom R^{**} precipitates Thon's variant—we may call it P_5—of the poverty measure satisfying this monotonic property.[10]

There remains, of course, the substantial issue as to whether a poverty measure *should* always register an increase whenever there is such a transfer, even when the transfer actually reduces the number of the poor.[11] In so far as the index of poverty is interpreted to represent the condition of the poor—how many and each precisely how poor—a good case can perhaps be made for permitting the possibility that a

10 $$P_5 = \{2/(n+1)n\pi\} \sum_{r(i)=1}^{q} (\pi - y_i)\, R(i).$$

This can be easily compared with the poverty measure P as expressed in (C13).

[11] The 'transfer axiom' considered (but not used in the derivation of P) in Sen (1976a) demanded: 'Given other things, a pure transfer of income from a person below the poverty line to anyone who is richer must increase the poverty measure' (p. 219). In Sen (1977a) this was modified to the less demanding requirement, corresponding to the weak transfer axiom considered here: 'Given other things, a pure transfer of income from a person below the poverty line to anyone richer must strictly increase the poverty measure unless the number below the poverty line is strictly reduced by the transfer' (p. 77) This contrast is the central one between P and P_5.

reduction of the prevalence of the poor might under some circumstances compensate a rise in the extent of penury of those who remain below the poverty line. The old measure P includes this possibility, while Thon's P_5 does not. If, however, the focus is on inequality or living standard and not specifically on the predicament of people in falling below the poverty line, then the unqualified transfer axiom would make a good deal of sense, since the poverty-alleviating role of crossing the poverty line would be then rendered less crucial.[12] Again, the variation proposed has merits that are conditional on the purpose for which the poverty measure is being sought.

Another interesting variant of the poverty measure P has been proposed by Takayama (1979), related to an approach that has been extensively explored by Hamada and Takayama (1978). From the actual income distribution a 'censured' income distribution is obtained by replacing the incomes that exceed the poverty line by incomes exactly equalling the poverty line (π). Takayama (1979) then takes the Gini coefficient G_c of the censured income distribution as the measure of poverty—we may call it P_6. Other measures of inequality are also applied to the censured distribution to derive corresponding measures of poverty in Hamada and Takayama (1978).

The approach has some clear merits. The Gini coefficient of the censured distribution is a much neater—and closer—translation of the Gini measure of inequality into a poverty measure. It doctors the income distribution itself by ignoring the information on the actual incomes of the people who are not poor, but counts them in with poverty line incomes. Takayama (1979) has also provided an interest-

---

[12] The unqualified 'transfer axiom' is, of course, essentially the same as the 'Pigou-Dalton condition' used in the measurement of inequality (see Atkinson, 1970), and of the living standard of a community (see Sen, 1976b, 1979a). The measurement of poverty is, however, quite a different type of exercise for which note must be taken of the 'poverty line', and the unqualified transfer axiom takes no note of this at all. An important result recently established by Kundu and Smith (1981) throws further light on this question. They show that no uniformly continuous poverty measurement function can satisfy simultaneously the unqualified 'transfer axiom' and 'population monotonicity axioms' demanding that an addition to the poor population (respectively, non-poor population), other things given, must increase (respectively, decrease) the poverty value. While Kundu and Smith's 'population monotonicity axioms' are really very demanding in this particular form, the conflict that they pinpoint is a more general one. The tension arises from the fact that the unqualified 'transfer axiom' takes no note whatever of the poverty line, whereas the 'population monotonicity axioms' treat that line as the great divider. Sensitivity to the poverty line is indeed an appropriate characteristic of axioms for poverty measurement, and this can be incorporated in many different ways. The 'week transfer axiom' used here (and in Sen, 1977a) takes note of the poverty line in the way already specified. It is this modified axiom—and not the unqualified 'transfer axiom'—that the measure P satisfies (see Sen, 1977a, p. 77), determining precise trade-offs through axioms R and A.

ing axiomatization of his measure of poverty G_c, and Hamada and Takayama (1978) have suggested derivations for similar poverty measures based on other inequality indexes applied to the censured distribution.

The main drawback of this approach lies in its robust violation of the monotonicity axiom, viz. that a reduction of income of anyone below the poverty line, given everything else, must increase the poverty measures. A person below the poverty line may still be among the relatively richer in the censured distribution of income with an income above the mean and the median of that distribution. A reduction of his income will in an obvious sense reduce the extent of inequality in the censured distribution, but in an equally obvious sense the community must now be having *more*—not less—poverty. So the simplicity of the formulae used by Takayama (1979) and Hamada and Takayama (1978) is achieved at some real cost—to wit, dropping the monotonic relation between the poverty measure and vector-dominance of deprivation of the poor.

While P has certain unique advantages, which its axiomatization brings out, several of the variants are certainly permissible interpretations of the common conception of poverty.[13] There is nothing defeatist or astonishing in the acceptance of this 'pluralism'. Indeed, as argued earlier (Chapters 2 and 3), such pluralism is inherent in the nature of the exercise. The variants are all in the same tradition as measure P, being concerned not merely with H and I, but also with the distribution among the poor.

[13] Osmani (1978) has also analysed several different poverty indicators, and has taken explicit note of multi-commodity issues.

Appendix D
Famine Mortality: A Case Study

In this Appendix[1] the size and pattern of mortality in the great Bengal famine of 1943 are studied. Mortality in the Bengal famine was a hotly debated issue during and just after the famine, and has, in fact, remained so. The pattern of mortality is worth studying also for the light it throws on the nature of the famine. The general features of the famine and its possible causation were studied in Chapter 6.

D.1. HOW MANY PER WEEK: 1,000, 2,000, 26,000, 38,000?

'The Secretary of State for India', wrote *The Statesman*, the Calcutta newspaper, on 16 October 1943,

> seems to be a strangely misinformed man. Unless the cables are unfair to him, he told Parliament on Thursday that he understood that the weekly death-roll (presumably from starvation) in Bengal including Calcutta was about 1000, but that 'it might be higher'. All the publicly available data indicate that it is very much higher; and his great office ought to afford him ample means of discovery.[2]

Sir T. Rutherford, the Governor of Bengal, wrote to the Secretary of State for India on 18 October 1943, two days after *The Statesman* editorial:

> Your statement in the House about the number of deaths, which was presumably based on my communications to the Viceroy, has been severely criticised in some of the papers. My information was based on what information the Secretariat could then give me after allowing for the fact that the death-roll in Calcutta would be higher owing to the kind of people trekking into the city and exposure to inclement weather. . . . The full effects of the shortage are now being felt, and I would put the death-roll now at no less than 2000 a week.[3]

Was this higher figure of 2,000 close to the mark?

The Famine Inquiry Commission (1945a) noted that 'from July to December 1943, 1,304,323 deaths were recorded as against an average of 626,048 in the previous quinquennium', and the difference attributed

---

[1] This Appendix draws heavily on Sen (1980b), written in memory of Daniel Thorner.

[2] 'The Death-Roll', editorial, *The Statesman*, 16 October 1943. See also Stephens (1966). Ian Stephens was the editor of *The Statesman*, a British-owned paper, which distinguished itself in its extensive reporting of the famine and its crusading editorials.

[3] Letter to Mr. L. S. Amery, no. L/E/8/3311; document no. 180 in Mansergh, (1973), vol. IV, pp. 397–8. The earlier communication referred to by Rutherford is document no. 158 in the same volume.

to the famine comes to a bit over 678,000.[4] This would make the average weekly death-roll in excess of 26,000 rather than 2,000.

The Famine Inquiry Commission went on to note that 'all public health statistics in India are inaccurate', and 'even in normal times deaths are not fully recorded'. In rural Bengal deaths were reported by the village *chowkidar* (village watchman), in addition to his other duties, and he was 'usually illiterate, and paid about Rs. 6 or Rs. 7 a month'. During the famine period, 'in certain places the salaries of *chowkidars* were not paid and they deserted their posts to obtain work on military projects and aerodromes', while 'some of them died'.

The replacement of dead and vanished *chowkidars* was no easy matter and several weeks and months might elapse before successors could be found, during which deaths presumably went unrecorded. Further, in the height of the famine thousands of people left their homes and wandered across the countryside in search of food. Many died by the roadside—witness the skulls and bones which were to be seen there in the months following the famine. Deaths occuring in such circumstances would certainly not be recorded in the statistics of the Director of Public Health.[5]

Taking note of all this, the Commission arrived at the conclusion that 'the number of deaths in excess of the average in 1943 was of the order of one million'—nearly all of it in the second half of the year.[6] On this estimate the death-roll in the second half of 1943 would seem to have been around 38,000 *per week*.

D.2 HOW MANY IN FACT?

No reason was given by the Commission for choosing the particular correction ratio that was used, except the thoroughly respectable one that it was arrived at 'after due consideration of the available facts' (1945a, p. 109). To this figure of one million deaths attributed to the famine of 1943, the Commission added the number of registered deaths in the first half of 1944 in excess of the previous quinquennial average without any correction. The reason for this asymmetry stemmed from the Commission's belief that there was 'an unquestionable improvement in the collection of mortality statistics' at the end of 1943 owing to efforts made by civil and military medical authorities (p. 109). The excess death registration for the first half of 1944 amounts to 422,371. Adding this to the estimate of one million for 1943, the Commission rounded off the mortality toll of the famine thus:

[4] Famine Inquiry Commission (1945a), p. 108. For the year as a whole the difference came to 688, 846.
[5] Famine Inquiry Commission (1945a), p. 109. See also *Census of India 1951*, vol. VI, part IB, pp. 1–2.
[6] Famine Inquiry Commission (1945a), pp. 108–9.

'about 1.5 million deaths occurred as a direct result of the famine and the epidemics which followed in its train' (p. 110).

Dr Aykroyd, a distinguished nutrition expert, who was a member of the Commission and who in fact made the Commission's estimates of mortality, has recently stated (as was quoted in Chapter 6) that he now thinks 'it was an under-estimate, especially in that it took too little account of roadside deaths, but not as gross an under-estimate as some critics of the Commission's report, who preferred 3 to 4 million, declared it to be' (Aykroyd, 1974, pp. 77). Who were these critics and how did they arrive at their figures?

The most quoted estimate—from the Anthropology Department of the Calcutta University—was based on a sample survey. The following estimates were released on 21 February 1944—much before the Famine Inquiry Commission had even been appointed:

The Anthropology Department of the University of Calcutta has carried out a sample survey of ten of the famine-affected districts of Bengal. The statistics for eight districts have so far been tabulated. They cover eight hundred sixteen-family units with a total membership of three thousand eight hundred and eighty. The total deaths in these groups during June–July 1943 and November–December 1943, has been three hundred eighty-six or ten per cent during six months (i.e. 100 per thousand). As the death rate for Bengal does not exceed thirty per thousand per annum, i.e., fifteen per thousand for six months, the excess mortality (100–15) of eighty-five per thousand, that is, eight and a half percent, has to be ascribed to famine and the pestilence that followed in its wake. As some areas in North Bengal were much less affected than Western or Central Bengal or the deficit areas of Eastern Bengal, some reduction has to be made to estimate the total mortality figures for Bengal. It will probably be an under-estimate of the famine to say that two-thirds of the total population were affected more or less by it. On this basis the probable total number of deaths above the normal comes to well over three and a half millions.[7]

The applicability of an excess mortality rate of $8\frac{1}{2}$ per cent to two-thirds of the population of Bengal is, in fact, a piece of *pure* guesswork—and an illegitimate one at that, since the sample that was surveyed was chosen from the worst affected areas in Bengal. Later the leader of the group, Professor K. P. Chattopadhyaya, himself pointed out limitations of this estimate, and proposed a figure of 2.2 million for excess deaths in 1943. Adding the half a million excess deaths taken by the Famine Inquiry Commission for 1944, Chattopadhyaya came to a 'minimum' estimate of 'total excess mortality' equalling 2.7 million.[8]

Between Chattopadhyaya's figure of 2.7 million and the Famine Inquiry Commission's 1.5 million (not to mention the minute estimates

---

[7] Reprinted in Ghosh (1944), Appendix G.
[8] Chattopadhyaya and Mukherjea (1946), p. 5.

in contemporary official statements in London and New Delhi[9]), there remains a wide gap. The lack of evidence on the representative nature of Chattopadhyaya's sample renders it dubious and the arbitrariness of Commission's correction factor makes it difficult to evaluate their estimate also.[10] But a more fundamental question concerns the time coverage of the mortality estimates. Both these figures cover up to June 1944. The acute starvation associated with the famine had ended around December 1943, even though 'the death rate remained high throughout the greater part of 1944' (Famine Inquiry Commission, 1945a, p. 1). When did the death rate, in fact, return to 'normal'? The Famine Inquiry Commission did not answer this question.

It could not have. At the time the Report was submitted in 1945, the death rate had not *yet* returned to normal. When did it do so? This is clearly one of the first things to ascertain, since the forces of post-famine epidemics to which the Commission refers in incorporating the excess deaths in the first half of 1944 in its total mortality estimate, went on raging for years.

For this, and indeed for any other year-to-year study, we have to rely on death registration data with suitable corrections. It is argued in the *Census of India 1951*, in its report on the 'Vital Statistics of West Bengal: 1941–50', that, while there are errors in registration, 'under-registrations are fairly uniform and do not take sudden leaps and bounds from year to year' (vol. VI, Part 1B, pp. 1–2).[11] While it seems most likely that the registration ratio did decline in 1943 and improved again in 1944, there seems to be little reason for assuming a radically different proportion of post-1944 registration compared with pre-1943 ratios.

For West Bengal, Jain's use of the reverse survival method yields an under-registration of deaths of 33.9 per cent in 1941–50. This makes the actual mortality 51 per cent higher on the average than registered

[9] There is something puzzling about the official statements on the minute size of mortality. Lord Wavell records in his 'journal' on 19 October 1943, when he became the new viceroy, that the outgoing viceroy, Lord Linlithgow, confessed to him that 'in July he expected that deaths in Bengal might be up to 1,000,000 or 1½ million, and that we looked like getting off better than he had thought possible' (Wavell, 1973, p. 34). Presumably the government had meanwhile persuaded themselves that the situation was *incomparably* better than had been 'thought possible'!

[10] Aykroyd (1974) is candid in acknowledging the arbitrariness of his estimate: 'at all events, the figure of 1.5 million deaths is in the history books, and whenever I come across it I remember the process by which it was reached' (p. 77).

[11] It is perhaps also worth remarking that, for India as a whole, the ratio of registered deaths to the estimated number of deaths obtained by using the 'reverse survival method' for 1941–50 by S. P. Jain (1954) is 0.73, while the same method had yielded a ratio of 0.74 for 1931–40. See Jain (1954), p. 44. The estimates for earlier decades are of Kingsley Davis: 0.74 for 1931–40, 0.72 for 1921–30, and 0.70 for 1911–20.

mortality. I shall use this ratio of correction uniformly, though it should be noted that this would tend to *underestimate* famine mortality, since registration was especially bad in 1943—the year of the famine and of peak death even in terms of registration data. There is, thus, a *downward* bias in our estimation of famine deaths.[12]

In Table D1 numbers of the registered deaths for each year from 1941 to 1950 are given for West Bengal. The time pattern is one of *monotonic* decline except for the one severe jump upwards in 1943. In fact, despite falling each year after 1943, annual mortality did not return to the 1942 level even by the end of the decade. Since the number of deaths had tended to fall each year, the Famine Inquiry Commission's procedure of taking the average mortality in the previous *quinquennium* as the 'normal' mortality may understate excess mortality for the famine years. Instead, I have made two sets of estimates: estimate A, with the 'normal' being taken to be the average of the deaths in 1941 and 1942, and estimate B, with the 1942 death rate being taken as the 'normal'. Estimate B yields, naturally, a higher series of 'excess deaths', which are presented for 1943–50 in Table D1 and Figure D1. However, even estimate B can be thought to be understating the magnitude of excess mortality, since the relevant comparison is not with the level in the *pre-famine* year, but with the level to which the expected death rates *would*

TABLE D1
Recorded Deaths in West Bengal, 1941–50

		Excess deaths	
	Deaths	A	B
1941	384,220		
1942	347,886		
1941–2 Average	*366,053*		
1943	624,266	258,213	276,380
1944	577,375	211,322	229,489
1945	448,600	82,547	100,714
1946	414,687	48,634	66,801
1947	387,165	21,112	39,279
1948	385,278	19,225	37,392
1949	372,559	6,506	24,673
1950	356,843	−9,210	8,957

Source: Based on death statistics from *Census of India 1951* vol. VI, part 1B, Table 6.

[12] A substantial *net* migration from East to West Bengal during the late 1940s would also tend to underestimate the actual death rate during 1941–50, and thus underestimate the under-registration of deaths, thereby underestimating famine mortality.

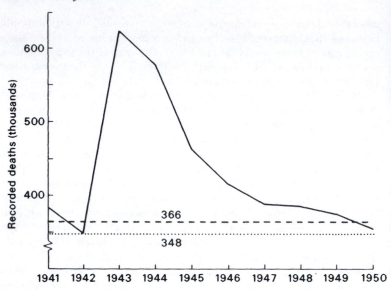

FIG. D1 Recorded Deaths during 1941–50 in West Bengal

have fallen in the post-famine years *but for* the intervention of the famine.[13]

The numbers of excess deaths under assumptions A and B respectively for each year are given in Table D1. The 'excess' becomes negative for A from 1950 onwards and for B—it can be checked from later data—from 1951 onwards; this is so with a stationary *total* death norm, which—as discussed above—*understates* the levels of excess mortality.

Adding up until the excess mortality is eliminated yields a total of excess mortality owing to the famine of 648,000 for Assumption A and 784,000 for assumption B. If the turmoil of the partition of Bengal in 1947 and the displacement resulting from it make us reluctant to read the impact of the famine in the excess mortality figures beyond 1946, we

---

[13] Note that the *absolute* number of deaths went on falling through the decades, despite the increase in the size of the population, which failed to increase only during the immediate famine years; see *Census of India 1951*, vol. VI, part 1B, pp. 2–4.

can be conservative and count the excess figures only during 1943–6.[14] This yields a total registration excess mortality of 601,000 under assumption A and 673,000 under B.

If Jain's (1954) estimate of under-registration in West Bengal during 1941–50 is applied uniformly, then these excess registration figures would have to be raised by 51 per cent to arrive at the actual excess mortality.[15] This yields 908 thousand and 1.016 million respectively under A and B.

All of this relates to West Bengal only. The famine was at least as serious in East Bengal—later East Pakistan, now Bangladesh.[16] Unfortunately, there is no 'reverse survival' estimate of under-registration for East Bengal comparable with Jain's calculation for the West of Bengal. I have not, therefore, tried to make an independent estimate of famine mortality in East Bengal. However, the Census of Pakistan 1951 reports an estimate, viz. a figure of 1.714 million, 'worked out from official statements, which as explained are largely estimates in the absence of reliable reports'.[17] Added to my estimates for West Bengal, this yields 2.622 million and 2.730 million respectively, under assumptions A and B. Note that the East Bengal figures given in the Pakistan Census take account of deaths only up to 1944 and not up to 1946, as in our West Bengal estimates. Taking note of the facts that (1) the population of what became West Bengal was almost exactly a third of the population of undivided Bengal in 1941; (2) the registered number of deaths in West Bengal tended to be around a third of the total number of deaths in Bengal before 1943; and (3) in the famine year the number of registered deaths in West Bengal was again almost exactly a third of that in Bengal as a whole,[18] if we feel bold enough to treat

[14] Note, however, that the strictly monotonic decline of the number of deaths continued right through 1947 (see Table D1). The *death rate per thousand* also underwent a strictly monotonic decline, since a declining number of deaths with an increasing population size implies a strictly monotonic fall of the death rate. Excess mortality figures beyond 1946 have, however, been ignored to avoid overestimating famine mortality, by biassing the procedures in the opposite direction.

[15] This may be compared with the Famine Inquiry Commission's correction of recorded excess mortality in 1943 of 688,846 to one million, which amounts to a correction factor of 45 per cent. (For some inexplicable reason the Commission notes the correction ratio to be 'some 40 per cent'—p. 109.) For 1944, however no correction was made by the Commission. A 'pilot survey' conducted by government of Bengal in 1948 found the correction factor to be 46.4 per cent (see Chaudhuri, 1952, p. 9).

[16] See Famine Inquiry Commission (1945a, pp. 114–15).

[17] *Census of Pakistan 1951*, Chapter III, p. 30. The arbitrary nature of this estimate is emphasized, and reference is also made to the fact that, 'according to popular belief, however, the deaths from famine in East Bengal were between two and two and a half million'.

[18] The number of registered deaths in 1943 was 624,266 for West Bengal and 1,873,749 for Bengal as a whole (see Famine Inquiry Commission, 1945a, p. 108, and *Census of India, 1951*, vol. VI, part IB, p. 21).

famine excess mortality in West Bengal to be a third of that in undivided Bengal, then the total Bengal famine mortality works out as 2.724 million and 3.048 million respectively under assumptions A and B.

These figures are put together in Table D2. Since the Famine Inquiry Commission and K. P. Chattopadhyaya both gave excess mortality figures separately for the famine year 1943, the results of our calculation with blow-up for Bengal are shown separately for 1943 also. It is interesting that Chattopadhyaya's over-all estimate comes fairly close to those presented here, but the coincidence is accidental, since his figure refers to mortality in 1943 and in the first half of 1944 only. In fact, for 1943 as such the estimates given here are quite close to those of the Famine Inquiry Commission. The bulk of the difference in our respective total estimates arise from (1) the longer time coverage in my estimates (using, however, the same logic as employed by the Commission itself in attributing high post-famine mortality to the famine), and (2) continued correction for under-registration of deaths even beyond 1943 (using results of corrections through the 'reverse survival' method).

TABLE D2
Estimates of Bengal Famine Mortality

	Excess mortality in 1943 (millions)	Total excess mortality due to the famine (millions)
Famine Inquiry Commission	1.00	1.50
K. P. Chattopadhyaya	2.20	2.70
Assumption A + Pakistan Census		2.62
Assumption B + Pakistan Census		2.73
Assumption A blown up for all Bengal	1.17	2.72
Assumption B blown up for all Bengal	1.25	3.05

Since there were several downward biases—as explained—built into the estimates presented here, we may be inclined to pick a figure around 3 million as the death toll of the Bengal famine. (It has also the merit of being a 'round' number—that arbitrary preference shown by our ten-fingered species captivated by the decimal system.) But what emerges most powerfully from our analysis is not so much the largeness of the size of total mortality, but its time pattern—lasting for years after the famine. This was largely due to the epidemics associated with the famine, and to this issue I now turn.

D.3 HOW DID THEY DIE?

In December 1943, Bengal reaped a harvest larger than any in the past. Curiously enough, it was also the month in which the death rate in Bengal reached its peak in this century. The famine in the form of starvation had by then come largely to an end—starvation deaths seemed to have peaked around September and October that year. Cholera mortality reached its maximum in October and November. Malaria peaked in December, and continued in its elevated position through the next year and later. Smallpox reached its height in March and April 1944, and a greater height still one year later. The starvation phase of the famine had given way to the epidemic phase.

Table D3 presents the yearly time series of registered deaths from some of the principal causes. The sharp jump upwards in 1943 of cholera, malaria, fever, dysentery, diarrhoea, etc., can be easily seen. For seasonal reasons the impact of smallpox was not felt until the following year since it hits primarily in early spring. Taking the average mortality in 1941 and 1942 as the 'normal' mortality for each disease respectively, 'excess mortality' from each disease has been calculated for the period 1943–6. The last row presents the inter-disease breakdown of excess mortality.

Before discussing the inter-disease pattern of excess mortality, it is worth commenting on the absence of starvation as a major reported cause of death during that great famine. One reason for this peculiarity is that starvation was not typically used as a separate category in reporting deaths. This was due partly to the habit of using traditional categories in reporting causes of death, but also to the fact that typical starvation deaths show other identifiable symptoms at the final stages, and these *proximate* 'causes' tend to fit well into the traditional categories. For example, it is common to die of starvation through diarrhoea (indeed, 'famine diarrhoea' is a well-known phenomenon) as well as dysentery—partly as a result of eating uneatable objects. Clearly, many of the deaths reported under 'dysentery, diarrhoea and enteric group of fevers' were, in fact, starvation deaths. The same holds for several other categories, including the general category of deaths owing to 'fever'.[19]

Excluding 'fever', which is a diverse basket of diseases varying from influenza and measles to cerebro-spinal fever and Kala-azar, the ranking of the main diseases in terms of their contributions to excess mortality were (in decreasing order): malaria, cholera, 'dysentery, diarrhoea and enteric group of fevers', and smallpox. The nature of these ailments as well as direct accounts suggest that the explosive

---

[19] Compare the problem of interpreting the large number of deaths from lethal scurvy during the Irish famine of 1845–6.

TABLE D3

Diseases and Deaths in West Bengal, 1941–6 Registrations

	Dysentery, diarrhoea, and enteric group of fevers	Cholera	Malaria	'Fever' (excl. malaria)	Smallpox	TB	Respiratory diseases other than TB	Total
1941	25,321	15,612	85,505	109,912	9,286	7,989	34,345	384,220
1942	23,234	11,427	85,078	97,764	1,023	6,734	32,847	347,886
1941–2 Average	*24,278*	*13,519*	*85,291*	*104,838*	*5,155*	*7,362*	*33,596*	*366,053*
1943	41,067	58,230	168,592	159,398	2,261	6,830	35,140	624,266
1944	36,040	20,128	166,897	176,824	19,198	7,318	37,052	577,375
1945	24,463	8,315	123,834	122,549	23,974	6,951	33,839	448,600
1946	25,651	9,774	102,339	121,391	4,971	7,227	31,926	414,687
Excess:								
1943–6	*30,109*	*42,371*	*220,498*	*164,810*	*29,784*	*–1,122*	*3,623*	*600,716*
Share of total excess (%)	5.0	7.1	36.7	27.4	5.0	–0.2	0.6	100.0

Source: Based on current registration data, reported in *Census of India 1951*, vol. VI, part 1B. Note that the 'enteric group of fevers' figure both under 'fever' and under 'dysentery, diarrhoea, and enteric group of fevers', but the overlap is quantitatively rather tiny.

outbursts of epidemics during and immediately following the famine were affected not merely by starvation and malnutrition, but also by other factors, e.g. the impact of the famine on sanitary arrangements, water supply, and other civic amenities, exposure to vectors through movements in search of food, as well as inability to receive medical attention owing to destitution and a breakdown of public health facilities.[20] In addition, infectious deseases can spread directly to people who may not have been affected otherwise by the famine. Epidemics do, of course, also have a rhythm of their own.[21] Once an epidemic occurs, its echo effects may last for quite a few years.

The diseases unleashed by the Bengal famine had the dual characteristics of being both (1) epidemic diseases associated with previous famines, and (2) endemic diseases in the region. Malaria had been associated with Indian famines at least from the nineteenth century,[22] and epidemics of cholera and smallpox had been observed in many previous famines, including the Bengal famine of 1770. Dysentery and diarrhoea are, of course, 'peculiarly famine diseases'—as the Famine Inquiry Commission described them. The same applies to the mixed bundle called 'fever' other then malaria. But all these diseases were also endemic in the region. Malaria and fevers, which are sometimes difficult to distinguish,[23] were the biggest killers in the pre-famine days, followed at quite some distance by 'dysentery, diarrhoea and enteric groups of fevers', cholera, and smallpox in that order. In the sharing of famine mortality, the relative positions are not very different, with malaria and fever being followed at a substantial distance by cholera, 'dysentery, etc.,' and smallpox, in that order.

Perhaps the most interesting case is that of the dog that did not bark, viz. respiratory diseases including TB. These diseases killed many more in the pre-famine period than any of the other group of diseases, with the exception of malaria and other fevers. But, remarkably, mortality from TB and from other respiratory diseases seem to have been hardly influenced by the Bengal famine (see Table D3). This experience is *not* unusual in the context of other Indian famines, in which TB and other respiratory diseases have not typically played a

[20] See Famine Inquiry Commission (1945a) on these disruptive consequences of the famine and on the large-scale trekking of destitutes in search of food. See also Ghosh (1944) and Das (1949). .

[21] See Bailey (1957). In fact, because of the spread effects of epidemics, the Bengal famine may also have contributed to deaths outside Bengal, especially in Orissa and Bihar. See Famine Inquiry Commission (1945a), pp. 104–5. See also *Census of India 1951*, vol. XI, part I, p. 41.

[22] See the Reports of the Indian Famine Commissions of 1898 and 1901. Also the findings of S. R. Christophers regarding the nineteenth-century famines, quoted in Famine Inquiry Commission (1945a), p. 122.

[23] On this see the Report of Indian Famine Commission of 1898.

prominent part, but there is something of a puzzle in this in a more general context. The linkage of TB and other respiratory diseases with malnutrition is well established (see Keys, 1950), and seems to be conceded even by those who dispute the influence of starvation as such on other diseases spread through infectious contagion (see, for example, Chambers, 1972, pp. 82–6).

Tuberculosis is, of course, slow to develop and is influenced more by chronic undernourishment than by a short period of severe starvation; this might suggest that the spread of tuberculosis would not be much enhanced by a famine. But famine-induced movements and sanitary breakdowns may help in the expansion of the infection. More importantly, since tuberculosis and other respiratory diseases were already widespread in Bengal, it would be natural to expect that starvation during the famine would convert morbidity into mortality on a substantial scale. That this was not reported as having happened during and immediately after the Bengal famine thus does leave one with an interesting and important problem. Attributing this counter-intuitive phenomenon comfortably to an assumed error of reporting is tempting, but this explanation would be convincing only with em-pirical evidence of the existence of such a bias in a large enough scale. Also, since TB and other respiratory diseases typically had rather undistinguished records in previous Indian famines *as well*, an *ad hoc* explanation for the Bengal famine of 1943 as such is not what is needed.

The Bengal famine killed mostly by magnifying the forces of death normally present in the pre-famine period—a magnifying role that other famines had played in the past. The universality of this endemic-to-epidemic relationship is, however, seriously affected by the apparent inertness of TB and other respiratory disease. This inertness also seems to contrast quite sharply with the view taken of these diseases in the international literature on famine-induced epidemics (see for example Keys, 1950, Foege, 1971, Chambers, 1972).

D.4 WHAT REGIONAL DISTRIBUTION?

Excess mortality can be estimated separately for each district in West Bengal on the basis of the registration data presented in the *Census of India 1951* (vol. VI, part IB). These are presented in Table D4, with the 'normal' level of mortality being taken to be the average of the figures for 1941 and 1942. The percentage excesses for the famine year 1943 and for the period 1943–6 are presented separately, and the ranks in the two orderings of excesses are also given. The inter-district variations are quite remarkable, even though for every district the excess is positive both for 1943 and for the period 1943–6.

There are some differences between the two rankings. Malda, which ends up as the most affected district over-all, was one of the less affected

TABLE D4

Excess Mortality in West Bengal: Breakdown by District

District	Average mortality, 1941–2 ('normal')	Excess mortality, 1943	Excess mortality, 1943–6	Percentage excess, 1943	Percentage excess, 1943–6 (annual)	Excess rank, 1943	Excess rank 1943–6	Intensity class according to Bengal Govt Revenue Dept	Intensity class according to Bengal Govt Dept of Industries
Malda	8,237	+3,080	+45,512	+37.4	+129.0	9	1	Slight	Slight
Howrah	18,842	+15,832	+52,444	+84.0	+69.6	3	2	Moderate	Slight
Murshidabad	32,382	+32,691	+87,869	+101.0	+67.8	2	3	Slight	Slight
Birbhum	23,007	+17,482	+51,369	+76.0	+55.8	5	4	Slight	Slight
Calcutta	30,385	+21,883	+61,588	+72.0	+50.7	6	5		
Midnapur	52,489	+72,250	+104,747	+137.6	+49.9	1	6	Severe	Severe
West Dinajpur	10,858	+1,600	+20,281	+14.7	+46.7	13	7	Slight	Slight
Nadia	21,819	+17,021	+31,914	+78.0	+36.6	4	8	Slight	Slight
24-Parganas	54,062	+37,151	+65,501	+68.7	+30.3	7	9	Severe	Severe
Jalpaiguri	20,171	+6,633	+21,062	+32.9	+26.1	11	10	Slight	Moderate
Hoogly	21,688	+5,868	+18,299	+26.8	+21.1	12	11	Moderate	Slight
Burdwan	35,401	+12,057	+26,382	+34.1	+18.6	10	12	Moderate	Slight
Bankura	26,212	+13,958	+15,953	+53.5	+15.2	8	13	Moderate	Slight
Darjeeling	10,495	+763	+1,779	+7.3	+4.2	14	14	Slight	Moderate

Source: Based on *Census of India* 1951, vol, VI, part 1B.

districts in the famine year itself. Similarly, Midnapur, which was most affected in the famine year, ends up in a somewhat moderate position for the whole period. The pattern of the epidemics that followed the famine re-ordered the districts in terms of mortality. However, the two rankings are not unrelated, and the value of Spearman's rank correlation coefficient is 0.60, which offers no problem in rejecting the null hypothesis that the two rankings are independent.

What is perhaps of greater interest is the fact that the Bengal government's diagnoses of the relative severity of the famines in the different districts differed quite substantially from the excess mortality rankings for 1943–6 as well as for 1943 itself. A five-category classification of the subdivisions was issued by the Revenue Department in 1944, and a four-category classification by the Department of Industries in the same year.[24] Putting together the classification of the subdivisions within each district, I have presented a broad three-class partitioning in Table D4 reflecting the two official views of 'degree of incidence of famines'. Both put Malda—ultimately the most affected district—in the lowest category of incidence. The two did the same to Murshidabad and Birbhum, but in fact both the districts had a high incidence of excess mortality in 1943 as well as in the period 1943–6. On the other hand, 24-Parganas, which neighbours Calcutta, and from where many destitutes trekked into Calcutta at the height of the famine,[25] was put in the highest category of incidence in both the official lists, despite being only moderately placed in the excess mortality rankings for the famine year as well as the post-famine period.[26] Since relief operations were strongly influenced by these diagnoses, the discrepancies are of a certain amount of practical interest.

Finally, a remark on the excess mortality in Calcutta is worth making. Most people who died in Calcutta from starvation and from related diseases in the famine year were destitutes who had moved into Calcutta in search of food; the regular residents of Calcutta were protected by various public and semi-public schemes of food distri-

[24] Quoted in Mahalanobis, Mukherjea and Ghosh (1946), pp. 11–14.

[25] A sample survey of the destitutes in Calcutta conducted in September 1943 revealed that nearly 82 per cent of the destitutes surveyed came from this one district (see Das, 1949, p. 58).

[26] Deaths occurring in Calcutta of people normally residing in 24-Parganas should, in fact, be attributed to the 24-Parganas itself. This correction would tend to raise somewhat the excess mortality rates of the 24-Parganas. The required corrections are difficult to estimate because of lack of precise data on 'normal residence' of those dying in Calcutta during the famine and post-famine years. But rough breakdowns would seem to indicate that the relative position of the 24-Parganas would not change drastically, especially for the period 1943–6. The contrast between the reality and the official perception will still hold, and the importance of being close to Calcutta in having one's distress officially observed will not disappear.

bution (see Famine Inquiry Commission, 1945a). Based on this observation, it has been frequently stated that the residents of Calcutta escaped the famine.[27] This is largely true as far as starvation is concerned, but in the epidemics that were induced by the famine, Calcutta had its own share of casualties, reflected by the excess mortality figures after 1943, i.e. after virtually all the famine destitutes from elsewhere had left or been repatriated.

D.5 WHICH OCCUPATION CATEGORY?

The death registration figures do not specify occupational backgrounds. We can, however, surmise something about probable death rates by examining the rates of destitution of different income groups. These were computed on the basis of a sample survey conducted by Mahalanobis, Mukherjea and Ghosh (1946), already used in Chapter 6 above, and are presented in Table D5 (taken from Table 6.7 above). In the second column the destitution rates are added up with the transition to the occupation of 'paddy husking' – a typical destitution syndrome for rural women with children. On this basis it would appear that the

TABLE D5

Destitution Rates of Different Occupation Categories in Bengal:
January 1943–May 1944

	proportion of destitution	*Proportion of destitution and transition to paddy husking*
Peasant cultivation and share-cropping	1.3	1.5
Part-time agricultural labour	1.4	2.0
Agricultural labour	4.6	6.1
Non-cultivating owners	1.6	2.4
Fishing	9.6	10.5
Craft	3.8	4.3
Husking paddy	4.7	–
Transport	6.0	6.9
Trade	2.2	2.6
Profession and services	2.1	2.6
Non-agricultural labour	3.7	4.5
Other productive occupations	4.6	4.6

Source: See Table 6.7 above.

[27] E.g., 'In the end not a single man died of starvation from the population of Greater Calcutta, while millions in rural areas starved and suffered' (Sir Manilal Nanavati's note, Famine Inquiry Commission, 1945a, p. 102).

most affected groups were fishermen, transport workers, and agricultural labourers. In terms of absolute numbers, agricultural labourers as an occupation group were dominant.

One of the few direct surveys of the occupational basis of famine mortality was presented by Mukerji (1965) for five villages in the Faridpur district in East Bengal; the survey was conducted in 1944. The results are presented in Table D6. In these villages the highest mortality category is agricultural labour. The importance of agricultural labour among the famine victims is brought out also by the survey of destitutes in Calcutta conducted in 1943 by T. Das (1949).

Our information on this crucial aspect of famine mortality is limited and somewhat haphazard. And we have virtually no information at all on the occupational composition of post-famine mortality in the epidemics.

TABLE D6

Distitution in Five Surveyed Villages in Faridpur

Occupation on 1/1/43	Proportion of destitution (%)	Proportion being 'wiped off' during 1943 (%)
Peasant cultivation and share-cropping	18.4	6.4
Agricultural labour	52.4	40.3
Artisan	35.0	10.0
Petty trader	31.8	14.0
Crop-sharing landlord	6.3	0.0
Priest and petty employee	27.3	27.3
Office employee	10.0	0.0
Landlord	0.0	0.0
'Unproductive'	44.4	16.7
Total	28.5	15.2

Source: See Table 6.8 above.

D.6 FAMINE MORTALITY AS MAGNIFIED NORMAL MORTALITY

Peculiarities in the pattern of famine mortality compared with normal mortality have been a subject of discussion for a long time. A supposedly lower impact of famines on women is one of the 'regularities' that has received some attention in India. Sir Charles Elliot, Famine Commissioner of Mysore in 1876 and Census Commissioner of India for the 1881 Census, summarized the general belief regarding nineteenth-century Indian famines: 'all the authorities seem agreed that women succumb to famine less easily than men'.[28]

Was this the case with the Bengal famine? Das (1949) found, in his survey of destitutes in Calcutta in September 1943, that 'for every dead woman there were nearly two dead men' (p. 93). In its Report the Famine Inquiry Commission referred to Das's findings—then available in unpublished form—and also noted that there was a higher proportionate increase in male deaths compared with female deaths in 1943.[29] The Commission referred to the contrary result from Mahalanobis's survey of 2,622 families which found a higher percentage of mortality among women, but went on to comment on the 'considerable irregularity' in the various subdivisions covered in the survey.

The sex breakdown of pre-famine 'normal' mortality given by the average of 1941 and 1942 as well as that of the excess mortality in 1943 and in the period 1943–6 are all presented in Table D7, based on registration data. The ratios seem remarkably stable through the famine. While the proportion of men in excess mortality in 1943 is a bit higher than in the pre-famine average, the difference is small, and over the larger period of famine mortality the proportionate breakdown of the excess is just the same as for the pre-famine average.[30]

There may, of course, be biases in the registration system, but this should apply to registrations both before and during the famine. In fact, it is more likely that there was a serious bias in Das's sample survey of destitutes in Calcutta which contained a large proportion of families that had 'lost their male earning members', and this bias would be reflected in the results of the survey, which asked respondents to recall which members of the family had died.[31] To what extent this type of observation bias was present also in the accounts of the nineteenth-century famines, I do not know, but certainly as far as the 1943 famine is concerned there is little need for going into the rather contrived explanations[32] that have been proposed to explain the supposed contrast of sex ratios.

[28] For this and other observations, see *Census of India 1911*, vol. I, part I, appendix to Chapter VI; and also Das (1949), pp. 93–6.

[29] Famine Inquiry Commission (1945a, pp. 110–11). The Department of Anthropology had noticed the same, and referred to it as 'a very sinister and significant feature' of the Bengal famine (see Ghosh, 1944, Appendix G, p. 183).

[30] The male population exceeded the female population in Bengal, and the recorded death rate per unit of population was higher for women in every year during the decade 1941–50 through the famine (see *Census of India 1951*, vol. VI, part IB, Tables 7 and 8, pp. 29–30).

[31] Das (1949), p. 93.

[32] My favourites are some of those proposed by Mr. W. C. Bennet, C. S.: 'Women find employment as maid-servants in the houses of rich men when men have no work to look

TABLE D7

Excess Mortality of Men, Women, Children, and the Old: West Bengal

	Average mortality, 1941–2		Excess mortality, 1943		Excess mortality, 1943–6	
	Numbers	Percentages of total	Numbers	Percentages of total	Numbers	Percentages of total
Men	191,943	52	140,439	54	315,282	52
Women	174,310	48	117,774	46	285,434	48
Children below 5	106,080	29	74,838	29	174,058	29
Old people above 60	57,044	16	40,212	16	93,600	16

Source: Based on current registration data, reported in *Census of India 1951*, vol. VI, part IB. Note that 'men' and 'women' include figures for all ages, and 'children below 5' and 'old people above 60' include those for both sexes.

Das (1949) also noted a much higher proportion of deaths among children, and opined that 'this will certainly cripple the next generation of the Bengalees'.[33] The Anthropology Department of Calcutta University had reported a similar bias in its press statement in 1944.[34]

Is this borne out by the registration data? The answer seems to be no. The data are given in Table D7. The proportion of children below five in average mortality in the immediate pre-famine period was 29 per cent, and that is also the percentage of children in excess mortality in the famine year (1943) as well as in the four-year period of famine mortality (1943–6).[35] The extraordinarily high level of mortality of children is, of course, an excruciating problem, but that is a characteristic not only of famine mortality but also of normal mortality in the absence of famine in this part of the world.

Table D7 also presents the mortality figures for the old people, those above sixty. Once again the proportions of famine mortality mirror the pattern of normal mortality.

I end this section with a final observation dealing with the monthly pattern of death at the height of the famine. Table D8 presents the monthly death registrations during June–July of 1943–4, when mortality was at its highest, and also the average monthly registrations in the preceding quinquennium.[36] The similarity between the two monthly patterns is striking.[37] This is brought out clearly by figure D2 as well. (For the benefit of the blind, I note that regressing monthly mortality y in the famine period on normal pre-famine monthly mortality x, by least-squares, yields a very high value of r^2. The estimated regression function, in fact, is $y = 3,175x - 122,535$, with r^2 having the convincing value of .95.) The famine seems to have worked by magnifying the forces of mortality each month, heightening the peak mortality relatively more.

---

for'; 'women possess ornaments of value which they may dispose for their own benefit whenever necessary'; 'the woman in a Hindu family always keeps the household stores, and has no scruple in availing herself of the advantage it gives her' (see *Census of India 1911*, vol. I, part I, appendix to Chapter VI, pp. 220–2).

[33] Das (1949), pp. 91–2.

[34] See Appendix G in Ghosh (1944).

[35] The Famine Inquiry Commission (1945a) noted a decrease in the number of deaths for infants under one month, but attributed this to a decrease in the number of births as well as to a reporting bias (p. 109). Adjustments for this group would not affect the total proportions of children in excess mortality by very much.

[36] The data come from Famine Inquiry Commission (1945a), p. 213.

[37] Cf. Jutikkala and Kauppinen's (1971) observation regarding 'catastrophic' and 'normal' mortality in pre-industrial Finland (1749–1850): 'The figures suggest that the seasonal distribution of deaths did not differ significantly between "catastrophic" and "normal" years' (p. 284).

TABLE D8

Mortality by Months during July 1943–June 1944 compared with Previous Quinquennial Average

	Deaths during 1943–4	Quinquennial average deaths: 1938–42
July	126,437	78,816
August	151,126	83,968
September	171,755	85,253
October	236,754	105,529
November	289,723	128,454
December	328,708	142,033
January	228,128	112,263
February	170,955	89,594
March	162,933	98,428
April	167,368	98,615
May	145,812	85,176
June	106,032	74,774

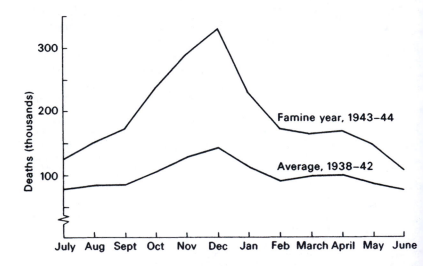

FIG. D2 Monthly Pattern of Recorded Mortality before and during the Famine

D.7 CONCLUDING REMARKS

While it is not possible to say at all precisely how many people were killed by the Bengal famine of 1943, there is evidence that an estimate of around 3 million would be closer to the mark than the figure of 1.5 million arrived at by the official Famine Inquiry Commission (and widely quoted in later works). The difference is largely due to:

1) continued high 'excess mortality' for several years after the famine, caused by famine-induced epidemics the impact of which the Commission considered only for 1943 and the first half of 1944;

(2) underestimation by the Commission of the actual extent of under-registration of deaths in official records.

Both these contrasts largely reflect differences between the data available to the Commission and those available now. Apropos(1), the Commission, working in late 1944 and early 1945, could hardly have gone beyond the first half of 1944 in its mortality coverage. Apropos (2), the Commission chose to use an arbitrary correction for under-registration, not having any way of estimating it directly or indirectly. In contrast, we can use the results of 'reverse survival' exercises based on Census data of 1951 *vis-à-vis* those of 1941 and the results of a direct sample survey held in 1948. There is thus no quarrel, only a very substantial difference in the respective estimates based on *current* information (see Section D.2).

While the gigantic size of excess mortality attributable to the famine is of a certain amount of interest, the *time pattern* of mortality is of possibly greater relevance. Very substantially more than half the deaths attributable to the famine of 1943 took place *after* 1943. The size of mortality did not return to the pre-famine situation for many years after the famine, and the epidemics of malaria and other fevers, cholera, smallpox, dysentery, and diarrhoea that sprung up during and immediately after the famine went on raging for a long time (see Tables D1 and D3 and Figure D1). This has obvious implications for health policy.

Regarding the regional pattern of famine mortality, the relative importance of different districts changed quite a bit between the starvation phase and the later epidemic phase (see Table D4). What is perhaps of greater interest is that the official diagnoses of the relative severity of the famine in the different districts differed substantially from the pattern emerging from the 'excess mortality' calculations, both for the starvation phase and for the later epidemic phase (see Section D.4). Since government relief and rehabilitation work was based on these official diagnoses, the contrasts were of practical import.

Information on the occupational pattern of mortality is very limited, but some general impressions emerge from a broadly based 1944 survey covering the occupational pattern of destitution, and two local 1943 surveys directly going into deaths related to occupations (see Section D5). In absolute terms, the most severe incidence of famine mortality during the famine itself fell almost certainly on the class of agricultural labourers. Their *relative incidence* was high too, but that applies also to other groups like fisherman, transport workers and non-agricultural labourers in rural areas. In Chapter 6 the nature and causation of the observed occupational pattern of destitution were analysed, relating them to the positions of the different groups in the structure of production and exchange in the economy.

Regarding the diseases that took most of the toll, they had the dual characteristics of being both (1) endemic diseases in the region, and (2) epidemic diseases in past famines (see Section D.3). Gigantic as the famine was, it killed mostly by adding fuel to the fire of disease and mortality normally present in the region. This possibly explains why the seasonal pattern of famine deaths even during the actual famine and its immediate aftermath was essentially the normal seasonal pattern—just linearly displaced severely upwards (see Table D 8 and Figure D2). The sex and age patterns of famine mortality also seem to show remarkable similarity with the normal pattern of mortality in pre-famine Bengal (see Table D7).

Bibliography

AALL, C. and HELSING, E. (1976), 'The Sahelian Drought', *Journal of Tropical Pediatrics and Environmental Child Health*, 22.

ABDEL-FADIL, M. (1975), *Development, Income Distribution and Social Change in Rural Eygpt (1952–1970)*, Cambridge: University Press.

ABDULLAH, A. A. (1976a), 'Land Reform and Agrarian Change in Bangladesh', *Bangladesh Development Studies*, 4.

ABDULLAH, A. A. (1976b), 'Agrarian Development and IRDP in Bangladesh', *Bangladesh Development Studies*, 4.

ABEL-SMITH, B. and TOWNSEND, P. (1965), *The Poor and the Poorest*, London: Bell.

ABUL FAZL (1592), *Ain-i-Akbari*, Agra. Translated by Blachmann and Jarrett, *Ain-i-Akbari*, 2nd edn. Calcutta, 1949.

ADELMAN, I. and MORRIS, C. T. (1971), 'The Anatomy of the Pattern of Income Distribution in Developing Countries', *American Economic Review*, 61.

ADELMAN, I. and MORRIS, C. T. (1973), *Economic Growth and Social Equity in Developing Countries*, Stanford: University Press.

ADELMAN, I. and ROBINSON, S. (1978), *Income Distribution Policy in Developing Countries: A Case Study of Korea*, Oxford: University Press.

ADNAN, S., KAMAL, A., KHAN, A. M. and MUQTADA, M. (1977), 'Differentiation and Class Structure in Char Shamraj', Working Paper no. 8, Village Study Group, Dacca University.

ADNAN, S. and RAHMAN, H. Z. (1978), 'Peasant Classes and Land Mobility: Structural Reproduction and Change in Rural Bangladesh', Working Paper no. 9, Village Study Group, Dacca University.

ADY, P. (1944), 'Inflation in India', *Bulletin of the Oxford Institute of Statistics*, 6.

Agro-Economic Research Centre for East India (1960), *Consumer Price Index and Wages for Agricultural Labourer in the Western Region of West Bengal*, Santiniketan: Visva-Bharati.

AHLUWALIA, M. (1976), 'Inequality, Poverty and Development', *Journal of Development Economics*, 3.

AHLUWALIA, M. (1978), 'Rural Poverty and Agricultural Performance in India', *Journal of Development Studies*, 14.

AHLUWALIA, M. (1979), 'Growth and Poverty in Developing Countries', World Bank Staff Working Paper no. 309.

AHMED, IFTIKHAR (1975a), 'The Green Revolution, Mechanisation and Employment', ILO Working Paper WEP 2–22/WP 12.

AHMED, IFTIKHAR (1975b), 'The Green Revolution in Bangladesh: Adoption, Diffusion and Distribution Questions', ILO Working Paper WEP 2–22/WP 16.

AHMED, IQBAL (1978), 'Unemployment and Underemployment in Bangladesh Agriculture', *World Development*, 6.

AHMED, RAISUDDIN (1979), *Foodgrain Supply, Distribution and Consumption Policies within a Dual Price Mechanism: A Case Study of Bangladesh*, Research Report no. 8, Washington DC: International Food Policy Research Institute.

ALAMGIR, M. (1976), 'Poverty, Inequality and Development Strategy in the Third World', mimeographed, Bangladesh Institute of Development Studies.

ALAMGIR, M. (1978a), *Bangladesh: A Case of Below Poverty Level Equilibrium Trap*, Dacca: Bangladesh Institute of Development Studies.

ALAMGIR, M. (1978b), 'Towards a Theory of Famine', Seminar Paper no. 103, Institute for International Economic Studies, University of Stockholm.

ALAMGIR, M. (1980), *Famine in South Asia—Political Economy of Mass Starvation in Bangladesh*, manuscript, Bangladesh Institute of Development Studies. Cambridge, Mass., Oelgeschlager, Gunn and Hain.

ALAMGIR, M., et al. (1977), *Famine 1974: Political Economy of Mass Starvation in Bangladesh, A Statistical Annex*. Dacca: Bangladesh Institute of Development Studies.

ALAVI, HAMZA (1973), 'Peasant Classes and Primordial Loyalties', *Journal of Development Studies*, 1.

AMBIRAJAN, S. (1978), *Classical Political Economy and British Policy in India*, Cambridge: University Press.

AMIN, SAMIR (1974), *Neo Colonialism in West Africa*, New York: Monthly Review Press.

AMIN, SAMIR (ed.) (1975), *L'Agriculture africaine et le capitalisme*, Paris: Anthropos-Idep.

AMIN, SAMIR (1977), *Unequal Development*, New York: Monthly Review Press.

AMIN, SAMIR and VERGOPOULOS, K. (1974), *La Question paysanne et le capitalisme*, Paris: Anthropos-Idep.

ANAND, S. (1977), 'Aspects of Poverty in Malaysia', *Review of Income and Wealth*, 23.

ANAND, S. (1978), *Inequality and Poverty in Malaysia: Measurement and Decomposition*, St Catherine's College, Oxford; to be published.

ARROW, K. and HAHN, F. (1971), *General Competitive Analysis*, Edinburgh: Oliver and Boyd.

ATKINSON, A. B. (1969), *Poverty in Britain and the Reform of Social Security*, Cambridge: University Press.

ATKINSON, A. B. (1970), 'On the Measurement of Inequality', *Journal of Economic Theory*, 2.

ATKINSON, A. B. (1975), *The Economics of Inequality*, Oxford: Clarendon Press.

AYKROYD, W. R. (1974), *The Conquest of Famine*, London: Chatto and Windus.

AZIZ, SARTAJ (ed.) (1975), *Hunger, Politics and Markets: The Real Issues in the Food Crisis*, New York: University Press.

AZIZ, SARTAJ (1977), 'The World Food Situation and Collective Self-Reliance', *World Development*, 5.

AZIZ, SARTAJ (1978), *Rural Development: Learning from China*, London: Macmillan.

BAIER, S. (1974), 'African Merchants in the Colonial Period: A History of Commerce in Damagaram (Central Niger) 1880–1968', PhD dissertation, University of Wisconsin.

BAILEY, N. T. J. (1957), *The Mathematical Theory of Epidemics*, New York.

BAISHYA, P. (1975), 'Assam: Man-Made Famine', *Economic and Political Weekly*, 10, 24 May.

BALL, N. (1976), 'Understanding the Causes of African Famine', *Journal of Modern African Studies*. 14.

BALOGH, T. (1966), *The Economics of Poverty*, London: Weidenfeld and Nicolson (2nd edn. 1974).

BALOGH, T. (1978), 'Failures in the Strategy against Poverty', *World Development*, 6.

BARAN, P. A. (1962), *Political Economy of Growth*, New York: Monthly Review Press.

BARAN, P. A., and SWEEZY, P. M. (1966), *Monopoly Capital*, New York: Monthly Review Press.

BARDHAN, P. K. (1970), 'On the Minimum Level of Living and the Rural Poor', *Indian Economic Review*, 6.

BARDHAN, P. K. (1971), 'On the Minimum Level of Living and the Rural Poor: A Further Note', *Indian Economic Review*, 6.

BARDHAN, P. K. (1973), 'On the Incidence of Poverty in Rural India', *Economic and Political Weekly*, February 1973; reprinted in Srinivasan and Bardhan (1974).

BARDHAN, P. K. (1974), 'The Pattern of Income Distribution in India: A Review', in Srinivasan and Bardhan (1974).

BARRACLOUGH, S. (1977), 'Agricultural Production Prospects in Latin America', *World Development*, 5.

BARTEN, A. P. (1964), 'Family Composition, Prices and Expenditure Pattern', in Hart and Mills (1964).

BATCHELDER, A. B. (1971), *The Economics of Poverty*, New York: John Wiley.

BAUER, P. T. (1971), *Dissent on Development*, London: Weidenfeld and Nicolson.

BECKERMAN, W. (1977), 'Some Reflections on "Redistribution with Growth",' *World Development*, 5.

BECKERMAN, W. (1978), 'Estimates of Poverty in Italy in 1975', ILO World Employment Programme Working Paper, WEP 2–23/WP 70.

BECKERMAN, W. (1979a), *The Impact of Income Maintenance Programmes on Poverty in Four Developed Countries*, Geneva: ILO.

BECKERMAN, W. (1979b), 'The Impact of Income Maintenance Payments on Poverty in Britain, 1975', *Economic Journal*, 89.

BELETE, S., GEBRE-MEDHIN, M., HAILEMARIAM, B., MAFFI, M., VAHLQUIST, B. and WOLDE-GABRIEL, Z. (1977), 'Study of Shelter Population in the Wollo Region', *Journal of Tropical Pediatrics and Environmental Child Health*, 23; republished from *Courrier*, (1976), 26.

BENGTSSON, B. (1979), *Rural Development Research: The Role of Power Relations*, SAREC Report, Stockholm: SIDA.

BENTZEL, R. (1970), 'The Social Significance of Income Distribution Statistics', *Review of Income and Wealth*, 16.

BERG, A. (1973), *The Nutrition Factor*, Washington, DC: Brookings Institution.

BERRY, L., CAMPBELL, D. J. and EMKER, I. (1977), 'Trends in Man–Land Interaction in West African Sahel'; in Dalby, Harrison Church and Bezzaz (1977).

BESHAH, T. W. and HARBISON, J. W. (1978), 'Afar Pastoralists in Transition and Ethiopian Revolution', *Journal of African Studies*, 5.

BHALLA, AJIT (1977), 'Technologies Appropriate for a Basic Needs Strategy', mimeographed, Geneva: ILO.

BHALLA, SHEILA (1979), 'Real Wage Rates of Agricultural Labourers in Punjab, 1961–77: A Preliminary Analysis', *Economic and Poltical Weekly*, 14, 30 June.

BHATIA, B. M. (1967), *Famines in India 1860–1965*, 2nd edn, Bombay: Asia.

BHATTACHARJEE, J. P. (1977), 'External Assistance and Agricultural Development in the Third World', *World Development*, 5.

BHATTACHARYA, N. and CHATTERJEE, G. S. (1974), 'Between-States Variation in Consumer Prices and Per Capita Household Consumption in Rural India', *Sankhyā*, 36.

BHATTACHARYA, N. and CHATTERJEE, G. S. (1977), 'A Further Note on

Between-States Variation in Level of Living in Rural India', Technical Report no. ERU/4/77, Indian Statistical Institute, Calcutta.

BHATTY, I. Z. (1974), 'Inequality and Poverty in Rural India', in Srinivasan and Bardhan (1974).

BLACKORBY, C. and DONALDSON, D. (1977), 'Utility vs. Equity: Some Plausible Quasi-orderings', *Journal of Public Economics*, 7.

BLACKORBY, C. and DONALDSON, D. (1978), 'Measures of Relative Equity and Their Meaning in Terms of Social Welfare', *Journal of Economic Theory*, 18.

BLACKORBY, C. and DONALDSON, D. (1980a), 'Ethical Indices for the Measurement of Poverty', *Econometrica*, 48.

BLACKORBY, C. and DONALDSON, D. (1980b), 'A Theoretical Treatment of Indices of Absolute Inequality', *International Economic Review*, 21.

BLIX, G., HOFVANDER, Y. and VAHLQUIST, B. (1971), *Famine: A Symposium Dealing with Nutrition and Relief Operations in Times of Disaster*, Uppsala: Swedish Nutrition Foundation.

BLYN, G. (1966), *Agricultural Trends in India 1891–1947: Output, Availability and Production*, Philadelphia: University of Pennsylvania Press.

BONDESTAM, L. (1974), 'People and Capitalism in the North-East Lowlands of Ethiopia', *Journal of Modern African Studies*, 12.

BOOTH, A., CHAUDHRI, D. P. and SUNDRUM, R. M. (1979), 'Income Distribution and the Structure of Production', mimeographed, Australian National University, Canberra.

BOOTH, C. (1889), *Life and Labour of the People in London*, London.

BORDA, J. C. (1781), 'Mémoire sur les élections au scrutin', in *Mémoires de l'Académie Royale des Sciences*.

BORGSTROM, G. (1969), *Too Many: An Ecological Overview of Earth's Limitations*, New York: Collier.

BORGSTROM, G. (1973), *World Food Resources*, New York: Intext Publishers.

BORKAR, V. V. and NADKARNI, M. V. (1975), *The Impact of Drought on Rural Life*, Bombay: Popular Prakashan.

BOURNE, G. H. (1943), *Starvation in Europe*, London: Allen and Unwin.

BOWLEY, A. L. (1923), *The Nature and Purpose of the Measurement of Social Phenomena*, London: P. S. King.

BRADLEY, P. N. (1977), 'Vegetation and Environmental Change in West African Sahel', in O'Keefe and Wisner (1977).

BRODER, I. E., and MORRIS, C. T. (1980), 'Socially Weighted Real Income Comparisons: An Application to India', mimeographed, American University.

BROWN, J. A. C. (1954), 'The Consumption of Food in Relation to Household Composition and Income', *Econometrica*, 22.

BROWN, L. R. and ECKHOLM, E. P. (1974), *By Bread Alone*, Oxford: Pergamon Press.

BROWN, W. R. and ANDERSON, N. D. (1976), *Historical Catastrophes: Famines*, Reading, Mass: Addison-Wesley.

BRUTON, H. J. (1965), *Principles of Development Economics*, Englewood Cliffs, N J: Prentice-Hall.

BURGER, G. C. E., *et al.* (1948), *Malnutrition and Starvation in Western Netherlands, September 1944–July 1945*, The Hague.

BURINGH, P. (1977), 'Food Production Potential of the World', *World Development*, 5.

BUTTS, R. E., and HINTIKKA, J. (eds) (1977), *Foundational Problems in the Special Sciences*, Dordrecht: Reidel.

CALDWELL, J. C. (1975), *The Sahelian Drought and its Demographic Implications*, Washington, DC.

CALDWELL, J. C. (1977), 'Demographic Aspects of Drought: An Examination of the African Drought of 1970–74', in Dalby, Harrison Church and Bezzaz (1977).

CANNON, T. G. (1978), 'The Role of Environmental Influence and "Natural" Disasters', mimeographed, Thames Polytechnic, London.

CASSEN, R. H. (1978), *India: Population, Economy, Society*, London: Macmillan.

Centre for Development Studies, Trivandrum (1975), *Poverty, Unemployment and Development Policy: A Case Study of Selected Issues with Reference to Kerala*, New York: United Nations.

Center for Disease Control (1973), *Nutritional Surveillance in Drought Affected Areas of West Africa (Mali, Mauritania, Niger, Upper Volta)*, Austin, Texas: US Public Health Service.

CHAKRAVARTY, SATYA (1980a), 'New Indices for the Measurement of Poverty', mimeographed, Indian Statistical Institute, Calcutta.

CHAKRAVARTY, SATYA (1980b), 'Some Further Results on the Measurement of Poverty', mimeographed, Indian Statistical Institute, Calcutta.

CHAKRAVARTY, S. and PAL, M. (1978), 'Some Results on Measurement of Inequality', Technical Report no. ERU/3/78, Indian Statistical Institute, Calcutta.

CHAKRAVARTY, SUKHOMOY and ROSENSTEIN-RODAN, P. N. (1965), *The Linking of Food Aid with Other Aid*, Rome: FAO.

CHAMBERS, J. D. (1972), *Population, Economy and Society in Pre-industrial England*, London: Oxford University Press.

CHATTERJEE, G.S. and BHATTACHARYA, N. (1974), 'On Disparities in Per Capita Household Consumption in India', *Sankhya: The Indian*

Journal of Statistics, 36, Series C; reprinted in Srinivasan and Bardhan (1974).

CHATTOPADHYAYA, K. P. and MUKHERJEA, R. (1946), 'A Plan for Rehabilitation', in Mahalanabis *et al.* (1946).

CHAUDHURI, D.G. (1952), *Vital Statistics Special Report on Pilot Survey: Incompleteness of the Birth and Death Registration in Urban and Rural Areas in the Province of West Bengal during 1948 with Recommendations for its Improvement*, Calcutta: Government of West Bengal.

CHAUDHURI, PRAMIT (1978), *The Indian Economy: Poverty and Development*, London: Crosby Lockwood Staples.

CHENERY, H., AHLUWALIA, M. S., BELL, C. L. G., DULOY, J. H. and JOLLY, R. (1974). *Redistribution with Growth*, London: Oxford University Press.

CHICHILNISKY, GRACIELA (1979), 'Basic Needs and Global Models: Resources, Trade and Distribution', mimeographed, Essex University.

CLARK, S., HEMMING, R. and ULPH, D. (1979), 'On Indices for the Measurement of Poverty', mimeographed, Institute for Fiscal Studies, London.

CLARKE, T. (1978). *The Last Caravan*, New York: G. P. Tutnam's Sons.

CLAY, E. J. (1976), 'Institutional Change and Agricultural Wages in Bangladesh', *Bangladesh Development Studies*, 4.

CLIFFE, L. (1974), 'Feudalism, Capitalism and Famine in Ethiopia', *Review of African Political Economy*, 1.

CLINE, W. R. (1973), 'Interrelationship between Agricultural Strategy and Rural Income Distribution', *Food Research Institute Studies*, 12.

CLINE, W.R. (1975), 'Distribution and Development: A Survey of the Literature', *Journal of Development Economics*, 2.

Club du Sahel (1977), *Strategy and Programme for Drought Control and Development in the Sahel*, Paris: OECD.

COHEN, J. M. and WEINTRAUB, D. (1975), *Land and Peasants in Imperial Ethiopia: The Social Background to a Revolution*, Assen: Van Goreum.

COLE, J. (1976), *The Poor of the Earth*, London: Macmillan.

COLLIER, P. (1980), 'Poverty and Growth in Kenya', World Bank Staff Working Paper 389.

Comité Information Sahel (1974), *Qui se nourrit de la famine en Afrique?* Paris: Maspéro.

COPANS, J. *et al.* (1975), *Sécheresses et famines du Sahel*, Paris: Maspéro.

CURREY, B. (1978), 'The Famine Syndrome: Its Definition for Preparedness and Prevention in Bangladesh', *Ecology of Food and Nutrition*, 7.

DAHL, G., and HJORT, A (1976), *Having Herds: Pastoral Herd Growth and*

Household Economy, Stockholm: University of Stockholm.

DAHL, G. and HJORT, A. (1979), *Pastoral Change and the Role of Drought*, Stockholm: SAREC.

DALBY, D. and HARRISON CHURCH, R. J. (1973), *Drought in Africa*, London: International African Institute.

DALBY, D., HARRISON CHURCH, R. J. and BEZZAZ, F. (1977), *Drought in Africa 2*, London: International African Institute.

DALTON, H. (1920), 'The Measurement of the Inequality of Incomes', *Economic Journal*, 30.

DALRYMPLE, D. (1964), 'The Soviet Famine of 1932–1934', *Soviet Studies*, 15.

DALRYMPLE, D. (1965), 'The Soviet Famine of 1932–1934, Some Further References', *Soviet Studies*, 16.

DANDEKAR, V. M. and RATH, N. (1971), *Poverty in India*, Poona: Indian School of Political Economy.

DAS, T. (1949), *Bengal Famine (1943)*, Calcutta: University of Calcutta.

DASGUPTA, A. K. (1950), 'The Theory of Black Market Prices', *Economic Weekly*, 2, reprinted in Dasgupta (1965).

DASGUPTA, A. K. (1965), *Planning and Economic Growth*, London: Allen and Unwin.

DASGUPTA, BIPLAB (1977a), *Village Society and Labour Use*, Delhi: Oxford University Press.

DASGUPTA, BIPLAB (1977b), *Agrarian Change and the New Technology in India*, Geneva: UNRISD.

DASGUPTA, P., SEN, A. and STARRETT, D. (1973), 'Notes on the Measurement of Inequality', *Journal of Economic Theory*, 6.

DEATON, A., and MUELLBAUER, J. (1980), *Economics and Consumer Behaviour*, Cambridge: University Press.

DEBREU, G. (1959), *The Theory of Value*, New York: John Wiley.

DE HAEN, H. (1978), 'Analysing the World Food Problem', *Options: A IIASA News Report*, Winter.

DHARM, NARAIN (1976), *Growth of Productivity in Indian Agriculture*, Occasional Paper no. 93, Cornell University.

DICKSON, H. (1977), 'Agricultural Policy in the World Market', Working Paper, Nationalekonomiska Institutionen, Göteborgs Universitet.

DODGE, C. P. and WIEBE, P. D. (1979), 'Famine Relief and Development in Rural Bangladesh', *Economic and Political Weekly*, 11, 29 May.

DONALDSON, D. and WEYMARK, J. A. (1980a), 'A Single-Parameter Generalization of the Gini Indices of Inequality', *Journal of Economic Theory*, 22.

DONALDSON, D. and WEYMARK, J. A. (1980b), 'Ethically Flexible Gini Indices for Income Distribution in the Continuum', Discussion Paper no. 8020, CORE, Louvain.

DORFMAN, R. (1979), 'A Formula for the Gini Coefficient', *Review of Economics and Statistics*, 61.

DREWNOWSKI, J. (1977), 'Poverty: Its Meaning and Measurement', *Development and Change*, 8.

DUTT, R. C. (1900), *Famines and Land Assessment in India*, London.

DUTT, R. C. (1901), *Indian Famines: Their Causes and Prevention*, London.

DUTTA, BHASKAR (1978), 'On the Measurement of Poverty in Rural India', *Indian Economic Review*, 13.

DUTTA, BHASKAR (1979), 'Intersectoral Disparities and Income Distribution in India: 1960–61 to 1973–74', Working Paper no. 209, Delhi School of Economics.

DWORKIN, RONALD (1977), *Taking Rights Seriously*, London: Duckworth (2nd edn. 1978).

EDEN, F. M. (1797), *The State of the Poor*, London.

EDQUIST, C. and EDQVIST, O. (1979), *Social Carriers of Techniques of Development*, Stockholm: SIDA.

EHRLICH, P. R. and EHRLICH, A. H. (1972), *Population Resource Environment: Issues in Human Ecology*, San Francisco: Freeman.

EL KHAWAS, M. (1976), 'A Reassessment of International Relief Programs', in Glantz (1976).

EMMANUEL, A. (1972), *Unequal Exchange*, New York: Monthly Review Press.

ENGEL, E. (1895), 'Die Lebenskosten belgischer Arbeiter-Familien früher und jetzt', *International Statistical Institute Bulletin*, no. 9.

ENGELS, F. (1892), *The Condition of the Working-Class in England in 1844*, London: Allen and Unwin.

ESHERICK, J. (1972), 'Harvard on China: The Apologetics of Imperialism', *Bulletin of Concerned Asian Scholars*, 4.

ESHERICK, J. (1976), *Reform and Revolution in China*, Berkeley: University of California Press.

Ethiopian Ministry of Agriculture (1973), *Final Report of the Crop Condition Survey for 1972–73 Harvest*, Addis Ababa: Imperial Ethiopian Government.

Ethiopian Ministry of Agriculture (1974), *A Photogrammatic Assessment of 1966 E. C. Harvest Conditions in Eritrea, Tigra, Wollo, Northern Shea and Harerghe*, Addis Ababa: Imperial Ethiopian Government.

Ethiopian Relief and Rehabilitation Commission (1975), [Report on the first] 1½ *years: May Starvation Cease–'Ethiopia Tikdem'*, Addis Ababa: Imperial Ethiopian Government.

ETIENNE, G. (1968), *Studies in Indian Agriculture: The Art of the Possible*, Berkeley: University of California Press.

ETIENNE, G. (1977a), *Bangladesh: Development in Perspective*, Geneva: Graduate Institute of International Studies.

ETIENNE, G. (1977b). 'Foodgrain Production and Population in Asia: China, India and Bangladesh', *World Development*, 5.

FAALAND, J. and PARKINSON, J. R. (1976), *Bangladesh: The Test Case for Development*, London: Hurst.

Famine Inquiry Commission, India (1945a), *Report on Bengal*, New Delhi: Government of India.

Famine Inquiry Commission, India (1945b), *Final Report*, Madras: Government of India.

FAROUK, and ALI, M. (1977), *The Hardworking Poor (A survey of how people use their time in Bangladesh)*, Dacca: Bureau of Economic Research, University of Dacca.

FAULKINGHAM, R. H. (1977), 'Ecological Constraints and Subsistence Strategies: The Impact of Drought in a Hausa Village, A Case Study from Niger', in Dalby, Harrison Church and Bezzaz (1977).

FEDER, E. (1977), 'Agribusiness and the Elimination of Latin America's Rural Proletariat', *World Development*, 5.

FIELDS, G. S. (1976), 'A Welfare Economic Approach to Growth and Distribution in a Dual Economy', Discussion Paper no. 255, Economic Growth Centre, Yale University.

FIELDS, G. S. (1980), *Poverty, Inequality and Development*, Cambridge: University Press.

FIELDS, G. S. and FEI, J. C. H. (1978), 'On Inequality Comparisons', *Econometrica*, 46.

FISHLOW, A. (1972), 'Brazilian Size Distribution of Income', *American Economic Review*, 62.

FLERI, L. F. (1979), *Bangladesh Health Conditions*, mimeographed, UNADPI.

FLOOD, G. (1975), 'Nomadism and its Future: The Afar', *Royal Anthropological Institute News (RAIN)*, 6; reprinted in Hussein (1976).

FOEGE, H. W. (1971), 'Famine, Infections and Epidemics', in Blix, Hofvandor and Vahlquist (1971).

FRANK, A. G. (1969), *Capitalism and Underdevelopment in Latin America*, New York: Monthly Review Press.

FRANKE, R. W., and CHASIN, B. H. (1979), *The Political Economy of Ecological Destruction: Development in the West African Sahel*, Montclair, NJ: Allanheld.

FRIEDMAN, M. (1952), 'A Method of Comparing Incomes of Families Differing in Composition', *Studies in Income and Wealth*, 15.

FURTADO, C. (1964), *Development and Underdevelopment*, Berkeley: University of California Press.

GADGIL, D. R. and SOVANI, N. V. (1943), *War and Indian Economic Policy*, Poona: Gokhale Institute.

GASTWIRTH, J. L. (1972), 'The Estimation of Lorenz Curve and Gini Index', *Review of Economics and Statistics*, 54.

GASTWIRTH, J. L. (1975), 'The Estimation of a Family of Measures of Economic Inequality', *Journal of Econometrics*, 3.

GEBRE-MEDHIN, M. (1974), 'Famine in Ethiopia', *Ethiopian Medical Journal*, 12.

GEBRE-MEDHIN, M., et al. (1974), *Profile of Wollo under Famine*, Addis Ababa: Ethiopian Nutrition Institute, 24/74.

GEBRE-MEDHIN, M., HAY, R., LICKE, Y. and MAFFI, M. (1977), 'Initial Experience of a Consolidated Food and Nutrition Information System. Analysis of Data from the Ogaden Area', *Journal of Tropical Pediatrics and Environmental Child Health*, 23.

GEBRE-MEDHIN, M. and VAHLQUIST, B. (1976), 'Famine in Ethiopia: A Brief Review', *American Journal of Clinical Nutrition*, 29.

GEBRE-MEDHIN, M. and VAHLQUIST, B. (1977), 'Famine in Ethiopia— The Period 1973–75', *Nutrition Reviews*, 35.

GEERTZ, CLIFFORD (1963), *Agricultural Innovation: the Process of Ecological Change in Indonesia*, Berkeley: University of California Press.

GEORGE, P. S. (1979), *Public Distribution of Foodgrains in Kerala—Income Distribution Implications and Effectiveness*, Washington, DC: International Food Policy Research Institute.

GEORGE, Susan (1976), *How the Other Half Dies: The Real Reasons for World Hunger*, Harmondsworth: Penguin.

GHAI, D., KHAN, A. R., LEE, E. and ALFTHAN, T. A. (1977), *The Basic-Needs Approach to Development*, Geneva: ILO.

GHAI, D., KHAN, A. R., LEE, E. and RADWAN, S., eds. (1979), *Agrarian Systems and Rural Development*, London: Macmillan.

GHAI, D., LEE, E. and RADWAN, S. (1979), 'Rural Poverty in the Third World: Trend, Causes and Policy Reorientations', ILO Working Paper, WEP 10-6/WP 23, Geneva.

GHAI, Y. P. (1976), 'Notes towards a Theory of Law of Ideology: Tanzanian Perspectives', *African Law Studies*, no. 13.

GHOSH, AJIT (1979), 'Short-term Changes in Income Distribution in Poor Agrarian Economies: A Study of Famines with Reference to Indian Sub-Continent', ILO Working Paper, WEP 10-6/WP 28, Geneva.

GHOSH, ARUN (1977), 'Prices and Fluctuations in Economic Activity in India 1861–1967', mimeographed, New Delhi.

GHOSH, K. C. (1944), *Famines in Bengal 1770–1943*, Calcutta: Indian Associated Publishing.

GINNEKEN, W. VAN (1976), *Rural and Urban Income Inequalities in Indonesia, Mexico, Pakistan, Tanzania and Tunisia*, Geneva: ILO.

GINNEKEN, W. VAN (1980), 'Some Methods of Poverty Analysis: An Application to Iranian Data, 1975–1976', *World Development*, 8.

GINNEKEN, W. VAN (1979a), 'Income Distribution in LDCs—A Survey of Current Research' mimeographed, Geneva: ILO.

GINNEKEN, W. VAN (1979b), 'Basic Needs in Mexico: Analysis and Policies', ILO Working Paper, WEP 2–23/WP 76.

GLANTZ, M. H. (ed.) (1976), *The Politics of Natural Disaster: The Case of the Sahel Drought*, New York: Praeger.

GLANTZ, M. H. and PARTON, W. (1976), 'Weather and Climate Modification and the Future of the Sahel', in Glantz (1976).

GOEDHART, T., HALBERSTADT, V., KAPTEYN, A. and VAN PRAAG, B. (1977), 'The Poverty Line: Concept and Measurement', *Journal of Human Resources*, 4.

GORMAN, W. M. (1956), 'The Demand for Related Goods', *Journal Paper J3129*, Iowa Experimental Station, Ames, Iowa.

GORMAN, W. M. (1976), 'Tricks with Utility Function', in M. J. ARTIS and A. R. NOBAY (eds), *Essays in Economic Analysis*, Cambridge: University Press.

GRAAFF, J. DE V. (1946), 'Fluctuations in Income Concentration', *South African Journal of Economics*, 14.

GRAAFF, J. DE V. (1977), 'Equity and Efficiency as Components of the General Welfare', *South African Journal of Economics*, 45.

GRANT, J.P. (1978), *Disparity Reduction Rates in Social Indicators*, Washington, DC: Overseas Development Council.

GRAY, M. (1979), *Man against Disease: Preventive Medicine*, Oxford: University Press.

GREENOUGH, P. R. (1979), 'Prosperity and Misery in Modern India: The Bengal Famine 1943–44', mimeographed, Department of History, University of Iowa; to be published.

GRIFFIN, K. (1976), *Land Concentration and Rural Poverty*, London: Macmillan.

GRIFFIN, K. (1978), *International Inequality and National Poverty*, London: Macmillan.

GRIFFIN, K. (1979), *The Political Economy of Agrarian Change*, 2nd edn, London: Macmillan.

GRIFFIN, K. and GHOSE, A. (1979), 'Growth and Impoverishment in the Rural Areas of Asia', *World Development*, 7.

GRIFFIN, K. and JAMES, J. (1979), 'Problems of Transition to Egalitarian Development', *Manchester School*, 47.

GRIFFIN, K. and KHAN, A. R. (eds.) (1977), *Poverty and Landlessness in Rural Asia*, Geneva: ILO.

GRIFFIN, K. and KHAN, A. R. (1978), 'Poverty in the Third World: Ugly Facts and Fancy Models', *World Development*, 6.

GULATI, I. S. and KRISHNAN, T. N. (1975), 'Public Distribution and Procurement of Foodgrains: A Proposal', *Economic and Political Weekly*, 10, 24 May.

GULATI, I. S. and KRISHNAN, T. N. (1976), 'Public Distribution and Procurement of Foodgrains: A Correction and Some Elucidations and Observations', *Economic and Political Weekly*, 11, 21 February.

GUPTA, A. P. (1977), *Fiscal Policy for Employment Generation in India*, Delhi: Tata McGraw-Hill.

HAALAND, G. (1977), 'Pastoral Systems of Production: the Socio-cultural Context and Some Economic and Ecological Implications', in O'Keefe and Wisner (1977).

HABIB, IRFAN (1963), *Agrarian Systems of Mughal India*, London: Asia Publishing House.

HAMADA, K. and TAKAYAMA, N. (1978), 'Censored Income Distribution and the Measurement of Poverty', *Bulletin of International Statistical Institute*, 47.

HAMILTON, C. (1975), 'Increased Child Labour—An External Dis-economy of Rural Employment Creation for Adults', *Asian Economies*, December.

HAMMOND, P. J. (1977), 'Dual Interpersonal Comparisons of Utility and the Welfare Economics and Income Distribution', *Journal of Public Economics*, 6.

HAMMOND, P. J. (1978), 'Economic Welfare with Rank Order Price Weighting', *Review of Economic Studies*, 45.

HANSEN, B. (1969), 'Employment and Wages in Rural Egypt', *American Economic Review*, 59.

HANSSON, B. (1977), 'The Measurement of Social Inequality', in Butts and Hintikka (1977).

HAQ, MAHBUBUL (1976), *The Poverty Curtain: Choices for the Third World*, New York: Columbia University Press.

HAQUE, W., MEHTA, N., RAHMAN, A. and WIGNARAJA, P. (1975), *Towards a Theory of Rural Development*, Bangkok: UN Asian Development Institute.

HARDIN, C. M. (ed.) (1969), *Overcoming World Hunger*, Englewood Cliffs, NJ: Prentice-Hall.

HARE, R. M. (1963), *Freedom and Reason*, Oxford: Clarendon Press.

HARLE, V. (ed.) (1978), *The Political Economy of Food*, Westmead: Saxon House.

HARRISON CHURCH, R. J. (1961), 'Problems and Development of the Dry Zone of Wes Africa', *Geographical Journal*, 127.

HARRISON CHURCH, R. J. (1973), 'The Development of the Water Resources of the Dry Zone of West Africa', in Dalby and Harrison Church (1973).

HART, HERBERT (1961), *The Concept of Law*, Oxford: Clarendon Press.

HART, OLIVER (1977), 'On the Profitability of Speculation', *Quarterly Journal of Economics*, 91.

HART, P. and MILLS, G. (1964), *Econometric Analysis for National Accounts*, London: Butterworth.

HARTMANN, B., and BOYCE, J. (1979), *Needless Hunger: Voices from a Bangladesh Village*, San Francisco: Institute for Food and Development Policy.

HARTWELL, R. M. (1972), *The Long Debate on Poverty*, London: Institute of Economic Affairs.

HAY, R. W. (1975), 'Analysis of Data from Ogaden—Hararghe Province', Consolidated Food and Nutrition Information System, Ethiopian Food and Nutrition Surveillance Programme, Addis Ababa.

HAY, R. W. (1978a), 'The Concept of Food Supply System—with Special Reference to Management of Famine', *Ecology of Food and Nutrition*, 7.

HAY, R. W. (1978b), 'The Statistics of Hunger', *Food Policy*, November.

HAY, R. W. (1980), 'The Food Accounting Matrix: An Analytical Device for Food Planning', mimeographed, Queen Elizabeth House, Oxford.

HAZLEWOOD, A. (1976), 'Kenya: Income Distribution and Poverty: An Unfashionable View', *Journal of Modern African Studies*, 16.

HELLEINER, G. K. (1966), *Peasant Agriculture, Government and Economic Growth in Nigeria*, Homewood, Ill.: Irwin.

HELWEG-LARSEN, P. *et al.* (1952), 'Famine Diseases in German Concentration Camps', *Acta Medica Scandinavia*, suppl. 274, Stockholm.

HEYER, JUDITH (1980), 'The Impact of Smallholder Rural Development Programme on Poverty in Tropical Africa', mimeographed, Queen Elizabeth House, Oxford.

HEYER, J., ROBERTS, P. and WILLIAMS, G. (eds) (1980), *Rural Development in Tropical Africa*, London: Macmillan.

HICKS, J. R. (1939), *Value and Capital*, Oxford: Clarendon Press.

HICKS, J. R. (1958), 'The Measurement of Real Income', *Oxford Economic Papers*, 10.

HICKS, J. R. (1979), *Causality in Economics*, Oxford: Basil Blackwell.

HIRSCH, F. (1976), *Social Limits to Growth*, Cambridge, Mass.: Harvard University Press.

HIRSCHMAN, A. O. (1977), *The Passions and the Interests*, Princeton, NJ: University Press.

HIRSCHMAN, A. O. and ROTHSCHILD, M. (1973), 'The Changing Tolerance for Income Inequality in the Course of Economic Development', *Quarterly Journal of Economics*, 87.

HOBSBAWM, E. J. (1957), 'The British Standard of Living, 1790–1850', *Economic History Review*, 10.

HOBSBAWM, E. J. (1968), 'Poverty', in *International Encyclopaedia of the Social Sciences*, New York.

HOBSBAWM, E. J., MITRA, A., RAJ, K. N., SACHS, I. and THORNER, A.(eds) (1980), *Peasants in History: Essays in Memory of Daniel Thorner*, Calcutta: Oxford University Press.

HOLT, J. and SEAMAN, J. (1976), 'The Scope of the Drought', in Hussein (1976).

HOLT, J. and SEAMAN, J. (1979), 'The Causes and Nature of Famine: A General Theory', mimeographed, International Disaster Institute, London.

HOLT, J., SEAMAN, J. and RIVERS, J. P. W. (1975), 'The Ethiopian Famine of 1973–74: 2. Harerghe Province', *Proceedings of the Nutritional Society*, 24.

HOPECRAFT, A. (1968), *Born to Hunger*, London: Pan Books.

HSIA, R. and CHAU, L. (1978), *Industrialisation, Employment and Income Distribution*, London: Croom Helm.

HUECKEL, G. (1973), 'War and the British Economy, 1815–1973: A General Equilibrium Analysis', *Explorations in Economic History*, 10.

HUQ, A. (ed.) (1976), *Exploitation and the Rural Poor*, Comilla: Bangladesh Academy of Rural Development.

HUSSEIN, A. M. (ed.) (1976), *Rehab: Drought and Famine in Ethiopia*, London: International African Institute.

HUTCHINSON, J. (1972), *Farming and Food Supply*, Cambridge: University Press.

ILO (1976a), *Employment, Growth and Basic Needs: A One-World Problem*, Geneva: ILO.

ILO (1976b), *Basic Needs and National Employment Strategies*, Background Papers, vol. I, Tripartite World Conference on Employment, Income Distribution and Social Progress and the International Division of Labour, Geneva, ILO.

IMPERATO, P. J. (1976), 'Health Care Systems in the Sahel before and after the Drought', in Glantz (1976).

Institute for Food and Development Policy (1979), 'The Aid Debate', Working Paper no. 1, San Francisco.

Interfutures (1979), *Facing the Future: Mastering the Probable and Managing the Unpredictable*, Paris: OECD.

ISENMAN, P. J. and SINGER, H. W. (1977), 'Food Aid: Disincentive Effects and Their Policy Implications', *Economic Development and Cultural Change*, 25.

ISHIKAWA, S. (1977), 'China's Food and Agriculture', *Food Policy*, May.

ISHIKAWA, S., KHAN, A. R., AHMED, I., NASEEM, S. M., WICKRAMASEKARA, P., LEE, E. and VAIDYANATHAN, A. (1980),

Employment Expansion in Asian Agriculture, Asian Employment Programme, Bangkok: ILO/ARTEP.

ISLAM, NURUL (1977), *Development Planning in Bangladesh: A Study in Political Economy*, London: Hurst.

ISLAM, RUSHIDAN (1977), 'Approaches to the Problem of Rural Development', Working Paper no. 10, Village Study Group, Dacca University.

JACKSON, D. (1972), *Poverty*, London: Macmillan.

JAIN, S. P. (1954), 'Computed Birth and Death Rates in India during 1941–1950', Annexure II, *Estimation of Birth and Death Rates in India during 1941–50*, 1951 Census of India, Paper no. 6, New Delhi, Government of India.

JODHA, N. S. (1975), 'Famine and Famine Policies: Some Empirical Evidence', *Economic and Political Weekly*, 10, October 11.

JOHNSON, B. L. C. (1975), *Bangladesh*, London: Heinemann.

JOHNSON, D. GALE (1967), *The Struggle against World Hunger*, New York: Foreign Policy Association.

JOHNSON, D. GALE (1973). 'Famine', in *Encyclopaedia Britannica*, 1973 edn.

JOHNSON, D. GALE (1975), *World Food Problems and Prospects*, Washington, DC: American Enterprises Institute for Public Policy Research.

JOHNSON, D. GALE (1976), 'Increased Stability of Grain Supplies in Developing Countries: Optimal Carryovers and Insurance', *World Development*, 4.

JOLLY, R. (1976), 'The World Employment Conference: The Enthronement of Basic Needs', *Overseas Development Institute Review*, no. 2.

JOSHI, NANDINI (1978), *The Challenge of Poverty: The Developing Countries in the New International Order*, Delhi: Vazirani and Arnold-Heinemann.

JOSLING, T. (1977), 'Grain Reserves and Government Agricultural Policies', *World Development*, 5.

JOY, L. and PAYNE, P. (1975), *Food and Nutrition Planning*, Nutrition Consultants Reports Series, no. 35; ESN: CRS/75/34, Rome: FAO.

JUTIKKALA, E. and KAUPPINEN, M. (1971), 'The Structure of Mortality during Catastrophic Year in Pre-Industrial Society', *Population Studies*, 25.

KAKWANI, N. (1977), 'Measurement of Poverty and Negative Income Tax', *Australian Economic Papers*, 16.

KAKWANI, N. (1980a), *Income Inequality and Poverty*, New York: Oxford University Press.

KAKWANI, N. (1979), 'Issues in Measurement of Poverty', Discussion Paper no. 330, Institute of Economic Research, Queen's University, Kingston, Ontario.

KAKWANI, N. (1980b), 'On a Class of Poverty Measures', *Econometrica*, 48.

KALDOR, NICHOLAS (1976), 'Inflation and Recession in the World Economy', *Economic Journal*, 86.

KAUTILYA (*circa* 320 BC), *Arthasastra*, Pataliputra (Patna); translated by R. SHAMASASTRY, *Kautiliya Arthasastra*, Mysore, 1909; 2nd edn, 1919; Bangalore, 1915; 2nd edn, 1923.

KEYS, A. (1950), *The Biology of Human Starvation*, Minneapolis.

KHALIFA, A. and SIMPSON, M. (1972), 'Perverse Supply in Nomadic Conditions', *Oxford Agrarian Studies*, 1.

KHAN, A. R. (1972), *The Economy of Bangladesh*, London: Macmillan.

KHAN, A. R. (1977), 'Poverty and Inequality in Rural Bangladesh', in Griffin and Khan (1977).

KHAN, A. R. (1979), 'The Comilla Model and the Integrated Rural Development Programme in Bangladesh: An Experiment in Cooperative Capitalism', *World Development*, 7.

KLOTH, T. I. (1974), *Sahel Nutrition Survey 1974*, Atlanta: US Public Health Service.

KLOTH, T. I. *et al.* (1976), 'Sahel Nutrition Survey: 1974', *American Journal of Epidemiology*, 103.

KNIGHT, C. G. and NEWMAN, J. L. (1976), *Contemporary Africa: Geography and Change*, Englewood Cliffs, NJ: Prentice-Hall.

KNUDSON, O. and SCANDIZZO, P. L. (1979), 'Nutrition and Food Needs in Developing Countries', World Bank, Staff Working Paper no. 328.

KOLM, S. Ch. (1969), 'The Optimal Production of Social Justice', in Margolis and Guitton (1969).

KOLM, S. Ch. (1976a), 'Unequal Inequalities: I', *Journal of Economic Theory*, 12.

KOLM, S. Ch. (1976b), 'Unequal Inequalities: II', *Journal of Economic Theory*, 13.

KONANDREAS, P., HUDDLESTON, B. and RAMANGKURA, V. (1979), *Food Security: An Insurance Approval*, Washington, DC: International Food Policy Research Institute.

KOOPMANS, T. C. (1957), *Three Essays on the State of the Economic Science*, New York: McGraw-Hill.

KORNAI, JÁNOS (1979a), *The Economics of Shortage*, mimeographed; to be published.

KORNAI, J. (1979b), 'Resource-constrained versus Demand-constrained Systems', *Econometrica*, 47.

234   *Bibliography*

KRELLE, W. and SHORROCKS, A. F. (1978), *Personal Income Distribution*, Amsterdam: North-Holland.

KRISHNAJI, N. (1976), 'Public Distribution and Procurement of Foodgrains: A Comment', *Economic and Political Weekly*, 11, 21 February.

KUMAR, DHARMA (1974), 'Changes in Income Distribution and Poverty in India: A Review of the Literature', *World Development*, 2.

KUMAR, S. K. (1979), *Impact of Subsidised Rice on Food Consumption in Kerala*, Washington, DC: International Food Policy Research Institute.

KUNDU, A., and SMITH, T. E. (1981), "On the Possibility of Poverty Indices", Working Paper 43, Regional Science and Transportation, University of Pennsylvania.

KUZNETS, S. (1966), *Modern Economic Growth*, New York: Norton.

LADEJINSKY, W. (1976), 'Food Shortage in West Bengal: Crisis or Chronic?', *World Development*, 4.

LAL, DEEPAK (1976), 'Agricultural Growth, Real Wages and the Rural Poor in India', *Economic and Political Weekly*, 11.

LANCASTER, K. J. (1966), 'A New Approach to Consumer Theory', *Journal of Political Economy*, 74.

LAPPÉ, F. M., and COLLINS, J. (1977), *Food First: Beyond the Myth of Scarcity*, New York: Houghton Mifflin (republished New York: Ballantine Books, 1979).

LAPPÉ, F. M. and COLLINS, J. (1978), *World Hunger: Ten Myths*, San Francisco: Institute for Food and Development Policy.

LARDY, N. R. (1978), *Economic Growth and Distribution in China*, Cambridge: University Press.

LEVINSON, F. J. (1974), *Morinda: An Economic Analysis of Malnutrition among Young Children in Rural India*, Cambridge, Mass.: Cornell–MIT International Nutrition Policy Series.

LIFSCHULTZ, L. (1975), 'The Crisis Has Not Passed', *Far Eastern Economic Review*, 5 December.

LIPTON, MICHAEL (1977), *Why Poor People Stay Poor: A Study of Urban Bias in World Development*, London: Temple Smith.

LIVINGSTONE, I. (1977), 'Economic Irrationality among Pastoral Peoples—Myth or Reality', *Development and Change*, 8.

LLOYD, E. M. H. (1956), *Food and Inflation in Middle East 1944–45*, Stanford: University Press.

LOFCHIE, M. F. (1975), 'Political and Economic Origins of African Hunger', *Journal of Modern African Studies*, 14.

LÖRSTAD, M. H. (1976), 'Nutrition Planning through Gaming', *Food and Nutrition*, 3.

LOVEDAY, A. (1916), *The History and Economics of Indian Famines*, London: G. Bell.

LUCE, R. D. and RAIFFA, H. (1958), *Games and Decisions*, New York: John Wiley.

LUNDHOLM, B. (1976), 'Domestic Animals in Arid Ecosystems', in Rapp, Le Houérou and Lundholm (1976).

MADISON, ANGUS (1970), 'The Historical Origins of Indian Poverty', *Banca Nazionale del Lavoro*, no. 92.

MAGDOFF, H. (1968), 'The Age of Imperialism', *Monthly Review*, 20.

MAHALANOBIS, P. C., MUKHERJE, R., and GHOSH, A. (1946), 'A Sample Survey of After-effects of the Bengal Famine of 1943', *Sankhya*, 7.

MAHALANOBIS, P. C., *et al.* (1946), *Famine and Rehabilitation in Bengal*, Calcutta: Statistical Publishing Society.

MALLORY, W. H. (1926), *China: Land of Famine*, New York: American Geographical Society.

MALTHUS, T. R. (1798), *Essay on the Principle of Population as It Affects the Future Improvement of Society*, London.

MALTHUS, T. R. (1800), *An Investigation of the Cause of the Present High Price of Provisions*, London.

MANETSCH, J. (1977), 'On the Role of Systems Analysis in Aiding Countries Facing Acute Shortages', *Man and Cybernetics*, 7 April.

MANN, H. H. (1955), *Rainfall and Famine*, Bombay: Indian Society of Agricultural Economics.

MANN, J. S. (1968), 'The Impact of Public Law 480 Imports on Prices and Domestic Supply of Cereals in India', *American Journal of Farm Economics*, 49.

MANSERGH, N. (ed.) (1971), *The Transfer of Power 1942-7*, vol. III, London: HMSO.

MANSERGH, N. (ed.) (1973), *The Transfer of Power 1942-7*, vol. IV, London: HMSO.

MARGLIN, S. A. (1974-5), 'What Do Bosses Do?' *Review of Radical Political Economics*, Part I, 6; Part II, 7.

MARGOLIS, J. and GUITTON, H. (eds) (1969), *Public Economics*, London: Macmillan.

MARNHAM, P. (1977), *Nomads of the Sahel*, London: Minority Rights Group.

MARRIS, R. and THEIL, H. 'International Comparisons of Economic Welfare', presented to A. E. A., Denver (1980), 'Towards a World Utility Function', mimeographed, Department of Economics, University of Maryland.

MARX, KARL (1857-8), *Grundrisse der Kritik der Politischen Okonomie*. Moscow: Marx-Engels-Lenin Institute, 1939 and 1941; English translation by M. Nicolaus (1973), *Grundisse: Foundations of the Critique of Political Economy*, Harmondsworth: Penguin; also part translation with supplementary texts of Marx and Engels, and with an Introduction by Eric Hobsbawm (1964), *Pre-Capitalist Economic Formations*, London: Lawrence and Wishart.

MARX, KARL (1859), *Zur Kritik der Politischen Ökonomie*, Berlin: Deitz Verlag, 1964; English translation by S. W. Ryazanskaya, with an Introduction by Maurice Dobb (1971), *A Contribution to the Critique of Political Economy*, London: Lawrence and Wishart.

MARX, KARL (1867), *Das Kapital*, vol. I; English translation by S. Moore and E. Aveling, edited by F. Engels (1887), *Capital: A Critical Analysis of Capitalist Production*, vol. I, London: Sonnenschein; republished by Allen and Unwin, 1938.

MASEFIELD, G. B. (1963), *Famine: Its Prevention and Relief*, Oxford: University Press.

MATHIAS, PETER (1972), 'Adam's Burden: Diagnoses of Poverty in Post-Medieval Europe and the Third World Now', Gildersleeve Lecture, Barnard College, Columbia University.

MATLOCK, W. G. and COCKRUM, E. L. (1976), 'Agricultural Production Systems in the Sahel', in Glantz (1976).

MAYER, JEAN (1975), 'Management of Famine Relief', *Science*, 5, 9 May.

McALPIN, MICHELLE (1976), 'The Demographic Effects of Famine in Bombay Presidency, 1871–1931: Some Preliminary Findings', mimeographed, Economics Department, Tufts University.

McHENRY, D. F. and BIRD, K. (1977), 'Food Bungle in Bangladesh', *Foreign Policy*, no. 27, Summer.

McLAREN, D. S. (1974), 'The Great Protein Fiasco', *Lancet*, 13 July.

MEADOWS, D. H., MEADOWS, D. L., RANDERS, J. and BEHRENS III, W. W. (1972), *The Limits to Growth*, Washington, DC: Potomac Associates.

MEILLASSOUX, C. (1972), 'From Reproduction to Production', *Economy and Society*, 1.

MEILLASSOUX, C. (1974), 'Development or Exploitation: Is the Sahel Famine Good for Business?' *Review of African Political Economy*, 1.

MEILLASSOUX, C. (1975), *Femme, greniers, et capitaux*, Paris: Maspéro.

MELLOR, J. W. (1976), *The New Economics of Growth: A Strategy for India and the Developing World*, Ithaca, NY: Cornell University Press.

MELLOR, J. W. (1978a), 'Food Price Policy and Income Distribution in Low-Income Countries', *Economic Development and Cultural Change*, 27.

MELLOR, J. W. (1978b), *Three Issues of Development Strategy: Food, Population, Trade*, Washington, DC: IFPRI.

MENCHER, J. P. (1978), 'Why Grow More Food?: An Analysis of Some Contradictions in the "Green Revolution" in Kerala', *Economic and Political Weekly*, 13.

MIA, AHMADULLAH (1976), *Problems of Rural Development: Some Household Level Indicators*, Dacca Integrated Rural Development Programme.

MILLER, D. S., and HOLT, J. F. J. (1975), 'The Ethiopian Famine', *Proceedings of the Nutritional Society*, 34.

MILLER, H. P. (1971), *Rich Man, Poor Man*, New York: Cromwell.

MILLER, S. M., REIN, M., ROBY, P. and CROSS, B. (1967), 'Poverty, Inequality and Conflict', *Annals of the American Academy of Political Science*.

MILLER, S. M. and ROBY, P. (1971), 'Poverty: Changing Social Stratification', in Townsend (1971).

MINHAS, B. S. (1970), 'Rural Poverty, Land Distribution and Development', *Indian Economic Review*, 5.

MINHAS, B. S. (1971), 'Rural Poverty and Minimum Level of Living', *Indian Economic Review*, 6.

MINHAS, B. S. (1974), 'Rural Poverty, Land Distribution and Development Strategy: Facts', in Srinivasan and Bardhan (1974).

MITRA, ASHOK (1977), *Terms of Trade and Class Relations: An Essay in Political Economy*, London: Frank Cass.

MONOD, T. (ed.) (1975), *Pastoralism and Development in Africa*, London: Oxford University Press.

MORAES, DOM (1974), *A Matter of People*, London: Deutsch.

MORAES, DOM (1975), 'The Dimensions of the Problem: Comment', in Aziz (1975).

MORAWETZ, D. (1977), *Twenty-five Years of Economic Development 1950 to 1975*, Baltimore: Johns Hopkins University Press.

MORRIS, M. D. (1974), 'What is Famine?', *Economic and Political Weekly*, 9, 2 November.

MORRIS, M. D. (1975), 'Needed—A New Famine Policy', *Economic and Political Weekly*, Annual Number, 10.

MORRIS, M. D. (1979), *Measuring the Condition of the World's Poor: The Physical Quality of Life Index*, Oxford: Pergamon Press.

MUELLBAUER, JOHN (1974a), 'Recent UK Experience of Prices and Inequality: An Application of True Cost of Living and Real Income Indices', *Economic Journal*, 84.

MUELLBAUER, JOHN (1974b), 'Household Composition, Engel Curves and Welfare Comparison between Households: A Duality Approach', *European Economic Review*, 5.

MUELLBAUER, JOHN (1974c), 'Inequality Measures, Prices and Household Composition', *Review of Economic Studies*, 41.

MUELLBAUER, JOHN (1975), 'Aggregation, Income Distribution and

Consumer Demand', *Review of Economic Studies*, 42.

MUELLBAUER, JOHN (1976), 'Community Preferences and the Representative Consumer', *Econometrica*, 44.

MUELLBAUER, JOHN (1977a), 'Cost of Living', in *Social Science Research*, London: HMSO.

MUELLBAUER, JOHN (1977b), 'Testing the Barten Model of Household Composition Effects and the Cost of Children', *Economic Journal*, 87.

MUELLBAUER, JOHN (1978), 'Distributional Aspects of Price Comparisons', in Stone and Peterson (1978).

MUELLBAUER, JOHN (1980), 'The Estimation of the Prais-Houthakker Model of Equivalent Scales', *Econometrica*, 48.

MUKERJI, K. (1952), *Socio-Economic Survey of 49 Villages*, Calcutta: Chatterjee and Co.

MUKERJI, K. (1957), *The Problems of Land Transfer*, Santiniketan: Visva-Bharati.

MUKERJI, K. (1965), *Agriculture, Famine and Rehabilitation in South Asia*, Santiniketan: Visva-Bharati.

MUKHERJEE, M., BHATTACHARYA, N. and CHATTERJEE, G. S. (1972), 'Poverty in India: Measurement and Amelioration', *Commerce* (Calcutta), 125.

MUNDLAK, Y. (1979), *Intersectoral Factor Mobility and Agricultural Growth*, Washington, DC: International Food Policy Research Institute.

MYINT, H. (1973), *The Economics of Developing Countries*, 4th edn, London: Hutchinson.

MYRDAL, GUNNAR (1957), *Economic Theory and Underdeveloped Regions*, London: Duckworth.

MYRDAL, GUNNAR (1968), *Asian Drama*, New York: Pantheon.

NAKAMURA, J. I. (1966), *Agricultural Production and the Economic Development of Japan 1873–1922*, Princeton, NJ: University Press.

NASH, V. (1900), *The Great Famine and Its Causes*, London: Longmans.

National Bank of Ethiopia (1976), *Eleventh Annual Report 1974/5*, Addis Ababa: Government of Ethiopia.

NEWMAN, J. L. (1975), *Drought, Famine and Population Movements in Africa*, Syracuse, NY: University Press.

NEWMAN, PETER (1977), 'Malaria and Mortality', *Journal of American Statistical Association*, 72.

NICHOLSON, J. L. (1976), 'Appraisal of Different Methods of Estimating Equivalent Scales and Their Results', *Review of Income and Wealth*, 22.

NOLAN, LIAM (1974), *The Forgotten Famine*, Dublin: Mercier Press.

NORTON, B. E. (1976), 'The Management of Desert Grazing Systems', in Glantz (1976).

NOZICK, ROBERT (1974), *Anarchy, State and Utopia*, Oxford: Basil Blackwell.

OECD Development Centre (1979), *Food Aid for Development*, Paris: OECD.

OHKAWA, K. and ROSOVSKY, H. (1960), 'The Role of Agriculture in Modern Japanese Economic Development', *Economic Development and Cultural Change*, 9.

OHKAWA, K. and ROSOVSKY, H. (1973), *Japanese Economic Growth*, Stanford: University Press.

OHKAWA, K., *et al.* (1957), *The Growth Rate of the Japanese Economy since 1878*, Tokyo: Kinokuniya Bookstore.

OJHA, P. D. (1970), 'A Configuration of Indian Poverty', *Reserve Bank of India Bulletin*, 24.

O'KEEFE, P. and WISNER, B. (1975), 'African Drought—The State of the Game', *African Environmental Special Report No. 1: Problems and Perspectives*. London: International African Institute.

O'KEEFE, P. and WISNER, B. (eds) (1977), *Landuse and Development*, London: International African Institute.

ORSHANSKY, M. (1965), 'Counting the Poor: Another Look at the Poverty Profile', *Social Security Bulletin*, 28.

ORSHANSKY, M. (1966), 'Recounting the Poor: A Five Year Review', *Social Security Bulletin*, 29.

ORSHANSKY, M. (1969), 'How Poverty is Measured', *Monthly Labor Review*.

OSMANI, S. R. (1978), 'Economic Inequality and Group Welfare: Theory and Application to Bangladesh'; to be published by Oxford University Press.

OXBY, C. (1975), *Pastoral Nomads and Development*, London: International African Institute.

PADDOCK, W. and PADDOCK, P. (1967), *Famine—1975!*, Boston: Little, Brown.

PALEKAR, S. A. (1962), *Real Wages in India 1939–1950*, Bombay: International Book House.

PALMER, INGRID (1972), *Food and New Agricultural Technology*, Geneva: UNRISD, United Nations.

PANIKAR, P. G. K., *et al* (1975), *Poverty, Unemployment and Development Policy*, New York: United Nations, ST/ESA/29.

PANKHURST, R. (1961), *An Introduction to the Economic History of Ethiopia from Early Times to 1800*, London: Lalibela House.

PANKHURST, R. (1966), 'The Great Ethiopian Famine of 1888–1892: A New Assessment', *Journal of the History of Medicine and Allied Sciences*, 21.

PANTULU, Y. V. (1980), 'On Sen's Measure of Poverty', mimeographed, Sardar Patel Institute of Economic and Social Research.

PATNAIK, P., RAO, S. K. and SANYAL, A. (1976), 'The Inflationary

Process: Some Theoretical Comments', *Economic and Political Weekly*, 11, 23 October.

PAUKERT, FELIX (1973), 'Income Distribution at Different Levels of Development: A Survey of Evidence', *International Labour Review*, 108.

PEN, J. (1976), *Income Distribution*, Harmondsworth: Penguin.

PENNY, D. H. (1966), 'The Economics of Peasant Agriculture: The Indonesian Case', *Bulletin of Indonesian Economic Studies*, no. 5, October.

PENNY, D. H. (1979), 'The Economics of Peasant Starvation', presented at the 1979 Conference of the Australian Agricultural Economics Society.

PERKINS, D. H. (1969), *Agricultural Development in China 1368–1968*, Chicago: Aldine.

PERKINS, D. H. (1978), 'Meeting Basic Needs in the People's Republic of China', *World Development*, 6.

PINSTRUP-ANDERSON, P., RAIZ DE LONDONA, N. and HOOVER, E. (1976), 'The Impact of Increasing Food Supply on Human Nutrition: Implications for Commodity Priorities in Agricultural Research and Policy', *American Journal of Agricultural Economics*, 58.

POLEMAN, T. T. (1977), 'World Food: Myth and Reality', *World Development*, 5.

POWER, J., and HOLENSTEIN, A. (1976), *World of Hunger*, London: Temple Smith.

PRABHAKAR, M. S. (1974), 'The Famine: A Report from Dhubri', *Economic and Political Weekly*, 9.

PRAIS, S. J. and HOUTHAKKER, H. S. (1955), *The Analysis of Family Budgets*, Cambridge: University Press (2nd edn 1971).

PYATT, GRAHAM (1976), 'On the Interpretation and Disaggregation of Gini Coefficients', *Economic Journal*, 86.

PYATT, GRAHAM (1980), 'Poverty and Welfare Measures Based on the Lorenz Curve', mimeographed, Development Research Center, World Bank, Washington, DC.

PYATT, G. and THORBECKE, E. (1976), *Planning for a Better Future*, Geneva: ILO.

RADHAKRISHNA, R. and SARMA, A. (1975), 'Distributional Effects of the Current Inflation', *Social Scientist*, 30–1.

RADHAKRISHNA, R. and SARMA, A. (1980), 'Intertemporal Welfare Comparisons of India', mimeographed, Sardar Patel Institute of Economic and Social Research.

RADO, E. and SINHA, R. (1977), 'Africa: A Continent in Transition', *World Development*, 5.

RAHMAN, ANISUR (1974a), 'Relief Tour of Shahbajpur, Brahmanbaria:

Daily Diary', mimeographed, Dacca University.

RAHMAN, ANISUR (1974b), 'Famine', mimeographed, Dacca University.

RAJARAMAN, INDIRA (1974), 'Constructing the Poverty Line: Rural Punjab, 1960–61', Discussion Paper no. 43, Research Program in Economic Development, Princeton University.

RAMACHANDRAN, L. (1977), *India's Food Problem: A New Approach*, New Delhi: Allied Publishers.

RANGASAMI, AMRITA (1974a), 'West Bengal: A Generation is Being Wiped Out', *Economic and Political Weekly*, 9, 30 November.

RANGASAMI, AMRITA (1974b), 'The Uses of "Drought" ', *Economic and Political Weekly*, 9, 14 December.

RANGASAMI, AMRITA (1975), 'The Paupers of Kholisabhita Hindupara: Report on a Famine', *Economic and Political Weekly*, Annual Number, 10.

RAPP, A., LE HOUÉROU, H. N. and LUNDHOLM, R. (eds) (1976), *Can Desert Encroachment Be Stopped?*, Ecological Bulletins, no. 24. Stockholm.

RASHID, S. (1980), 'The Policy of Laissez-faire during Scarcities', *Economic Journal*, 90.

RATH, N. (1973), 'Regional Variation in Level and Cost of Living in Rural India', *Artha Vijnana*, 15.

RATUIM, A. M. A. (1974), 'An Analysis of Smuggling in Bangladesh', *Bangladesh Bank Bulletin*, 14.

RAWSKI, T. G. (1979), *Economic Growth and Employment in China*, Oxford: University Press.

RAYNAUT, C. (1977), 'Lessons of a Crisis', in Dalby, Harrison Church and Bezzaz (1977).

REDDAWAY, W. B. and RAHMAN, M. (1975), 'The Scale of Smuggling Out of Bangladesh', Research Report no. 21, Bangladesh Institute of Development Studies, Dacca.

REES, J. D. (1901), *Famines: Facts and Fallacies*, London.

REIN, M. (1971), 'Problems in the Definition and Measurement of Poverty', in Townsend (1971).

Relief and Rehabilitation Commission, Ethiopia (1976), 'Relief and Rehabilitation for Famine Victims in Ethiopia', in Hussein (1976).

RETZLAFF, R. H. (1978), 'Structural Change: An Approach to Poverty in Asian Rural Development', *Economic and Political Weekly*, 13, 22–30 December.

REUTLINGER, S. (1977), 'Malnutrition: A Poverty or a Food Problem', *World Development*, 5.

REUTLINGER, S. (1978), 'Food Insecurity: Magnitude and Remedies', *World Development*, 6.

REUTLINGER, S. and SELOWSKY, M. (1976), *Malnutrition and Poverty:*

Magnitude and Policy Options, Baltimore: Johns Hopkins University Press.

RICARDO, DAVID (1822), Text of speech in Parliament on 10 July: published in P. Sraffa (ed.), *The Works and Correspondence of David Ricardo*, vol. V, 'Speeches and Evidence', Cambridge: University Press.

RISKIN, CARL, (1975), 'Incentives for Industrial Workers', in Joint Economic Committee, *People's Republic of China: A Reassessment of the Economy*, Washington, DC: US Government Printing Office.

RIVERS, J. P. W., HOLT, J. F. J., SEAMAN, J. A. and BOWDEN, M. H. (1976), 'Lessons for Epidemiology from the Ethiopian Famines', *Annales Société belge de Médecine Tropicale*, 56.

RODGERS, G. B. (1976), 'A Conceptualisation of Poverty in Rural India', *World Development*, 4.

ROGERS, K. D., SRIVASTAVA, U. K. and HEADY, E. O. (1972), 'Modified Price, Production and Income Impacts of Food Aid under Market Differentiated Distribution', *American Journal of Farm Economics*, 54.

ROTHSCHILD, M. and STIGLITZ, J. E. (1973), 'Some Further Results on the Measurement of Inequality', *Journal of Economic Theory*, 6.

ROWNTREE, S. (1901), *Poverty: A Study of Town Life*, London: Macmillan.

RUDRA, ASHOK (1978), *The Basic Needs Concept and Its Implementation in Indian Development Planning*, Bangkok: ILO/ARTEP.

RUNCIMAN, W. G. (1966), *Relative Deprivation and Social Justice*, London: Routledge & Kegan Paul.

SARMA, J. S. (1978), 'India—A Drive toward Self-Sufficiency in Food Grains', *American Journal of Agricultural Economics*, 60.

SARMA, J. S., ROY, S. and GEORGE, P. S. (1979), *Two Analyses of Indian Foodgrains Production and Consumption Data*, Washington, DC: International Food Policy Research Institute.

SARRIS, A. H., ABBOTT, P. C. and TAYLOR, L. (1977), *Grain Reserves, Emergency Relief and Food Aid*, Washington, DC: Overseas Development Council.

SASTRY, S. A. R. (1977), 'Poverty, Inequality and Development: A Study of Rural Andhra Pradesh', *Anvesak*, 7.

SASTRY, S. A. R. (1980), "Poverty: Concepts and Measurement," *Indian Journal of Economics*, 61.

SASTRY, S. A. R. and SURYANARAYANA, T. (1980), 'Optimum Diet and Poverty Lines', National Seminar on Employment, Levels of Living on Public Policy, Sardar Patel, Institute of Economics and Social Research, Ahmedabad.

SCASE, R. (1974), 'Relative Deprivation: A Comparison of English and Swedish Manual Workers', in Wedderburn (1974).

SCHOVE, D. J. (1977), 'African Droughts and the Spectrum of Time', in Dalby, Harrison Church and Bezzaz (1977).

SCHULTZ, T. W. (1960), 'Value of U.S. Farm Surpluses to Under-developed Countries', *Journal of Farm Economics*, 42.

SCHULTZ, T. W. (1964), *Transforming Traditional Agriculture*, New Haven: Yale University Press.

SCITOVSKY, TIBOR (1976), *The Joyless Economy*, New York: Oxford University Press.

SEAMAN, J., and HOLT, J. (1980), 'Markets and Famines in the Third World', *Disasters*, 4.

SEAMAN, J., HOLT, J., RIVERS, J. and MURLIS, J. (1973), 'An Inquiry into the Drought Situation in Upper Volta', *The Lancet*, 6 October.

SEAMAN, J., HOLT, J. and RIVERS, J. (1974), *Harerghe under Drought*, Addis Ababa, Ethiopian Relief and Rehabilitation Commission.

SEAMAN, J., HOLT, J. and RIVERS, J. (1978), 'The Effects of Drought on Human Nutrition in an Ethiopian Province', *International Journal of Epidemiology*, 7.

SEASTRAND, F., and DIWAN, R. (1975), 'Measurement and Comparison of Poverty and Inequality in the United States', presented at the Third World Econometric Congress, Toronto.

SELOWSKY, M. and TAYLOR, L. (1973), 'The Economics of Malnourished Children: An Example of Disinvestment in Human Capital', *Economic Development and Cultural Change*, 22.

SEN, A. K. (1960), *Choice of Techniques*, Oxford: Basil Blackwell (3rd edn 1968).

SEN, A. K. (1966) 'Peasants and Dualism with or without Surplus Labour'; *Journal of Political Economy*, 74.

SEN, A. K. (1967a), 'Isolation, Assurance and the Social Rate of Discount', *Quarterly Journal of Economics*, 81.

SEN, A. K. (1967b), 'Surplus Labour in India: A Critique of Schultz's Statistical Test', *Economic Journal*, 77.

SEN, A. K. (1970), *Collective Choice and Social Welfare*, Edinburgh: Oliver and Boyd; reprinted by North-Holland, Amsterdam.

SEN, A. K. (1973a), *On Economic Inequality*, Oxford: Clarendon Press.

SEN, A. K. (1973b), 'Poverty, Inequality and Unemployment: Some Conceptual Issues in Measurement', *Economic and Political Weekly*, 8, Special Number.

SEN, A. K. (1974), 'Informational Bases of Alternative Welfare

Approaches: Aggregation and Income Distribution', *Journal of Public Economics*, 4.

SEN, A. K. (1975), *Employment, Technology and Development*, Oxford: Clarendon Press.

SEN, A. K. (1976a), 'Poverty: An Ordinal Approach to Measurement', *Econometrica*, 44.

SEN, A. K. (1976b), 'Real National Income', *Review of Economic Studies*, 43.

SEN, A. K. (1976c), 'Famines as Failures of Exchange Entitlements', *Economic and Political Weekly*, 11, Special Number.

SEN, A. K. (1976d), *Poverty and Economic Development*, Second Vikram Sarabhai Memorial Lecture, Ahmedabad, Vikram A. Sarabhai AMA Memorial Trust.

SEN, A. K. (1977a), 'Social Choice Theory: A Re-examination', *Econometrica*, 45.

SEN, A. K. (1977b), 'Starvation and Exchange Entitlements: A General Approach and Its Application to the Great Bengal Famine', *Cambridge Journal of Economics*, 1.

SEN, A. K. (1977c), 'On Weights and Measures: Informational Constraints in Social Welfare Analysis', *Econometrica*, 45.

SEN, A. K. (1978a), 'On the Labour Theory of Value: Some Methodological Issues', *Cambridge Journal of Economics*, 2.

SEN, A. K. (1978b), 'Ethical Measurement of Inequality: Some Difficulties', in Krelle and Shorrocks (1978).

SEN, A. K. (1979a), 'The Welfare Basis of Real Income Comparisons: A Survey', *Journal of Economic Literature*, 17.

SEN, A. K. (1979b), 'Issues in the Measurement of Poverty', *Scandinavian Journal of Economics*, 81.

SEN, A. K. (1980a), 'Description as Choice', *Oxford Economic Papers*, 32.

SEN, A. K. (1980b), 'Famine Mortality: A study of the Bengal Famine of 1943', in Hobsbawm *et al.* (1980).

SEN, A. K. (1980c), 'Famines', *World Development*, 8.

SEN, A. K. (1980d), 'Economic Development: Objectives and Obstacles', in R. F. Dernberger, ed., *China's Development Experience in Comparative Perspective*, Cambridge, Mass.: Harvard University Press.

SEN, A. K. (1981), 'Ingredients of Famine Analysis: Availability and Entitlements', *Quarterly Journal of Economics*, 95.

SEN, S. R. (1971), *Growth and Instability in Indian Agriculture*, Calcutta: Firma K. L. Mukhopadhyay.

SEN, SUNIL (1979), *Agrarian Relations in India 1793–1947*, New Delhi: People's Publishing House.

SHANIN, T. (1972), *The Awkward Class*, Oxford: Clarendon Press.

SHEAR, D. and STACY, R. (1976), 'Can the Sahel Survive? Prospects for Long-term Planning and Development', in Glantz (1976).

SHEARS, P. (1976), 'Drought in South-Eastern Ethiopia', in Hussein (1976).

SHEETS, H. and MORRIS, R. (1976), 'Disaster in the Desert', in Glantz (1976).

SHEPHERD, J. (1975), *The Politics of Starvation*, New York: Carnegie Endowment for International Peace.

SHUKLA, ROHIT (1977), 'Employment Behaviour in Labour Surplus Economy in a Famine Situation: A Study of Gujarat', *Anvesak*, 7.

SHUKLA, ROHIT (1979), *Public Works Policy during Droughts and Famines and Its Lessons for an Employment Policy*, Ahmedabad: Sardar Patel Institute of Economic and Social Research.

SINGER, H., and ANSARI, J. (1977), *Rich and Poor Countries*, London: Allen and Unwin.

SINGH, A. (1965), *Sectional Price Movements in India*, Benares: Benares Hindu University.

SINGH, AJIT (1978), 'The "Basic Needs" Approach to Development vs. the New International Economic Order: The Significance of Third World Industrialization', mimeographed, Department of Applied Economics, Cambridge University.

SINGH, INDERJIT (1979), 'Small Farmers and the Landless in South Asia', World Bank Staff Working Paper no. 320.

SINGH, K. SURESH (1975), *The Indian Famine 1967: A Study in Crisis and Change*, New Delhi: People's Publishing House.

SINHA, RADHA (1976a), *Food and Poverty: The Political Economy of Confrontation*, London: Croom Helm.

SINHA, RADHA (1976b), 'The World Food Security', *Journal of Agricultural Economics*, 26.

SINHA, RADHA (1977), 'The World Food Problem: Consensus and Conflict', *World Development*, 5.

SINHA, R., and GORDON DRABEK, A. (1978), *The World Food Problem: Consensus and Conflict*, Oxford: Pergamon.

SINHA, R., PEARSON, P., KADEKODI, G. and GREGORY, M. (1979), *Income Distribution, Growth and Basic Needs in India*, London: Croom Helm.

SMITH, ADAM (1776), *An Inquiry into the Nature and Causes of the Wealth of Nations*.

SOBHAN, REHMAN (1979), 'Politics of Food and Famine in Bangladesh', *Economic and Political Weekly*, 14.

SRINIVASAN, T. N. (1977a), 'Poverty: Some Measurement Problems', in *Conference Proceedings*, 41st Seminar of the International Statistical Institute, held at New Delhi.

SRINIVASAN, T. N. (1977b), 'Development, Poverty and Basic Human Needs: Some Issues', *Food Research Institute Studies*, 16.

SRINIVASAN, T. N. (1979), 'Malnutrition: Some Measurement and Policy Issues', mimeographed, World Bank, Washington, D.C.

SRINIVASAN, T. N. and BARDHAN, P. K. (1974), *Poverty and Income Distribution in India*, Calcutta: Statistical Publishing Society.

SRIVASTAVA, H. S. (1968), *The History of Indian Famines 1858–1918*, Agra: Sri Ram Mehra.

STEIN, Z., SUSSER, M., SAENGER, G. and MAROLLA, F. (1975), *Famine and Human Development: The Dutch Hunger Winter of 1944–1945*, London: Oxford University Press.

STEPHENS, I. (1966), *Monsoon Morning*, London: Ernest Benn.

STEPHENS, I. (1977), *Unmade Journey*, London: Stacey International.

STEWART, F. and STREETEN, P. (1976), 'New Strategies for Development: Poverty, Income Distribution and Growth', *Oxford Economic Papers*, 28.

STIGLER, G. J. (1945), 'The Cost of Subsistence', *Journal of Farm Economics*, 27.

STIGLITZ, J. E. (1974), 'Incentives and Risk Sharing in Share Cropping', *Review of Economic Studies*, 41.

STONE, R. (1970), *Mathematical Models of the Economy and Other Essays*, London: Chapman and Hall.

STONE, R., and PETERSON, W. (eds) (1978), *Econometric Contributions to Public Policy*, New York: Macmillan.

STREETEN, PAUL (1972), *The Frontiers of Development Studies*, London: Macmillan.

STREETEN, PAUL (1977), 'The Constructive Features of a Basic Needs Approach to Development', mimeographed, World Bank, Washington, DC.

STREETEN, P. and BURKI, S. J. (1978), 'Basic Needs: Some Issues', *World Development*, 6.

SUKHATME, P. V. (1977), *Nutrition and Poverty*, New Delhi: Indian Agricultural Research Institute.

SUKHATME, P. V. (1978), 'Assessment of Adequacy of Diets at Different Income Levels', *Economic and Political Weekly*, 13, Special Number.

SUMMERS, R. S. (1978), 'Two Types of Substantive Reasons: The Core of a Theory of Common-Law Justification', *Cornell Law Review*, 63.

SVEDBERG, PETER (1978), 'World Food Sufficiency and Meat Consumption', *American Journal of Agricultural Economics*, 60.

SVEDBERG, PETER (1979), 'The Price Disincentive Effect of Food Aid Revisited: A Comment', *Economic Development and Cultural Change*, 28.

SUBRAMANIAN, V. (1975), *Parched Earth: The Maharashtra Drought 1970–73*, New Delhi: Orient Longmans.

SWIFT, J. (1977a), 'Sahelian Pastoralists—Underdevelopment, Desertification, and Famine', *Annual Review of Anthropology*, 6.

SWIFT, J. (1977b), 'Desertification and Man in the Sahel', in O'Keefe and Wisner (1977).

SZAL, R. J. (1977), 'Poverty: Measurement and Analysis', ILO Working Paper, WEP 2–23/WP60.

TADESSE, K. (1976), 'Health Problems Resulting from Famine', in Hussein (1976).

TAKAYAMA, N. (1979), 'Poverty, Income Inequality and Their Measures: Professor Sen's Approach Reconsidered', *Econometrica*, 47.

TAYLOR, LANCE (1975), 'The Misconstrued Crisis: Lester Brown and World Food', *World Development*, 3.

TAYLOR, LANCE (1977), 'Research Directions in Income Distribution, Nutrition, and the Economics of Food', *Food Research Institute Studies*, 16.

TAYLOR, L. and SARRIS, A. (1976), 'Cereal Stocks, Food Aid and Food Security for the Poor', *World Development*, 4.

THEIL, H. (1967), *Economics and Information Theory*, Amsterdam: North-Holland.

THEIL, H. (1976), *Theory and Measurement of Consumer Demand*, 2 vols., Amsterdam: North-Holland, volume I (1975), and volume II (1976).

THOM, R. (1975), *Structural Stability and Morphogenesis: An Outline of a General Theory of Models*, Reading: Benjamin.

THON, D. (1979), 'On Measuring Poverty', *Review of Income and Wealth*, 25.

THON, D. (1980), "A Contribution to the Axiomatic Approach to the Measurement of Income Inequality and Poverty", Ph.D. thesis, Toronto University.

TOUPET, C. (1977), 'La Grande Sécheresse en Mauritanie', in Dalby, Harrison Church and Bezzaz (1977).

TOWNSEND, PETER (1954), 'The Meaning of Poverty', *British Journal of Sociology*, 5.

TOWNSEND, PETER (1971), *The Concept of Poverty*, London: Heinemann.

TOWNSEND, PETER (1974), 'Poverty as Relative Deprivation: Resources and Styles of Living', in Wedderburn (1974).

TOWNSEND, PETER (1979), *Poverty in the United Kingdom*, Harmondsworth: Penguin.

TUDGE, COLIN (1977), *The Famine Business*, London: Faber and Faber.

TYDINGS, J. D. (1970), *Born to Starve*, New York: William Morrow.

UNRISD (1975), 'Famine Risk in the Modern World', mimeographed, United Nations, Geneva.

UNRISD (1976), 'Famine Risk and Famine Prevention in the Modern World: Studies in Food Systems under Conditions of Recurrent Scarcity', mimeographed, United Nations, Geneva.

US President's Commission on Income Maintenance (1969), *Poverty amid Plenty*, Washington, DC: US Government Printing Office.

VAIDYANATHAN, A. (1974), 'Some Aspects of Inequalities of Living Standards in Rural India', in Srinivasan and Bardhan (1974).

VENKATARAMANI, M. S. (1973), *Bengal Famine of 1943: The American Response*, Delhi: Vikas.

WAGSTAFF, HOWARD (1976), *World Food: A Political Task*, London: Fabian Society.

WALFORD, C. (1878), 'On the Famines of the World: Past and Present', *Journal of Statistical Society*, 41.

WALLACE, R. (1900), *Lectures on Famines in India*, Edinburgh.

WAVELL, ARCHIBALD, 1st Earl (1973), *The Viceroy's Journal*, ed. P. Moon, Oxford: University Press.

WECKSTEIN, R. S. (1977), 'Food Security: Storage vs. Exchange', *World Development*, 5.

WEDDERBURN, DOROTHY (ed.) (1974), *Poverty, Inequality and Class Structure*, Cambridge: University Press.

WEDDERBURN, D. and CRAIG, C. (1974), 'Relative Deprivation in Work', in Wedderburn (1974).

WEISBROD, B. A. (ed.) (1965), *The Economics of Poverty*, Englewood Cliffs, NJ: Prentice-Hall.

WIDSTRAND, C. G. (1975), 'The Rationale of the Nomad Economy', *Ambio*, 1.

WILES, P. (1974), *Distribution of Income: East and West*, Amsterdam: North-Holland.

WILKINSON, R. G. (1973), *Poverty and Progress*, London: Methuen.

WINSTANLEY, D. (1976), 'Climatic Changes and the Future of the Sahel', in Glantz (1976).

WISEBERG, L. (1976), 'An International Perspective on the African Famines', in Glantz (1976).

WOOD, A. P. (1976), 'Farmers' Responses to Drought in Ethiopia', in Hussein (1976).

WOOD, G. D. (1976), 'Class Differentiation and Power in Bangladesh', in Huq (1976).

WOODHAM-SMITH, CECIL (1962), *The Great Hunger: Ireland 1845–9*, London: Hamish Hamilton (republished in new edition, London: New English Library, 1975).

World Bank (1975), *Ethiopia—Grain Storage and Marketing*, Washington, DC: World Bank.

World Bank (1980), *The World Development Report 1980*, Washington, DC: World Bank.

WRIGLEY, E. A. (1969), *Population and History*, London: Weidenfeld and Nicolson.

YITZHAKI, S. (1979), 'Relative Deprivation: A New Approach to the Social Welfare Function', *Quarterly Journal of Economics*, 93.

ZEEMAN, E. C. (1977), *Catastrophe Theory: Selected Papers 1972–77*, Reading, Mass.: Addison-Wesley.

ZEWDE, B. (1976), 'A Historical Outline of Famine in Ethiopia', in Hussein (1976).

ZIA BARANI (1291), *Tarikh-i-Firozshāhī*, Delhi.

Subject Index

Name index*

Aall, C., 217
Abbott, P. C., 242
Abdel-Fadil, M., 217
Abdullah, A. A., 151, 217
Abel-Smith, B., 29, 32, 217
Abul Fazl, 39, 217
Adelman, I., 24, 217
Adnan, S., 147, 151, 217
Ady, P., 217
Ahluwalia, M., 24, 32, 37, 217, 223
Ahmed, Iftikhar, 217, 218
Ahmed, Iqbal, 217, 231
Ahmed, R., 217
Alamgir, M., viii, 37, 39, 43, 63, 132, 134–
    47, 151, 217
Alavi, H., 217
Alfathan, T. A., 24, 227
Ali, M., 226
Ambirajan, S., 160, 217
Amin, S., 104, 217
Anand, S., viii, 37, 186, 189, 218
Anderson, N. D., 114, 155, 222
Ansari, J., 245
Arrow, K., 49, 173, 218
Artis, M. J., 228
Atkinson, A. B., 15, 22, 29, 191, 193, 219
Aykroyd, W. R., 39, 43, 52, 86, 160, 197,
    198, 219
Aziz, S., 7, 8, 42, 83, 158, 159, 219

Baier, S., 127, 219
Bailey, N. T. J., 205, 219
Baird-Smith, Col., 160
Baishya, P., 219
Ball, N., 126, 219
Balogh, T., 24, 219
Baran, P. A., 104, 219
Bardhan, P. K., 13, 28, 32, 219, 246
Barraclough, S., 158, 219
Barten, A. P., 30, 220
Batchelder, A. B., 33, 220
Bauer, P. T., 220
Beckerman, W., 24, 33, 186, 189, 220
Behrens III, W. W., 236

Belete, S., 94, 95, 97, 98, 100, 101, 102, 220
Bell, C. L. G., 24, 32, 223
Bengtsson, B., 220
Bennet, W. C., 211–213
Bentzel, R., 22, 220
Berg, A., 220
Berry, L., 120, 122, 126, 127, 220
Beshah, T. W., 220
Beveridge, Lord, 13
Bezzaz, F., 224
Bhalla, A., 24, 220
Bhalla, S., 220
Bhatia, B. M., 39, 55, 58, 160, 161, 220
Bhattacharjee, J. P., 220
Bhattacharya, A., viii
Bhattacharya, N., 26, 32, 220, 222, 238
Bhatty, I. Z., 32, 37, 221
Bird, K., 135–6, 236
Blackorby, C., 15, 37, 191, 221
Blix, G., 39, 42, 221
Blyn, G., 58, 221
Bondestam, L., 104, 105, 221
Booth, A., 221
Booth, C., 32, 221
Borda, J. C., 36, 187, 221
Boyce, J., 151, 230
Borgstrom, G., 158, 221
Borkar, V. V., 221
Bourne, G. H., 221
Bowden, M. H., 86, 88, 100, 105, 242
Bowley, A. L., 33, 221
Bradley, P. N., 114, 115, 122, 221
Broder, I. E., 187, 221
Brown, J. A. C., 30, 221
Brown, L. R., 83, 158, 222
Brown, W. R., 114, 155, 222
Bruton, H. J., 222
Burger, G. C. E., 222
Burki, S. J., 24, 246
Buringh, P., 158, 222
Butts, R. E., 222

Caldwell, J. C., 116, 120, 121, 122, 127, 222
Campbell, D. J., 120, 122, 126, 127, 220

*The index refers also to the bibliography which includes—*inter alia*—contributions relevant to this work but not specifically cited in the text.

254   *Index*

Khalifa, A., 121, 233
Khan, A. M., 217
Khan, A. R., 24, 47, 151, 152, 227, 228, 231, 233
Kloth, T. I., 116, 119, 121, 233
Knight, C. G., 233
Knudson, O., 233
Kolm, S. C., 15, 22, 191, 233
Konandreas, P., 159, 233
Koopmans, T. C., 172, 233
Kornai, J., 155, 233
Krelle, W., 234
Krishnaji, N., 234
Krishnamurti, J., viii
Krishnan, T. N., 228, 229
Kumar, D., 32, 234
Kumar, S. K., 234
Kundu, A., 193, 234
Kuznets, S., 234
Kynch, J., viii

Ladejinsky, W., 234
Lal, D., 32, 234
Lancaster, K. J., 24, 234
Lappé, F. M., 118, 136, 158, 159, 234
Lardy, N. R., 234
le Honerou, H. N., 129, 241
Lee, E., 24, 227, 231
Levinson, F. J., 234
Licke, Y., 87, 100, 106, 109, 227
Lifschultz, L., 234
Lipton, M., 43, 234
Livingstone, I., 234
Lloyd, E. M. H., 234
Lofchie, M. F., 118, 119, 234
Lörstad, M. H., 159, 234
Loveday, A., 43, 235
Luce, R. D., 128, 235
Lundholm, B., 129, 235, 241

Madison, A., 235
Maffi, M., 87, 98, 100, 102, 106, 109, 220, 227
Magdoff, H., 104, 235
Mahalanobis, P. C., 58–9, 67, 70–1, 73, 77, 96, 208, 209–10, 211, 235
Majumdar, M., viii
Mallory, W. H., 39, 164, 235
Malthus, T. R., 63, 160, 174–9, 235
Manetsch, J., 159, 235
Mann, H. H., 159, 235
Mansergh, N., 79, 80, 81, 82, 83, 195, 235

Marglin, S. A., 235
Margolis, J., 235
Marnham, P., 118, 121, 235
Marolla, F., 20, 43, 246
Marris, R., 30, 187, 235
Marx, K., 5, 15, 18, 235, 236
Masefield, G. B., 39, 83, 236
Mathias, P., 236
Matlock, W. G., 113, 114, 115, 119, 236
Mayer, J., 40, 236
McAlpin, M., 50, 236
McHenry, D. F., 135–6, 236
McLaren, D. S., 236
Meadows, D. H., 236
Meadows, D. L., 236
Mehta, N., 134, 229
Meillassoux, C., 120, 126, 236
Mellor, J. W., 236
Mencher, J. P., 237
Mia, A., 142–3, 237
Mill, J. S., 175
Miller, D. S., 86, 101, 237
Miller, H. P., 237
Miller, S. M., 14, 237
Mills, G., 230
Minhas, B. S., 32, 237
Mitra, A., viii, 48, 231, 237
Monod, T., 237
Moraes, D., 164, 237
Morawetz, D., 24, 237
Morris, C. T., 24, 187, 217, 221
Morris, M. D., 24, 40, 237
Morris, R., 115–17, 119, 121, 245
Muellbauer, J., viii, 29, 30, 224, 237, 238
Mukerji, K., 70, 73–4, 210, 238
Mukherjea, R., 67, 70–1, 72–3, 77, 96, 197, 208, 209–10, 223, 235
Mukherjee, M., 32, 238
Mundlak, Y., 238
Muqtada, M., 217
Murlis, M., 116, 120, 243
Myint, H., 238
Myrdal, G., 238

Nadkarni, M. V., 221
Nakamura, J. I., 41, 238
Naseem, S. M., 231
Nash, V., 238
Newman, J. L., 116, 233, 238
Newman, P., 238
Nicholson, J. L., 30, 238
Nobay, A. R., 228
Nolan, L., 238